PARADISE OF SPORT

PARADISE OF SPORT

THE RISE OF ORGANISED SPORT IN AUSTRALIA

RICHARD CASHMAN

Melbourne

OXFORD UNIVERSITY PRESS

Oxford Auckland New York

OXFORD UNIVERSITY PRESS AUSTRALIA

Oxford New York
Athens Auckland Bangkok Bombay
Calcutta Cape Town Dar es Salaam Delhi
Florence Hong Kong Istanbul Karachi
Kuala Lumpur Madras Madrid Melbourne
Mexico City Nairobi Paris Singapore
Taipei Tokyo Toronto
and associated companies in
Berlin Ibadan

OXFORD is trade mark of Oxford University Press

© Richard Cashman, 1995
First published 1995

National Library of Australia
Cataloguing-in-Publication data:
Cashman, Richard, 1940– .
Paradise of sport: the rise of organised sport in Australia.
Bibliography
Includes index.
ISBN 0 19 553298 8.

Edited by Venetia Somerset
Text design by Perdita Nance
Cover design by Steve Randles
Cover photograph from Duane Hart/Sporting Images
Typeset by Kimberly Williams, Victoria
Printed by Australian Print Group
Published by Oxford University Press,
253 Normanby Road, South Melbourne, Australia

CONTENTS

PREFACE

Social commentators, from within Australia and outside, have long declared that the country is a paradise of sport. They have argued that many Australians have an obsession with sport and that sporting culture is central to Australian life. Some have said that the Australian passion for sport is distinctive and even unique.[1] Because these cultural assertions have been taken as axiomatic, few questions have been raised about Australian sporting culture. Why, when and how was a sporting paradise established? Who created it and for whom? What kind of paradise was it? What are the implications of a sporting paradise for other forms of culture? In answering these questions this book explores the rise and consolidation of organised sport in Australia, focusing on the period 1850–1914, the critical era when Australian sporting culture was formed.

The study of sport is a relatively recent phenomenon. Brian Stoddart was one of the first to attempt a critical history of Australian sport when he wrote *Saturday Afternoon Fever* (1984). Since then, there has been a boom in sports history research, with a number of important monographs on individual sports, clubs and institutions, particular themes along with regional histories.[2] *The Oxford Companion to Australian Sport* was published in 1992, a revised version appeared in 1994, and a Cambridge history, *Sport in Australia*, was published in 1995. Many theses on sports history have been written, and *Sporting Traditions*, the journal of the Australian Society for Sports History, has appeared for more than a decade. A history of Australian sport in the 1990s also needs to take notice of new work and approaches in Australian history itself. Inspired by Richard Holt's masterly *Sport and the British*, the present book draws on much recent research on Australian sporting history. Those who wish to research particular aspects of Australian sport in greater detail will be able to consult the notes and bibliography.

A definition of organised sport and the context in which it emerged is provided in Chapter 1. A more commercialised and professional sport began to appear in Britain in the late eighteenth century when greater press coverage and codification led to a more visible sporting culture. While the focus of this book is more on high-profile sport—mass-spectator, gate-money sport—every effort has been made to include material on more informal, junior and country sport. Because there has been limited research on non-élite sport, less is known about it and its relationship to élite high-profile sport.

A central assumption of this book is that sport does not merely reflect other social and political processes: it is an active and powerful agent in forming social and cultural values. Some sports clubs, according to Melbourne film critic, academic and football fan Deb Verhoven, 'are probably the most racist, sexist, homophobic spaces in [our] cultural community'.[3] Conservative and even reactionary values, clothed in the garb of tradition, continue to flourish in some arenas because sport, more than any other institution, is regarded by the general public as Australia's sacred cow. But it is also true, as Rick Gruneau has reminded us, that sport is a cultural terrain involving contests between individuals and groups over land, resources, institutions, values and ideology. Issues involving power, class, gender, race and ethnicity are fought out regularly both on and off the field.[4]

The task of the social historian is to relate sport to broader social, economic and political structures. A primary aim of this book is to encourage a more critical scrutiny of sporting institutions and ideologies from what has been labelled the cultural progressive perspective.[5] Because the institution of sport has largely been above criticism, there is a need to subject it to constructive criticism. Since sport has largely been dominated and used by conservative purposes, there is a need both to document this point and to explore other perspectives and uses of sport. The approach in this book is eclectic in that the author draws on a number of social theories and approaches rather than relying on a single overarching theoretical interpretation. To keep a plethora of scholarly names and theories out of view, for the general reader's sake, intellectual debt is mostly acknowledged in the notes and not in the text.

However, while criticism is welcome and necessary, it appears that some Australian commentators have felt a great deal of ambivalence about sport and its popularity. Some academic works present a bleak and unrelievedly negative view of the operation of contemporary sport in Australia, which is seen as totally unprogressive and possibly beyond redemption.[6] This book starts from a different premise. For better or worse, sport is central to the business of being Australian and appeals to many Australians. Sport is immensely popular and will continue to be so in the future. Nothing is likely to be achieved by labelling sport as undesirable or politically incorrect; instead, something so significant in Australian life deserves all the scrutiny we can give it.

ACKNOWLEDGEMENTS

Much of the credit for this book must go to my colleagues in the Australian Society for Sports History (ASSH) and British and North American sports historians. *Paradise of Sport* draws considerably on their research over the past two decades. My debts to various individuals are acknowledged in the notes. ASSH has provided me with a supportive network of researchers with a strong commitment to sports history.

Teaching a subject, 'The Rise of Organised Sport in Australia', at the University of New South Wales over the past decade has helped me develop and refine my ideas on the subject. Many undergraduate and postgraduate students have contributed through tutorial discussions and by writing essays and theses. A number of colleagues at my university have also encouraged me in many ways.

Many individuals have provided information, answered queries, and commented on drafts. These include Ray Bailey, Bill Baker, Roger Bell, Douglas Booth, Richard Broome, Kristine Corcoran, Braham Dabscheck, Nick Doumanis, Marina Duncan, Rae Frances, Sandra K. Hall, Roy Hay, Max Howell, Tony Hughes, John Hughson, Ian Jobling, Damien McCoy, Katharine Moore, Phil Mosely, Bill Murray, John Nauright, John O'Hara, Patrick O'Farrell, Virginia O'Farrell, Vicky Paraschak, Bruce Scates, Geoff Sherington, Max Solling, Bob Stewart, Brian Stoddart, Richard Stremski, Colin Tatz, Wray Vamplew, Ray Webster, Bernard Whimpress and Peter Yeend.

A number of persons have assisted by providing illustrative material. Thanks are due to the Batrouney family, Sean Brawley, Shayne Breen, John Daly, Tom Dunning, Lynne Embrey, Elery Hamilton-Smith, Tony Hughes, Rob Lynch, Warwick Norfolk, Heather Rose, Richard Stremski, Peter L. Swain, Laurie Woodman and Peter Yeend. Illustrations are published courtesy of Action Graphics, Australian Coaching Council, Australian Soccer Federation, The *Bulletin,* Collaroy Surf Lifesaving Club, Corporation of the City of Adelaide, Department of Education (NSW), Hakoah Club, Hawaii State Archives, *Herald-Sun* Pictorial Library, John Oxley Library, Launceston Reference Library,

Marrickville Library, Melbourne Cricket Club, New South Wales Department of Education, Newington College Archives, Australian Softball Archives, South Australian Museum, St George Historical Society, Sydney King's, The King's School, Victorian Football League.

I also wish to thank Peter Rose for his constructive criticism and general encouragement, and the staff of Oxford University Press who have been helpful. The manuscript has been considerably improved through the professional copy-editing of Venetia Somerset.

Lastly I wish to thank Margaret for her support and encouragement.

ABBREVIATIONS

AAA   Amateur Athletic Association
ABC   Australian Broadcasting Commission (now Corporation)
ACB   Australian Cricket Board
ADB   *Australian Dictionary of Biography*, MUP, 1966–
AFL   Australian Football League (formerly VFL)
AGPS   Australian Government Publishing Service
AJC   Australian Jockey Club
ALP   Australian Labor Party
ANU   Australian National University
AOC   Australian Olympic Committee
AOF   Australian Olympic Federation (since 1990)
ASC   Australian Sports Commission
ASSH   Australian Society for Sports History
ATSIC   Aboriginal and Torres Strait Islanders Commission
CAS   Confederation of Australian Sport
CUP   Cambridge University Press
GAA   Gaelic Athletic League
GPS   Great Public School
IOC   International Olympic Committee
MCC   Melbourne Cricket Club
MCG   Melbourne Cricket Ground
MLA   Member of the Legislative Assembly
MUP   Melbourne University Press
NASSH   North Americal Society for Sport History
NBL   National Basketball League
NES   non-English-speaking
NSW   New South Wales
NSWCA   New South Wales Cricket Association
NSWUP   New South Wales University Press
NWFU   North West Football Union
OCAS   *The Oxford Companion to Australian Sport*, 2nd edn, ed.
         Vamplew et al., OUP, Melbourne, 1994

OUP	Oxford University Press
QAAA	Queensland Amateur Athletic Association
RSPCA	Royal Society for the Prevention of Cruelty to Animals
SACA	South Australian Cricket Association
SBANSW	Surf Bathing Association of New South Wales
SCG	Sydney Cricket Ground
SP	starting price
STC	Sydney Turf Club
TAB	Totalisator Agency Board
TFL	Tasmanian Football League
UQP	University of Queensland Press
UWAP	University of Western Australia Press
VFA	Victorian Football Association
VFL	Victorian Football League (until 1990)
WASP	White Anglo-Saxon Protestant
WATC	Western Australian Turf Club
WSC	World Series Cricket
YMCA	Young Men's Christian Association

1
THE BRITISH INHERITANCE

The European colonisation of Australia took place at an important juncture in the development of organised sport in Britain. It coincided with the reshaping of sporting culture, which was becoming both more fashionable and more popular than before. Although this culture in Britain evolved progressively from the twelfth century, organised sport proper emerged in the second half of the eighteenth century,[1] when a new wave of popularity gave rise to a more urban and commercial culture of sport. The changes in sport at this time laid the groundwork for the spectacular expansion of sporting culture in the second half of the nineteenth century, variously referred to as the 'games revolution', the 'great sports craze' and the 'scramble for sport'.[2]

Organised sport was very much present at the birth and growth of European Australia. Just one year before Captain Phillip set foot on Sydney Cove in 1788, the famous Marylebone Cricket Club was established. Many important horse-racing traditions were of recent origin as well. Three of the classic horse-races began in the previous decade: the St Leger in 1776, the Oaks in 1779 and the Derby in 1780. The Jockey Club, based at Newmarket, had emerged from obscure origins to become the governing authority of the sport from 1751. A horse dealer, Richard Tattersall, founded a club in 1776 which took his name and became a focus for the betting fraternity and a London headquarters for the Jockey Club. Two great golf institutions, the Honourable Company of Edinburgh Golfers and the club of St Andrews later to become known as the Royal & Ancient, were founded in Scotland in 1744 and 1754 respectively. Another great sport of the eighteenth century, pugilism, had made considerable advances and was enjoying something of a boom in the 1780s.

Sport in the eighteenth century changed from the holding of an occasional and largely local event centred on informal conventions to more formal and regular competition based on codified rules and played over wider areas. The development of written rules reflected a greater standardisation. The Articles of Agreement set up by the Duke of Richmond were followed by the cricket laws of 1744, 1755, 1771, 1774 and 1788, by which time the core rules of modern cricket were in place. Although Jack Broughton's Rules of Boxing of 1743 were developed for his particular amphitheatre, they were soon recognised as the best rules of the time and helped to lay the foundations of boxing. The rise of the Jockey Club was of equal importance in racing as the club reduced regional variations in the rules and became the recognised authority on them.[3]

There were larger audiences for sport as the century progressed. Boxing crowds of 10 000 were recorded from the 1730s, and cricket drew comparable crowds at the London Artillery Ground in the next decade. The popular Hambledon Cricket Club attracted more than 20 000 spectators to some matches on Broad Halfpenny Down, Hampshire, in the 1770s and 1780s. Gate-entry charges were introduced partly to take advantage of the growing popularity of sport. Horse-racing, in particular, was becoming an industry which would employ thousands by the next century.

Sport became the vogue for the fashionable of Georgian England. The Prince of Wales, Frederick Louis, was a mad-keen cricketer in the 1730s and 1740s and became a leading patron of the game in Kent before he died at an early age from a cricket injury. Princes were also prominent in sports such as horse-racing, boxing and cock-fighting. Aristocrats spent huge sums of money in creating and supporting an attractive culture of sport. Ovals and racecourses were carved out of country estates. And sport became a central element in the calendar of élite social life, with balls and dinners the regular accompaniment of race days and fox-hunting meets.

During this century sport fired the imagination of aristocrats like Sir Horatio Mann, who created a cricket ground at his Bishopbourne estate in Kent and had a number of skilled players on his payroll. Although Mann was a member of five successive parliaments, representing Sandwich from 1774 to 1807, his obituary in the *Gentlemen's Magazine* stated that 'his life was rather dedicated to pleasure than business'. The Earl of Sandwich was a like-minded soul who did not let business interfere with sport. When summoned to attend a meeting of the Admiralty Board he replied: 'I'll be at your board when at leisure from cricket'.[4]

There is no better demonstration of the growing love of sport in this era than the rise of sporting art designed to adorn the great houses of the country. David Frith's fine collection of cricket illustrations of this era in *Pageant of Cricket* testifies to this and shows how greatly the game was romanticised: cricket matches were set in idyllic rural surroundings.

Such a link with nature, clearly an evocation of the pastoral tradition, as well as their own rural base, betrayed the backward-looking vision of men hankering after some rural utopia which was vanishing before their eyes as England became more industrial and urban. There was a world of difference between the romanticism of sporting artists—and landscape painters who often included a cricket match as an element of the rural scene[5]—and the realism of their famous contemporary William Hogarth. While the former conveyed the notion of bucolic bliss, Hogarth's art expressed the hustle of urban life, the vibrant turbulence of city mobs. Hogarth also depicted some of the darker passions associated with sport: the intensity and raucousness of the crowd at the cockpit and the many forms of plebeian cruelty to animals.

The gentry in the forefront of the sports revolution appeared to be hell-bent on swimming against the economic tide. In an era when the urban bourgeoisie became increasingly conscious of the value of saving and investment, many sporting patrons, such as Sir Horatio Mann, spent recklessly and conspicuously on sport. John O'Hara explains: 'For the [British] gentry, gambling, whether gaming or betting, was important as a show of wealth rather than an attempt to increase that wealth or to add force to their opinions.'[6] While they may have been out of step with the new economic realities, these Tory upholders of a vanishing order were, ironically, laying the foundations of a new culture of entertainment which was to find its home more in an urban environment. The codification of rules in cricket provides an interesting illustration of this. While the immediate purpose of the Articles of Agreement was to safeguard the bets of the gentry, the long-term effect was to lay the foundation of an organised mass sport.

There is an element of nostalgia in much sporting ideology. Nostalgia can be used to 'resist rapid changes' in society and to 'challenge new ways of thinking' promoted by élite groups. Nostalgia can also be constructed by dominant groups to promote 'a sense of cultural security' for society as a whole.[7] One form of nostalgia that has been overstated is the yearning for some past era when men were viewed as warriors. A related explanation for the popularity of sport is that it is a substitute for war. With the stress on the last explanation, there has been little recognition of sport as theatre and as an integral part of the emerging mass entertainment industry. One study of boxing has found close links between sport and theatre.[8] The literary and theatrical worlds were well represented at boxing matches staged in London amphitheatres in the first half of the eighteenth century and there was also the possibility that prize-fighting could have been incorporated into a broader program of entertainment.

While the impetus for organised sport came from the city, it drew on the edifice of popular rural-based sports such as cricket, football, horse-racing and many other long-established popular recreations. Rural sports, which were occasional and irregular and part of the festival cycle, provided many traditions for urban emulation and refinement. Some of the wealthiest and most influential patrons were based in

London, attached to the court or parliament. Newspapers, which helped build up a greater audience for sport, emanated from cities and towns. The city provided a larger audience for sport and it was here that many of the larger sporting venues were established. Some sports were more urban than others. Boxing and cricket were more London-based than horse-racing, which was 'spread very widely over the country'[9] and which had established its headquarters in a rural area, at Newmarket. Even so there were many important courses within convenient travelling distance from London, and the Newmarket Jockey Club also met at the Star and Garter Inn in London.

In these more urban surroundings, the growth of organised sport in the eighteenth century was part of a broader commercialisation of leisure which in turn was associated with what has been called a 'consumer revolution'.[10] Along with playing a variety of sports, more affluent Englishmen could enjoy greater travel to the emerging leisure towns, such as Tunbridge Wells, Bath and Scarborough; they could indulge in hobbies such as gardening, afford to keep pets, and purchase a greater range of children's toys. There was also a greater variety and volume of prints, magazines, books and newspapers which could be bought, borrowed or taken off the racks in a coffee house or tavern.

The majority, who could not afford to buy toys or pay for travel to leisure towns, could not pay to sit in a grandstand or enclosure. And money was not the only barrier. Those who could not read—and in the eighteenth century this was approximately 60 per cent of women and 40 per cent of men—were excluded from many facets of sporting culture. Newspaper reporting of sport increased as the century progressed to include advertisements of forthcoming events, scores and reports of particular matches, and stories and anecdotes about sporting stars. Leisure had traditionally been thought to be the preserve of the wealthy, who were often referred to as the 'leisure or leisured classes'.[11]

The introduction of gate-entry charges was an important development in the rise of a more commercialised sport in the eighteenth century. In 1700 sport took place on public land and was free of charge. Gate-entry charges emerged in horse-racing from the 1720s and in cricket and boxing by the 1740s. The extent of commercialism was limited, however, as charges were levied only at some events and affected only that section of the crowd which entered a stand or enclosure. Entry money was collected to defray the costs of running a particular event and often represented a minor portion of the organiser's income. Race organisers gained a larger amount of income from ground rentals—the leasing of booths for entertainment and refreshment—and from race subscriptions and donations from the local gentry.

Entrepreneurs later in the century were beginning to make a better fist out of profiting from sport. A shrewd businessman, Thomas Lord (1755–1832), was engaged to develop a cricket ground for his patrons, the founders of the Marylebone Cricket Club. Lord constructed a high wooden fence around the first Lord's ground at Dorset Square to restrict it from public view. When crowds continued to turn up to watch the gentlemen of the club play cricket, it didn't take Lord too long to recognise the commercial potential of this enclosed ground. He set about tapping this market by providing spectator facilities, including a grandstand, and by attracting all manner of entertainment. When there were not enough cricket matches, Lord hired out the ground for foot-races, pigeon-shooting, hopping matches and military exercises.

The commercialisation of sport could only proceed if the masses could afford to pay gate-money. Entrepreneurial activities like Lord's coincided with the beginnings of a rise in real income, which in effect meant the rise of a new leisured class. The growth of urban population was another factor making this commercialisation possible. The population of London jumped from approximately 200 000 in 1600 to 900 000 in 1800, and to 2.3 million by 1851. And with the advent of industrialisation city-dwellers were coming to represent a greater proportion of the English population than ever before. Whereas 80 per cent of people lived in the countryside in 1700, by 1801 33.8 per cent of the population were urban and by 1851 54 per cent lived in cities. But although this change was a dramatic one—as was the rise in the population of England and Wales from 5 million in 1700 to 18 million by 1851—the urban/rural dichotomy should not be exaggerated. There was less of a demarcation between city and country in the eighteenth century than at later times.[12]

The city provided a huge potential audience for spectator sport, as demonstrated by the massive crowds which turned up to public executions in London in the eighteenth century. An estimated 80 000 people—about one Londoner in ten—gathered at Moorefields to witness a hanging in 1767. The potential of this market was hardly recognised in the eighteenth century, though some 'spectators' were charged to sit in the stand to watch executions at Tyburn.

Cities also altered the spatial dimensions of sport. Whereas there was plenty of unalienated land for all manner of recreations in rural areas, available land in the cities was more restricted and, as time went on, more regulated by local authorities. Land in London was much more sought after; it was also more highly priced and more densely developed. City life therefore encouraged a more intensive and specialist development of land for sport.

All these changes appeared gradually in cities. At first all the cricket games and horse-racing events took place on unalienated land both in the city and the countryside. Most cricket games in London in the eighteenth century were played on commons such as Kennington and Ealing, parks such as Hyde Park, and greens such as Parsons Green. Playing facilities at these venues were temporary. The common at Kennington, for instance, was 'roped off for the accommodation of spectators'.[13]

Cricket's move to the ground of the Honourable Artillery Company (known as the Artillery Ground) represented a new tradition of the use of sporting space. This ground at Finsbury was probably enclosed (or partly enclosed), and gate-entry was charged at cricket games. The first game of cricket was in 1725 and cricket was played there regularly from the 1730s to the 1770s, during which time the ground became the leading cricket venue in London and the country.

The establishment of the first Lord's cricket ground in 1787 was an important development. Not wanting to continue to play on public land at Islington in north London, the gentlemen who formed the Marylebone Cricket Club leased a suitable tract of land for a private cricket ground. As the owners of this land the club was able to develop facilities specifically for cricket: Thomas Lord erected a hut where cricket equipment could be stored permanently and created a turf wicket.

Sport conducted on common land had to make do with temporary facilities which were dismantled at the end of each event. The enclosure of racecourses did not take place until later in the century when many racing clubs obtained a more permanent control over the land on which their sport took place. Some of the first golf links in Scotland were on open and uncultivated land bordering the sea which was shared with the general public who dried washing on gorse bushes, caught rabbits and practised archery.

Access to appropriate urban space accentuated the hierarchy of sports. The more privileged sports, such as cricket, backed by men of power and affluence, were able to secure choice privately owned or leased lots, where the specific needs of the sport could be catered for. Sports with less social and political clout gained access to public areas such as commons. When each event or carnival was completed the tents, booths and ropes were all packed away and removed until the next sporting occasion.

There were other sports, which came to be regarded as 'degraded' and 'disorderly' by the authorities, which were in the process of being marginalised in eighteenth-century London. These fringe sports, which included dog-fighting, badger-baiting and setting dogs on ducks, were pushed to the rough areas on the fringe of the city, such as Long Fields, behind Montague House.

Improvements in communications and transportation also contributed to the growth of organised sport. The beginnings of newspaper coverage of sport and the rise of a specialised sporting press helped to advertise particular events, to encourage the wider organisation of games, and to whet the appetites of urban populations for sport.

The newspaper was a comparatively recent innovation, first appearing in London in 1607. While there was some growth in newspapers during the seventeenth century, their size and circulation were small and their focus was narrow. Newspapers catered to wider tastes in the eighteenth century, including many matters of popular interest. There were regular press advertisements for racing events from the 1720s, along with notices of cricket matches and details of theatre and concert programs. The occasional notices of sporting events in the first half of the century were replaced by more regular and lengthy reporting of sport in the second half of the century. The activities of leading sportsmen were commented on at length. Vivid accounts of prize-fights, focusing on some of the emerging stars, became more common.

The development of a specialist sporting literature catered even more for those who wished to consume sport. One of the first to appear in 1733 was a fortnightly publication, *Historical List of all Horse-Matches Run*. Followers of the turf were able to purchase issues of the *Racing Calendar* from 1769. Costing 4d, it appeared fortnightly during the racing season. Newspapers devoted exclusively to sport date from the 1780s. *The World* appeared in the late 1780s, followed by the *Sporting Magazine*, which enjoyed a long career, in 1793. *Bell's Weekly Magazine* started in 1796.

Although the press grew in the eighteenth century, circulation figures were still minuscule. London daily newspapers had an average daily circulation of just 1500 in 1794, which was a tiny figure for a city approaching a population of one million. While illiteracy excluded half the population from reading papers, cost was an even more critical factor: a succession of Stamp Acts from 1712 had substantially increased the price of newspapers.

Travel in the seventeenth century was slow, uncomfortable and expensive. Limited transport facilities restricted the development of sport before 1700 to competition between one village and another or to contests within a region or a county. Horses competed in carnivals within their locality as they had to be walked to race-meetings. With a limited number of thoroughbreds available in a particular locality, race-meetings often consisted of a pot-pourri of events which could include races for thoroughbreds, half-breeds and hunters along with events for ponies, donkeys and even cows.

Sufficient improvements occurred in transport in the eighteenth century to make travel more feasible for the élite. From the 1740s rural cricket XIs made their way to London to play on the Artillery Ground. The Duke of Richmond brought his well-credentialled team from Slindon Parish, Sussex, to London in the 1740s. The Hambledon Cricket Club were regular visitors to the city later in the century and London teams travelled to Broad Halfpenny Downs. From the 1740s games were also played between teams representing counties.

From the 1740s teams were put in the field as 'all England'. Although none of the national or even the county teams were truly representative and were selected by an established governing body—they were put together by individual patrons—they often consisted of men from a variety of localities, as many as six counties.

Even more than the team, the club is the core unit of sport. Belonging to a particular team or joining a club either as a player or supporter is a point of primary allegiance for many sports followers. While some people develop a love for a particular sport or even sport in general, the majority of sports enthusiasts are more passionate about a particular team or club. The more complex and stratified societies of cities encouraged the creation of new social groupings, giving rise to social and sporting coteries and clubs. Within the city it became possible to share space with 'people of like minds, like incomes and from a similar social band'.[14]

Clubs were an early feature of organised sport. One of the first newspaper references to cricket is to a 1718 game between eleven London and eleven Kentish gamesters, the latter calling themselves the Punch Club Society. Sport for the Kent team was clearly an extension of a drinking group, an XI which must have enjoyed each other's company on and off the field. The existence of individual teams and clubs which competed against each other led to the emergence of another type of club, a governing authority or association, to organise competition between teams and to arbitrate on the rules from one venue to another.

Both types of club emerged in the eighteenth century, when there were about 1000 cricket clubs in England and Wales.[15] Most of these clubs were based on localities, the most famous being the Hambledon Cricket Club, which existed from 1756 to 1791. The Hambledon Club included aristocrats, yeoman farmers, respectable tradesmen and plebeian players and amounted to an acceptable blend of 'aristocratic patronage and local enthusiasm'. A tradition of success—the club won twenty-nine out of fifty-one matches against England from 1771 to 1781—was a potent factor in the club's cohesiveness. The deeds of the club were celebrated far and wide and more than half the county flocked to see their matches. The ethos of the club inspired its historian John Nyren later to publish one of the first classics of cricket, expressing 'authentic peasant portraits in their [own] language'.[16]

The club success was also built on an administrative structure which provided a prototype for other clubs. Hambledon had a central administrator, a president, and other officers to collect arrears. Members had to pay an annual subscription of three guineas. Playing members had to appear on practice days, which was when teams were selected, or risk a fine of 3d. The club even undertook to defray travel expenses of those who lived outside the immediate vicinity. The Bat and Ball Inn, run by the club president Richard Nyren, was the focal point for post-match dinners, musical evenings and an annual dinner.

The 'London Club', which dated from the 1730s, was a coterie of influential aristocrats headed by the Prince of Wales and including Lords Strathavon, Montford and Waldegrave. It was a forerunner of the Marylebone Cricket Club as members not only organised their own matches at the Artillery Ground but established the group as the administrative hub of the game. It was this club which produced the 1744 rules, the first rules for the game in general rather than for a particular match, and which was responsible for setting up many important fixtures at the Artillery Ground in the 1740s.

It was inevitable that London should become the focal point of cricket and many other sports. With the court and parliament located there, London had the greatest collection of influential patrons. The crowds which turned up at the Artillery Ground indicated the large potential audience for sport in the expanding metropolis. The founders of the Marylebone Cricket Club, like those of the London Club, were men of superior social status who dined at the Star and Garter Inn, Pall Mall.

These two clubs soon became the the supreme arbiters and organisers in their respective sports. The Jockey Club was issuing rules and hearing disputes a few years after its rise to prominence. The men who ran both clubs willingly assumed the mantle of authority; other, lesser, clubs acceded to their authority. The pattern of a dominant club was repeated in other sports: the Royal & Ancient became the supreme authority in golf, as did the Cumberland Society in sailing and the Portland Club in cards. Given the great variety of local rules in the various sports of the mid-eighteenth century, there was clearly a need for some group to create more national rules and standards. The greater amount of competition in the eighteenth century was another incentive for a centralised authority to emerge. Individual sports, such as horse-racing, looked for a focal point even before 1750: Newmarket was then to be seen as the headquarters of racing.

Competition in sports such as horse-racing was irregular and occasional in 1700. Because of a lack of thoroughbred horses in many localities, public interest was sustained by the practice of running a succession of heats before a winner was determined. By the end of the century horse-racing events were more regular and specialised. The practice of running heats had been abandoned by the 1780s and, there were more particular events such as a race for 3-year-olds at Newmarket in the 1750s and one for 2-year-olds in the 1770s. Handicap and weight-for-age races were introduced by the 1790s. By 1787 there were 61 meetings and 167 race days in England. *The Racing Calendar*, newspapers and stud books all provided information about wider competition along with details of standards and records.

Other sports, such as cricket and boxing, developed more slowly.[17] The number of quality matches in cricket, attracting large crowds and gates, varied from season to season. The fluctuation in the number of cricket matches was partly related to whether there was a dominant club in existence. Cricket was strongest in the heyday of the London Club, 1735–50 and the golden era of the Hambledon Club in the 1770s and 1780s. Even after the Marylebone club was established, there were some periods of relative stagnation in cricket, such as between 1790 and 1815.

Although cricket waxed and waned, there was clearly a continuing growth in the number of clubs and the forms of competition throughout the century. There were 30 reported cricket matches in the 1730s, 150 in the 1740s and 230 in the 1750s, but this may have reflected an increase in the press reporting of cricket.[18] There was also a broader range of clubs formed: clubs representing a village, a county, several counties, and even teams touted as 'all England'.

Increased competition was not limited to the major sports of the eighteenth century. There was a rapid growth in various forms of boat-racing from about 1780. Watermen—there were some 40 000 licensed watermen in Chelsea and Windsor in 1700—who had raced informally on the Thames for centuries competed for Doggett's Coat and Badge from 1715, an annual prize donated by an Irish comedian. This contest for six young watermen just out of apprenticeship is one of the oldest events with a continuing history in British sport. The first recorded regatta for watermen was organised on the Thames in 1775 and the sport also introduced a championship. A title bout was arranged when a challenger could get enough financial backing to make a contest attractive for the title-holder.[19]

School and university competition, along with many forms of amateur sport, did not emerge until the early nineteenth century. During the eighteenth and preceding centuries educational authorities had shown limited interest in sport, tolerating it as an extra-curricular activity. The students at Eton, who were left to pursue their own sporting inclinations, developed their own sports. The Eton ram hunt was a barbarous ceremonial, which took place from late Stuart times until 1747, in which a ram was chased around the local town or a schoolyard and then beaten to death, after which the club members were 'blooded'. Pupils at a number of schools were allowed to organise cock-fights on Shrove Tuesday afternoon. The Eton wall game, which evolved out of folk football, was played alongside a wall 11 feet (3.4 m) high and 118 yards (108 m) long, which had been built (though not for the game) in 1717. The first recorded game was in 1766. Another game developed at Eton in the nineteenth century, a handball game known as Eton 'fives', also made use of existing buildings, in that it was played alongside three adjacent walls outside the school chapel. Attitudes towards sport in educational institutions altered as sport became more organised, regulated and respectable.

Ideology is a central element of organised sport and serves many purposes. It provides a moral basis justifying some sports while undermining the character of others. It defines the social purpose of a particular sport, demarcating sport as territory occupied by a specific class or gender and creating the broader culture in which a sport functioned. With the expansion of the media in the eighteenth century sporting ideology became more developed. Fox-hunting, for instance, developed an elaborate and quite self-conscious justification. It was claimed that the sport was beneficial in that it reduced the fox population, brought business to local communities and provided a colourful spectacle for the local population. In broader terms fox-hunters saw themselves as preserving enduring rural traditions and promoting healthy outdoor recreation and good horsemanship.[20]

With the development of a more elaborate and sophisticated ideology, sport became more male-dominated in the nineteenth century than before, though one writer believes that British sport had always been a male preserve 'with its own language, its initiation rites, and models of true masculinity, its clubbable jokey cosiness. Building male friendships and sustaining large and small communities of men have been the prime purpose of sport. Women have been banished to the sidelines both literally and metaphorically.'[21] The ideal of manliness was a much-touted nineteenth-century concept which developed many wider meanings and associations.

Sport has always been associated more with male than with female culture. Medieval sports such as archery and jousting, which were linked with military endeavour, were largely male. Women also took little part in the more violent sports such as folk football. In the eighteenth century and before, however, many sports were far less gender-specific than they later became. Women participated, though never as much as men, in a number of pre-nineteenth-century sports including cricket, stool ball, trap ball, golf, foot-races, pugilism, rowing, sword-fighting, swimming and dancing.

Female monarchs had set the lead for aristocratic women in that they were prominent in sport as patrons, participants and spectators. Elizabeth I, Anne and Mary Queen of Scots were noted hunters. Anne Boleyn was an archer and Mary Queen of Scots was also fond of playing golf. Queen Anne, a great lover of horses, played some part in the laying out of the Ascot course. Other women followed the royal example: the Marchioness of Salisbury won a national reputation as a daring rider and was a master of the Hertfordshire foxhounds from 1775 to 1819.

At the popular level there was a sizeable female involvement in many sports. There were almost as many smock races for women, where women ran in long dresses, as there were running contests for men. From the 1740s to the 1770s there were many inter-village cricket games, particularly in the counties of Surrey and Sussex. With an increasing number of teams, clubs and competitions, the rise of more organised cricket for women paralleled that of the men's game, though on a smaller scale.[22]

Women's games were also played in a similar spirit to the male version. The scene at women's matches of this time was 'robust, colourful, boisterous, sometimes rowdy and certainly often inelegant, with spectators of both sexes drinking, shouting, swearing and gambling'.[23] There are many hints that women cricketers achieved more acceptance in this century than later. The leading matches were advertised in the press, gate-entry was charged and sizeable crowds watched. Women's matches were scheduled on the leading arena of the country, the Artillery Ground. Some of the leading patrons of the men's game, such as the 3rd Earl of Dorset, were sympathetic to women playing cricket.

Besides creating greater social stratification, the city sharpened gender differences. Expanding communications media helped redefine gender roles for a more complex urban society. This involved new definitions of male and female and also new attitudes towards homosexuality, which became seen as the antithesis of 'manly' behaviour.[24]

Behind the emerging facade of organised sport stood the long-established edifice of popular rural-based sport. Although there were links between organised and popular sport, in general they were traditions that ran parallel. Unlike organised sport, popular sports were irregular and occasional and usually part of annual wakes which took place in the slack periods in the rural work season: most occurred in late spring and early summer, after the summer crop was sown, or late summer and early autumn, after the harvest was brought in. While village feast days featured in many established sports, there was a measure of improvisation and spontaneity in the popular recreations. Sports such as boxing and wrestling existed side by side with recreations such as chasing the greased pig or grinning through a collar. Sports were just one part of an extended celebration lasting days and even weeks when there was good eating, abundant drinking, music and dancing. There was little commercialisation in locally organised popular sports, which involved whole communities.

Folk football, which was played in England from the twelfth century if not before, provides a good illustration of popular sport. A description of a match, which had been played from 'time immemorial' between two neighbouring parishes in Derby on Shrove Tuesday, conveyed the spirit of play. As there was no restriction on the number of participants, hundreds and even more than a thousand would line up on each side to

> join in the rough mêlée after the ball was thrown up in the market-place, and from there surged at random through the streets, down alleyways, across gardens, in and out of the River Derwent, with the object of reaching the goals situated at the opposite ends of the town. Victory was seldom achieved before six or more hours of rough horseplay and brawling, leaving a trail of physical injuries, petty vandalism, assaults and much heavy drinking.[25]

In some parts of the country this impromptu and ill-defined game was beginning to acquire some degree of organisation. Matches were advertised in the press, with each side limited to a specific number, from eight to thirty. Some forms of football developed particular rules restricting players to kicking the ball or permitting them to pick up the ball and run. Strutt, in 1801, referred to football games played on a defined field with the goals 80 to 100 yards apart.[26]

Violence was part of folk football as it was with many other popular sports. Without a referee to control play and to define acceptable behaviour, participants were free to kick shins, break bones, crack heads and even slaughter their opponents. Under the guise of football long-running scores were settled between one community and another. When the village of Chesterton took on the students of Cambridge the former were clearly spoiling for a fight as they hid sticks in a convenient church porch before the start of the match. Soon after the game began the villagers picked a fight with the students, brought out their sticks and beat their opponents.

The many forms of animal cruelty associated with sport have been well documented.[27] There were many elaborate forms of teasing animals: bull-running was a free-for-all bullfight without weapons and in which a whole community employed various methods of 'sporting' at the bull's expense before it was slaughtered in the evening. There were other sports, when one animal was set upon another, such as cock-fighting and bull, bear and badger-baiting. Throwing-at-cocks was yet another variation in which individuals threw objects at a cock tied to a stake, attempting to knock it to the ground.

There were many reasons why there was so much cruelty in popular sport involving humans and animals. Life was short, insecure and violent. The sight of the condemned on gibbets was a familiar one. There were regular and fearful outbreaks of epidemics. Sport, too, was largely rural-based and there was an attitude of indifference to the fate of wild animals and of domestic animals about to be slaughtered for human consumption.

Most popular sports took place on a village green, churchyard or market-place or adjacent to an alehouse or inn. The publican was one of the first to provide sporting facilities for local communities. It became a common practice in the seventeenth century for tippling houses to provide cards, card-tables and gaming equipment for customers. By the eighteenth century publicans had an expanded range of sporting equipment on hand for customer use: footballs, ninepins, quoits, skittles and darts. Sporting facilities were developed in many alehouse yards or in close vicinity to a public house: a Milton (Kent) alehouse had a (covered) ninepin alley in the yard by the stables with a 'set of nine pins and a frame and a ball'.[28]

There was an even greater development of sporting facilities at the more respectable inns patronised by the local gentry and located more in provincial towns and cities. Cockpits, which required a greater capital outlay than the alleys at alehouses, were built at a number of urban inns. A pit consisted of a small amphitheatre, with a raised platform in the centre, which in turn was surrounded by tiered benches for gamblers.

Many popular sports were changing in the late eighteenth century. There was a diminished gentry presence as many aristocrats were drawn towards the more sophisticated city culture. The enclosure movement in the countryside and industrial growth in cities restricted the amount of space available for sport. Even more important were changes in the time and work discipline of the emerging labour force. Gone for many factory workers were the task-oriented bouts of hard labour followed by extended periods of slack time and an ample number of holidays when multi-purpose festivals could last for days and even weeks. Industrial workers were soon to be tied to fixed daily labour from Monday to Saturday. Some of the old habits carried into the city, such as the St Monday holiday, when many workers enjoyed an extra unscheduled day of leisure, a Sunday–Monday weekend. Monday was a popular day for sport as it was the closest day to the last wage paid on a Saturday.[29]

Organised sport, as we now know it, became more prominent and recognisable in the eighteenth century. Existing forms of sporting culture were transformed into mass entertainment which became fashionable and popular. New sports emerged and existing ones were enhanced and embellished. With the expansion of gate-money sport, greater codification and media coverage, extended ideology and improved facilities, sport became a more central and recognisable part of British culture than before.

European colonisation of Australia coincided with this expansion. Sport, as much as religion or any other form of tradition and culture, was highly regarded by those who colonised Australia. Though it occupied no part of the initial purpose of British settlement, establishing a sporting culture in Australia came to be viewed as an important means of maintaining British culture in the Antipodes. Sport was a potent force present in the formative stages of European Australia.

2

AN UNLIKELY PARADISE

Australia was an unlikely future sporting paradise when Europeans first settled there with the objective of establishing a penal colony.[1] Survival in an alien and seemingly hostile environment was a primary concern. Recreation was far from the minds of those who arrived on the First Fleet. Very few bats, clubs, racquets, balls and racehorses were brought to Australia in the first decades of European settlement. It may be that the dearth of sporting opportunities in the first penal settlements created a greater appetite for sport and leisure. David Collins recorded in 1794 that a number 'made a daily practice of gaming' and that some of the convicts participated in it 'to the fullest extent'.[2] Ex-convict George Barrington, who became Principal Superintendent of Convicts at Parramatta, believed in c.1794 that convicts were gambling excessively, with some continuing after losing their 'provisions, money, and spare cloathing' to part with 'the very clothes from their backs'.[3]

The informal sport which existed in the first penal settlements was an important part of survival. Catching fish and shooting game added to the scarce resources of the colony in the struggle for physical survival. The role of sport in mental survival was perhaps even more important. Informal races between one longboat and another reduced the tedium of a drab and harsh existence. While gambling was often an end in itself, much of colonial betting was linked with sport. Gambling on a horse or boat-race, a game of cards, or a boxing or wrestling bout, or whatever diversion struck the fancy of an assembled crowd, also served the same purpose.

The origin of sport in Australia raises a number of questions. Did the original inhabitants have a 'sporting culture' before white settlement? Was Australia before the 1850s more of a sporting backwater than the sporting paradise it became afterwards with the increased wealth and population that followed the discovery of gold? Why, and in what form,

did a sporting culture appear? Were sporting developments in this era
of any significance for the later development of sport?

ABORIGINAL TRADITIONS OF SPORT

The original inhabitants of Australia, the Aborigines, had their own
traditions of sport. There were many forms of physical contests when
bands met: wrestling, spear-throwing contests, sham fights, primitive
forms of football involving possum-skin balls, spinning discs and stick
games. A recently published history of South Gippsland has the following charming description of a ball game of the original Kurnai people

> in which the leathery scrotum of a kangaroo was stuffed with grass, greased
> and used as a handball. Two teams were formed and the game was played
> by keeping the ball from the other side by throwing it from one team member
> to another. With shouts of laughter and the dingoes rushing in and out, the
> game sometimes went on for hours. The dingoes were treated very fondly,
> with the children caressing and playing with them a good deal.[4]

There were also forms of sport associated with tracking and hunting
which were part of the Aboriginal economy. Most coastal Aborigines,
both men and women, were adept at swimming, fishing and canoeing.

Aboriginal 'sport', unlike imported British sport, did not exist as a
separate compartment of life. Sport was inseparable from ritual and
daily life, whether it was part of hunting and gathering or during the
long periods of 'leisure' when one Aboriginal band met another and
took part in many games, pastimes and ceremonies. Hunting, which
was sometimes done in a leisurely fashion and had some elements of
play, was exclusively neither work nor leisure. Although there was
plenty of physical activity and contests in Aboriginal society, the notion
of organised sport which had developed in Britain did not exist.

The sport imported from Britain was based on notions of a division
between work and leisure quite alien to Aboriginal culture. It was in the
process of establishing itself as a separate compartment of life—apart
from work and as relaxation from work—with its own rules, times,
venues and culture. Michael Salter, one of the few to analyse Aboriginal
sport and games at some length, has concluded that Aboriginal games
were played primarily for enjoyment—though games may also have
been the means of teaching skills—and whole communities were
encouraged to participate. There was also little competition and relatively few rules.[5]

The arrival of Europeans proved disastrous to Aboriginal communities, their culture and economy. Imported disease was the initial killer,
but Europeans decimated their culture in one way and another: directly
through cultural genocide and more indirectly through seizing their land
and denigrating their culture. Europeans drew no inspiration from
Aboriginal culture.

While Aborigines later played a large role in some of the imported sports, particularly athletics, football and boxing, they did so primarily on European terms—there were few other avenues of cultural activity in white Australia (see ch. 8). There appears, for all the above reasons, no established continuity between sport in Aboriginal society and that in European, though it has been argued recently that Australian football had Aboriginal origins, a claim that has yet to be accepted.[6] Boomerang-throwing, which has emerged as a sport in recent times—ironically performed rather more by non-Aborigines—is one Aboriginal cultural contribution to contemporary sport. Organised sport as we know it, however, was an entirely imported phenomenon.

It is also very difficult to generalise about the nature of sport and play in Aboriginal culture before 1788 because of the diversity of that culture, which has been pointed out in a study of sport and play among the Pitjantjatjara.[7] There is also the problem that anthropological descriptions of Aboriginal sports and pastimes were produced by Europeans long after 1788. Research on Aboriginal wrestling has suggested that there may have been some elements of competition in Aboriginal sport in that wrestling, which involved young males, was organised both within and between bands. However, whether this was a feature of Aboriginal 'sport' before 1788 has yet to be established, since most of the sources are drawn from the nineteenth century.[8] As for reports of the existence of stick or ball games that resemble imported games, it is not clear whether these sports pre-date 1788 or whether they represent an Aboriginal modification of European games.

CONVICTS

Convicts made up the bulk of the population at penal settlements at Sydney (1788), Hobart (1803) and at Moreton Bay, later Brisbane (1824). From 1788 to 1820, 28 410 persons were transported, compared with a mere trickle of about 4500 free settlers. The convicts were of Anglo-Celtic origin, with Ireland contributing about a third of the immigrants. Most of the convicts were male: by 1820 there were more than three males to every female. Although this imbalance was reduced after the 1820s, males outnumbered females throughout the nineteenth century.

Convicts were familiar with sporting traditions. Some convicts had previously mingled in crowds which attended cricket matches, watched boxing bouts and attended horse-racing meetings in Britain and Ireland. The crime of pickpocket George Barrington, transported in 1791, was stealing a gold watch and chain on the Enfield racecourse. Gambling was the reason another convict, by the name of McKoy, was transported. Convicts were more likely to be found on the rougher edges of organised sport, involving themselves in the more informal recreations around the public house or in clandestine meeting-places away from the prying eyes of the authorities. Gambling on boxing matches, cock-fights or almost any sporting event became one of the earlier diversions for convicts.

It used to be thought that life for convicts was unrelievedly harsh and cruel, but recently some historians have suggested that working conditions for convicts were not as severe as formerly believed. They have argued that convict workers were not worse off than other early industrial workers and generally lived a better life.[9] There has been limited study as yet of convict leisure time though some work on Tasmanian convicts in the 1840s suggests that while 'non-working hours of Vandemonian penal society' did not produce a rich culture it did 'allow the convicts to transcend the system for short periods of time'.[10]

The informal sports which flourished initially among the convict population were the rougher and more violent ones, such as cock-fighting, bare-knuckle boxing and wrestling. These were also the recreations which required least resources. Blood sports were some of the first to be reported at any length in the semi-official *Sydney Gazette*—though this may have partly reflected the concern of the authorities with recreations associated with disorder. There was one such report of a cock-fight in the Brickfields in the *Gazette* of 11 August 1805 between 'Bone-a-part', 'a powerful party coloured pile', and 'Sir Sydney', 'a ginger of true English breed', which took place in front of a 'numerous concourse of persons'. The bout was scarcely over when a party of military and police broke up the gathering and arrested some of the participants.

The first reference to any sport in the *Sydney Gazette* was a 'desperate conflict' between a butcher and a blacksmith. Pugilism was another fringe sport which was only partly tolerated by authorities, and bouts were frequently broken up by the magistrates. This sport, while legal, was frowned on because of its perceived link with disorderly behaviour.

Not all sport was violent. Fishing was a popular recreation and David Bevan was auctioning rods by 1807. Boat-races for a stake of £50 were reported by 1810. Swimming and bathing were popular from the very first days of settlement and an enclosure on Sydney Harbour was constructed by the Marines as early as 1788; the first enclosure was at Darling Harbour at the bottom of Erskine Street. Bathing appears to have been a popular recreation as some swam 'all hours of the day' outside the enclosures at places such as the Government Wharf and the Dockyard. This practice led to an 1810 proclamation of Governor Macquarie warning that those who indulged in this 'very indecent and improper custom' of nude bathing would be prosecuted.[11]

MILITARY OFFICERS AND COLONIAL LEADERS

Convicts were supervised by the military. For the officers, who came from the ranks of the landed gentry, sport was an integral part of life and a means of defining their social status. Lieut. George Johnston— reputedly the first European to land at Port Jackson in 1788—was a prominent breeder of horses. Another influential citizen, Captain Piper, who arrived in Sydney in 1792 and became harbour master and collector of customs, also bred racehorses and promoted horse-racing. Tasmania's first chaplain, Rev. Robert Knopwood, had been part of 'the shooting and hunting set of the young Viscount Clermont' in his youth and had lost none of his love for sport in the colonies. He attended the track frequently and his diaries establish his great love of horse-racing.[12] Dr Robert Wardell (1793–1834), who became a leading barrister and editor after arriving in Sydney in 1824, attempted to emulate the life of an English country gentleman. His 2000-acre estate at Marrickville was fenced and included a gatehouse and gatekeeper. Wardell stocked his property with deer for the enjoyment of his hunting parties.

The military had the resources and interest to promote sport. The army in late eighteenth-century Britain was drawn from two main groups: officers from the landed gentry and the ranks from the working class. Sport for the officers was an expression of class status, part of being a gentleman. It was also, along with drilling and exercising, one of the few activities for regiments posted to far-flung settlements. Life for the British troops in places such as Australia and India was 'boring, brutish and hot', for there was a limit to the amount of training and military manoeuvres that could be undertaken.[13] Sport enhanced physical fitness, was a crucial boost to morale and provided an outlet for physical needs. It was, as one former India hand put it, the 'one great weapon against boredom'; the answer was 'sport, sport, sport'.[14] Sport between units, battalions and regiments also did much to cement army solidarities. Recognising its value, the army encouraged sport in many ways. Officers and ranks were given time off to play; equipment was provided, and the resources of the army were used to create suitable playing fields and racecourses.

Many regiments developed strong traditions of sport. The first bat-talion of the 73rd Regiment, which arrived in New South Wales in 1809, had supported horse-racing in India. This regiment was the moving force behind the Hyde Park racing carnival of 1810. The three-day carnival was run by the officers who laid out the racecourse on Hyde Park. Meetings to appoint stewards, to draft the rules of the course and to organise the event were held in the officers' mess. Most of the two dozen horses which raced in the carnival belonged to the officers.

The carnival was patronised by Governor Macquarie, who attended each of the race days. Official support was a reaction to the enthusiasm of the officers of the 73rd Regiment to stage a major sporting event. It was also an effort by the Governor to bring 'some order into colonial recreation by confining it to specified [annual] periods'.[15] His aim, in addition, was to civilise sport and society by supporting a properly conducted racing carnival which he hoped would replace the spontaneous, haphazard and often disorderly sport—a safety valve for a leisure-starved society.

During the first two decades of settlement many officers who remained in New South Wales had great opportunities to acquire wealth through land grants, convict labour and the sale of rum. They formed a wealthy caste and looked to sport as one way of enhancing their gentlemanly status. Several years before the Hyde Park races they had established a private club whose facilities included a billiard table.

The 73rd Regiment organised carnivals in 1811, 1812 and 1813. A Racing Kalendar was published in 1811 and a carefully drafted set of rules was published the following year. Unfortunately for Sydney horse-racing, the regiment was transferred to Ceylon after 1813 and the annual carnival lapsed until it was resumed, on a modified scale, in 1819.

The military continued to play an important role in the establishment of organised traditions and in bolstering some of the first civilian sporting initiatives. A regiment stationed in Adelaide augmented numbers at the Adelaide Hunt.[16] The military helped cricket to develop in many ways. Although the first cricket club in Sydney was a civilian one, the Australian Cricket Club, military teams played an important part in the beginnings of club cricket in Sydney, Hobart and Melbourne. The first fully recorded match was between the 17th and 39th Regiments on 7 May 1832 at Hyde Park. The match generated considerable interest among civilian cricketers and a subsequent match was organised between the 'Military' and 'Civilians'.[17]

Eventually the regiments stationed at Victoria Barracks combined to form a more permanent club, the Garrison Club, when a ground was opened at that location in February 1854. The establishment of a permanent ground, the Garrison Cricket Ground, dedicated exclusively to sport, was the greatest legacy of the military to Sydney sport. The ground behind Victoria Barracks later became the site of the Sydney Cricket Ground.

Military and naval personnel also contributed to the establishment of many other sports. The 'First Australian Regatta' was organised on 28 April 1827 by Captains Rous and Sterling of HMS *Rainbow* and HMS *Success*. Rous, who had arrived in Sydney the previous February, won the first race, a rowing event. Of the nine who started in the second event, sailing, four were naval personnel.[18]

Unmarried and 'fancy-free' officers and ranks undoubtedly contributed to a bachelor sporting subculture. They participated in all manner of sport, both the rough and the respectable. The *Australian* of 25 July 1827 referred to the 'naval and military bucks who fomented and kept the sport [of cock-fighting] alive [and who] enjoyed the game wonderfully'. The *Monitor* of 1 December 1830 reported that a 'main of cocks was fought at the Soldiers' Bathing House, Cockle Bay, backed by two officers, for fifty pounds a side'.

The military also played an important part in the rise of rugby in Sydney in the 1860s.[19] The Civil and Military Club was one of the earlier clubs in Sydney. When there were comparatively few teams organised there in the late 1860s games against the personnel of visiting naval ships provided much-needed competition.

The proposal to raise colonial militias in the 1860s, which stimulated volunteer rifle corps, cavalry regiments and martial display, had an impact on sport because this movement was a counter-attraction which tapped into the same leisure market. Sport and the volunteer corps overlapped: they both involved discipline, team-work and display, and often shared common venues such as Moore Park and the Domain. Martial fashion even influenced the character of sporting costume. The Geelong Football Club, for instance, was decked out in 1862 in a red, white and blue cap and a flannel shirt of solferino (bright crimson), a colour derived from a battle in North Italy in 1859.[20] British regiments were influential in Australian sport until their departure in 1870 when colonial defences were handed over to local troops. Matches between the red-coats and civilian teams in Melbourne in the 1860s featured 'rough and tumble play' with the soldiers kicking the shins of their opponents with their heavy boots. Recent migrants probably barracked for the soldiers while the Australian-born supported the local team.[21]

FREE SETTLERS

The arrival of greater numbers of free settlers from the 1820s created an environment in which the institutions of organised sport emerged in a more sustained manner. Convict settlements at Sydney and Hobart began to be transformed into bustling towns from the 1820s. The availability of cheap land and the growth of export industries, notably wool, created prosperity for larger landowners and merchants who exported raw materials back to Britain. Brisbane, which was not opened to free settlement until 1841, grew more slowly.

In the 1840s there was considerable population growth in the free settlements of Port Phillip (which became Victoria in 1851) and South Australia, though the population of Western Australia remained small until the 1890s. The white Australian population jumped from 36 968 in 1821[22] to 437 665 by 1851. By the middle of the century most Australian societies were 'free'.

Settled entirely by British and Irish stock, the towns of Australia became 'suburbs' of Britain linked by sailing ships and later by steam. Australia established productive export industries and in return imported British manufactured goods and culture. As a more complex and prosperous society emerged, Australia imported British urban ideals, including the culture of organised sport, along with equipment, practices, codes, constitutions and ideals.

The coming of free settlers provided an environment in which organised sport could emerge. There were from the 1820s a greater number of men, and a few women, of wealth and status—they made money from land, pastoral industries and trade within Australia or came from well-established British families—who had the finance and political clout to establish sporting institutions. Sir John Jamieson (1776–1844) in New South Wales and Frederick Armand Powlett (1811–65) in Victoria were both important in establishing sporting institutions.

Jamieson, the son of Thomas Jamieson who arrived on the First Fleet as surgeon's mate, became the complete colonial gentleman whose family made its fortune in New South Wales. After joining the navy and serving in many parts of the world, John Jamieson returned to Sydney and by the 1820s had become one of the most wealthy and influential landowners in the colony. Jamieson 'lived like a genial and prosperous English squire', took a keen interest in the turf and was an importer of bloodstock.[23]

Powlett, who arrived in Port Phillip in 1838, was born in England, the son of a chaplain to the Prince Regent and a descendant of the last Duke of Bolton. He moved in the right circles from the time of his arrival at Port Phillip. He was a confidant of Lieut.-Governor La Trobe and agent for his property. He was initially a police magistrate, then commissioner for the Westernport district, and later became the first gold commissioner for the colony. Powlett was a keen sportsman who was a 'renowned cricketer, race-horse owner and huntsman'.[24] As with their English forebears, sport provided men like Jamieson and Powlett with a means of demonstrating their gentlemanly status.

'PUB'-BASED SPORT

While regiments came and went, the public house became the focal point for all manner of sports. Daryl Adair has suggested the importance of the public house to colonial South Australia. When Adelaide was a tiny frontier settlement in the late 1830s public houses were the first buildings of substance erected, catering to the basic needs of new arrivals for food, drink and accommodation. The fourteen public houses in 1837 had expanded to sixty-three in 1840 and serviced a population of 6657: there was one public house to 105 adults.

With the dearth of public buildings and the limited urban infra-structure, public houses performed very wide roles. Besides providing food and drink for their immediate society they dealt with the needs of travellers, a lamp at the entrance representing one of the few sources of light in dark streets. A public house was a convenient transport stop. A variety of political events took place in public houses: district councils were founded there, council offices established, union meetings and elections held. All manner of meetings took place there: business groups and voluntary associations and celebratory dinners. Reading rooms and theatres were established in some public houses.

The first drinking establishments were modest and primitive. Grog shops, licensed to sell porter, appeared in Sydney and Parramatta as early as 1792, and the Rocks early became a focal point for taverns. Taverns offered food, drink and entertainment, mainly to itinerant patrons, and were far less imposing buildings than the more respectable hotels and inns.

Some of the publicans who built hotels in Sydney and Hobart in the 1820s and 1830s, and in Adelaide and Melbourne in the late 1830s and 1840s, were innovative and enterprising. To attract the largest possible clientele they promoted a wide variety of popular entertainment. The citizens of Adelaide were offered a great deal of entertainment: a small zoo, a singing room and semi-weekly musical evenings, live theatre, Aboriginal spear-throwing contests, card-playing, casino games and backgammon.

It was all manner of sport which entertained the largely male audience which frequented the public house. Many sports took place in or near a public house: cricket, foot-races, billiards, bowling, quoits, skittles, pigeon-shooting, boxing and wrestling. Trotting races either took place on the road in front of a public house or began at one and finished at another. One enterprising Adelaide publican announced that a Cornish Wrestling Championship, beginning on Easter Monday 1851, would last three days and nights.[25] The hotel organised seating, alongside the hotel building, for 2000 spectators.

The strong link between the public house and sport further strengthened the nexus already established between sport and male culture. While women attended entertainment at more respectable inns and while there were (in Adelaide) a few establishments which advert-ised themselves as 'family hotels', most were bastions of male culture. Women who frequented most houses were there to work as hostesses, barmaids and prostitutes.

The public house provided a congenial location for sport until the mid-nineteenth century, since sport was drink-based and linked with gambling. The first Sydney cricket clubs were all attached to public houses, and meetings and club dinners were held there. The publican played an important role in organising a cricket team, often helping to put up the stake-money for a match. George Buckingham, of the Odd

Fellows' Arms, advertised in the *Commercial Journal* of 17 January 1838 that he had secured a stock of bats, balls and wickets 'which he intends letting by the hour'.

Sydney had a long and impressive list of innkeeper-cricketers who were both organisers and players.[26] Some of the more prominent administrators of this era—Edward Flood, Richard Driver Senior and William Tunks—were publicans. By the 1840s some publicans were organising, and investing, in sport on a substantial scale. Thomas Shaw, publican of the Woolpack Inn, Petersham, was a keen sports promoter who established one of the first bowling greens in the country in 1845. The Petersham Racecourse was established on land, which he probably leased, behind his inn. During the 1840s the Petersham course was second only to Homebush as the premier course in Sydney; the annual post-Christmas carnival there, which lasted for two or three days, attracted crowds as large as 10 000.

Many publicans were involved in the organisation of the Petersham carnival. Horses were entered, and their fees paid, at the Sportsman Inn in the city. A number of other publicans set up booths and stalls on the course itself. Mrs Allison of the Queens Arms Inn, South Head Road, advertised in *Bell's Life* on 22 December 1849 that she would provide a 'Splendid Spread in her usual and approved style' at the Petersham races. Shaw himself benefited directly from gate-entry charges: the only permitted entrance was a gate opposite the Woolpack.

The role of publicans as influential sports promoters and entrepreneurs declined in the second half of the nineteenth century. As sport became more organised and required more expensive and sophisticated facilities, many publicans lacked the resources to organise large-scale sport. Governing bodies, boards of directors and State associations took over the larger task of running a sport and raising the large sums of capital needed to establish permanent facilities. With the rise of the middle-class sporting ideologies of athleticism and amateurism (see ch. 4) there was also a move to dissociate sport from the public house.

Publicans did not stop promoting sport. It appears that they continued to have a close link, particularly with working-class and gambling sports. Individual hotels continued to patronise particular sports. Australia's first game of lawn bowls was played at Beach Tavern, Hobart, on 1 January 1845. The British Hotel in North Adelaide became the promoter of the Adelaide Rifle Company. The first formal rules for Australian football of 1859 were drawn up at the Parade Hotel in East Melbourne. Many important racing clubs were established in public houses: the Victorian Racing Club at Scott's Hotel in 1864 and the Victorian Amateur Turf Club at Craig's Hotel in 1875. The Botany Hotel in Sydney was famous for its organisation of pedestrianism in the 1880s. Publicans recognised the value of advertising and sponsored races such as Publicans' Plates and Innkeepers' Purses at organised race-meetings at major racecourses.

A few enterprising publicans moved into the emerging entertainment industry. With the help of a public subscription of £1000 the proprietor of the Eagle Tavern in Melbourne built a theatre adjoining his hotel in 1840. The billiard room in the Temple Tavern in Adelaide must have been very substantial because it was later converted to the New Queen's Theatre, which seated 7000.

CLUBS AND ASSOCIATIONS

Creating a club was a self-conscious decision to organise a sport on a more permanent and continuing basis. City, colonial, State and national associations were only built on the foundation of clubs and interclub competition. There were few,[27] if any, sporting clubs in Australia before 1825, but the establishment of the Sydney Turf Club in 1825 set a precedent which was repeated in many other sports and cities. Turf clubs were set up in Tasmania (1826), Melbourne and Adelaide (1838), Moreton Bay (1843). There was a similar expansion in the number of cricket clubs after the formation of the Australian Cricket Club in 1826: the Hobart Town Cricket Club was formed in 1832, Melbourne Cricket Club in 1838 and Adelaide Cricket Club in 1839. Aquatic, hunt, regatta, rifle and yacht clubs were also formed at this time.[28]

The establishment of sporting clubs after 1825 reflected the changed character of Australian society. A wealthy élite, with pretensions to becoming a colonial aristocracy, was prominent in founding all manner of clubs: social, dining and sporting. Gentlemen's clubs, the Australian (Sydney), Melbourne and Adelaide clubs, were established in 1838. There were also dining clubs such as the Beef-steak Club for card-playing which operated at Odd Fellows' Arms in Sydney in the 1830s. The immediate object was to meet and fraternise with gentlemen of similar social standing—an activity essential to maintaining respectable society in the nineteenth century.

The initiative for the creation of the Sydney Turf Club seems to have come from Sir John Jamieson. It began with the patronage of Governor Brisbane and its first chairman was John Mackaness, sheriff of the colony. The club attracted many of the prominent citizens of New South Wales including John Piper and William Wentworth. An entrance fee of £5 and an annual subscription of £4 effectively screened the potential membership, which was set at sixty.

The social importance of club-founding was even more evident in Melbourne, where a common core of establishment individuals formed the influential Melbourne Club (1838), the Melbourne Cricket Club (1838) and the Port Phillip Turf Club (1841). Those who created these institutions represented an 'inner circle' who 'by default were the actual leaders of Melbourne society'. The first two clubs were complementary: the Melbourne Club provided accommodation and indoor activities, while the focus of the Melbourne Cricket Club was on outdoor recreation. This tightly knit group virtually ran the town in its early years: they 'served on the welcoming committees, ran the clubs, acted as stewards at balls, organised regattas, and directed banks, business ventures and charitable and philanthropic organizations'.[29]

Such clubs had a political dimension. The object of the Tasmanian Turf Club, founded in 1847, was 'to bestow class on racing, and to make it clear who had control'. This club, one of a number to emerge in Tasmania, was concerned to set standards, establish rules and create uniformity. It was open only to gentlemen: there was a £2 subscription and potential members had to pass the blackball test.[30]

Hunt clubs, which were formed in various colonies, also defined gentlemanly status. The establishment of such clubs was 'an ambitious attempt to emulate the gentry at home'.[31] Only a 'very select' number of persons from the Adelaide gentry joined in the Adelaide Hunt Club, which held winter meetings from 1842. 'The baying of the hounds, the sound of the horn and the wearing of "the pink" were not only of symbolic value to the upper classes, [but] reminded them of "home" and reassured them of their status in the antipodes'.[32]

Clubs also reflected the growing political complexity of Australian society from the 1820s. The central issue from this time was how fast colonies should dismantle the trappings of penal settlements. A political group in New South Wales, known as the 'emancipists', favoured enlarged rights for former convicts and lobbied for constitutional and liberal reform. They branded their opponents 'exclusives', which was a term of abuse for those higher ranks of landowners, merchants and officials who were opposed to the platform of the emancipists.

The political divisions in New South Wales led to a serious split in the Sydney Turf Club in 1827 which had very little to do with horse-racing. The controversy surfaced at a Turf Club dinner on 9 November 1827 when prominent emancipist William Wentworth unfavourably compared the conservative Governor Darling, whom many regarded as autocratic, with his predecessor Governor Brisbane. This speech led to the withdrawal of the Governor's patronage and the creation of a rival club, the Australian Racing and Jockey Club. Since the Sydney Turf Club was both a sporting club and a meeting place for the colonial élite, it was not surprising that politics should spill over into sport. While both clubs survived for a few years, the split was injurious to Sydney horse-racing because the colony had insufficient resources to support two élite racing clubs.

The greater complexity of Australian society provided an incentive for others to establish sporting clubs. The founding members of the Australian Cricket Club (ACC), formed in 1826, were native-born who identified with the emancipist cause. Innkeeper Edward Flood, club organiser and player, became a successful politician committed to the emancipist cause. The club's emblem was the cornstalk, the emblem of the native-born and the emancipist cause. Currency, which first played in 1844, was another club of the 'native-born'. The Australian-born were referred to as 'Currency lads' (and lasses) as distinct from the British-born 'Sterling'.[33] Added interest was provided for interclub competition when clubs such as the Australian and Currency were pitted against Mary-le-bone, Union and Victoria, which were made up of British-born players. While a flag featuring the cornstalk fluttered over the tent of the ACC, the latter teams played under the Union Jack.

The reasons for forming a sports club were different from those involved in founding an association to govern a sport. The players who joined the ACC were young males, unlike the mature individuals who joined the Sydney Turf Club. It is likely that members of the ACC placed a rather higher priority on companionship with males of similar age and background. One of the members of the club later wrote that through the club 'the bond of good acquaintance became more strongly cemented' and that their meetings and progress were marked by 'conviviality'.[34]

North American historians, interested in analysing the rise of organised sport, have stressed its role in the bonding of young single males in urban environments when it became more possible to share recreational space with people of like minds, incomes and social background. Clubs were given added meaning because they became extensions of workplace allegiances. It was logical to drink with and play sport with work-mates after hours. Sporting clubs also provided an outlet for rivalry between one trade or occupation group and another. They also 'gave a sense of status, stability and affirmation of their worth in increasingly anonymous cities'.[35] So sport came to provide social cohesion for the working classes, in rather a different way from the upper-class show of status.

From the 1830s and 1840s sport began to cater for a wider range of specific interest groups. Besides clubs for the native-born and British-born, there was a Drapers' Club at Homebush which organised a drapers' race-meeting. Annual carnivals organised by groups of tradesmen represented an innovation in Sydney horse-racing, a sport which had previously been largely the preserve of the aristocracy.[36]

A much-publicised split in the Australian Cricket Club in 1835 demonstrated the importance of club identity. The split occurred after the British-born, Cambridge-educated Hardy brothers arrived in New South Wales in 1832 and joined the predominantly native-born ACC. The immediate cause of dissension was that the brothers bowled in the round-arm style, a style of bowling the colonials were not yet ready to accept. The public heat generated by the split suggests that the more educated and refined Hardy brothers did not get on well with their colonial club-mates.

The very public debate about the issue in 1835 was intriguing for the passion with which 'Tom the Native' (Thomas Stubbs) argued that the

Hardys had wrecked the 'bond of good acquaintance' in the club. His disgust was conveyed by sexist language and a pun when he stated that 'the natives [of the Club] will play these *hardy*, immaculate, lady batsmen, £100 to £50'. While Stubbs argued vehemently in favour of an exclusive club, the British-born 'A Player' preferred a more cosmopolitan club.

IDEOLOGY AND THE PRESS

Although there was far less organised sport in Australia than in Britain or North America, there was a tolerance of sport in Australia, both rough and respectable, similar to that in British pre-industrial society. In pre-1850 Australia there was limited criticism of the links between sport and gambling, drinking and animal cruelty. Lobby groups—temperance, Sabbatarian interests and the Royal Society for the Prevention of Cruelty to Animals (RSPCA)—which were reforming sport in Britain, were not prominent in the colonies because of the relative weakness of the colonial bourgeoisie. Sport was therefore free to flourish in whatever way it could.

The local press was, however, aware of the inadequacy of recreational facilities in the 1820s. The *South-Asian Register* noted in April 1828 that there was a dearth of public amusements in New South Wales.[37] The editor of the *Sydney Gazette and NSW Advertiser* argued, on 18 February 1830, that Sydney 'is greatly in want of gymnastic amusements' and added that a bowling green would be a 'desirable acquisition'. Australia lacked patrons, organisers and consumers of sport. Many had to settle for more informal and less organised sport.

The slow development of the sporting press effectively illustrates this point. Until 1824 the Australian press consisted of semi-government newspapers, the *Sydney Gazette* (1803), with limited circulation, and a similar newspaper in Tasmania, the *Hobart Town Gazette* (1810). While the *Sydney Gazette* gave considerable space to the 1810 horse-racing carnival, sport was given no regular coverage. It was not until the removal of press restrictions in 1824 that an independent and more diverse press provided more coverage. Sports journalism burgeoned in Sydney in the 1830s, when some of the editors and even proprietors of newspapers were sportsmen.[38] For the first time, cricket scorecards, match reports, advertisements and general features on sport were published.

Press coverage of sport, however, remained limited until the 1850s. Australia's first sporting newspaper, the weekly *Bell's Life in Sydney and Sporting Reviewer*, first appeared in 1845, and journals bearing a similar name appeared in other colonies. It was based on the model of *Bell's Life in London*, begun in 1822. Costing 6d, its circulation was restricted. *Bell's Life in Sydney* included reports of theatre, concerts and politics; Australian sport was not yet large enough to sustain a weekly newspaper.

In the 1830s there were some initial attempts to articulate bourgeois sporting ideologies which linked sport with moral uplift. Cricket was frequently extolled in the colonial press as a 'manly', 'healthy', 'scientific' and 'noble' game.[39] But the dominant role of publicans in the 1830s and 1840s suggests that the reality was more to do with entertainment, a rather higher priority in sports based on drink and gambling.

Sport in colonial Australia was decidedly masculine and the role of women in the emerging sporting culture was limited. Their one assured role was to provide a spectator backdrop 'to enliven the scene' and to encourage male players to perform better. There was the occasional exception to the rule, such as Mrs Smith, who owned horses which raced in Tasmania in the 1840s. In male-dominated colonial society there was little scope for women to participate directly in sport.

While women were virtually excluded from playing sport, a few made money by providing recreational facilities for women. A bathing machine was built at Hobart by 1827; Adelaide had its Marine Baths by 1839 and advertised that 'a respectable married female previously accustomed to baths in England' was on hand.[40] A Mrs Bigges established baths in the 1830s which were open to both men and women, and by 1842 there were separate ladies' baths at Woolloomooloo Bay. There are hints that colonial women were keen to become involved in sport. One commentator noted as early as 1828 that 'Currency lasses' were 'all fond of frolicking in the water, and those living near the sea can usually swim and dive like water-hens'.[41]

TIMES AND PLACES

Sport before the 1850s was an occasional event largely confined to feast and festival days—public holidays such as Boxing, New Year's, Anniversary (now Australia) days, Easter and Whit Monday, as was the pattern in pre-industrial England. Apart from these, Monday was the most popular day for sport. In choosing to play early in the week players were following the custom of eighteenth-century England already referred to:

> Saturday, as pay day, was the day when there was the sharpest awareness of both the size of the week's wage and of the need to be present to collect it at the end of the day's work ... Conversely, Monday was the nearest day to the last wage and the work day furthest away from the wage yet to come. It was the day on which freedom from work was easiest to envisage and one which, for large groups of workers, was regarded as a more or less regular holiday. The phenomenon of St. Monday and of a weekend which covered Sunday and Monday has been generally recognised.[42]

As Table 1 shows, Monday was the most popular day for cricket in Sydney from the 1830s, though play on Saturday was becoming more common in the 1850s.

Table 1: Days of play in Sydney cricket, 1831–56

	1831–32/ 1839–40	1840–41/ 1849–50	1850–51/ 1855–56
26 Dec. to 1 Jan.	7	7	4
Monday	18	44	23
Tuesday	2	8	2
Wednesday	3	3	5
Thursday	4	3	1
Friday	2	1	1
Saturday	3	3	17
Sunday	0	0	0

Source: Scorecards listed in Scott, Early Cricket in Sydney.

The total absence of areas designated for sport in pre-1850 Australia was another indication of the limited development of sport, which took place on practically any available open space: on the town common, in town squares, in paddocks, on public roads, besides creeks, on beaches and in the water itself. Hyde Park, proclaimed on 13 October 1810 by Governor Macquarie, contained the first designated sports area in Sydney, though it served as a sports ground, recreation area and town common all in one. Situated to the west of town, Hyde Park had already become a popular venue for sport and recreation, as reflected in its previous names: 'Exercising Ground', 'Cricket Ground' and 'Race Course'. Hyde Park was the first home of Sydney horse-racing, from 1810 to 1825, and serious cricket was played there from the 1830s to 1856 on a ground marked out on the north-western portion. Other sports such as quoits, hurling and rugby were also played there.

Although Hyde Park was a convenient location for sport, there was always a problem there in that it was both a sports area and a park. Cricketers, for instance, complained regularly that they did not have exclusive right to their particular part of Hyde Park: they had to share the park with the military, who drilled there; the general public, which cut paths across the cricket ground; other sports, which did not respect the sacred turf; and stray cattle, sheep and goats. The quoit-players, who practised close to the cricket pitch and sometimes damaged it, were a particular bane of the cricketers.

The lack of space for sport in Sydney, a densely developed 'walking' city, profoundly affected the later shape of sport in the colony. The town of Melbourne, which developed in a way similar to North American New Frontier cities, had plenty of available space for sport (see ch. 3). Reflecting the changing priorities of a free settlement, horse-racing was established on a permanent site at Flemington as early as

1840, and the Melbourne Cricket Club site was selected by 1853, two
and a half decades before the Sydney Cricket Ground.

THE CHARACTER OF EARLY AUSTRALIAN SPORT

Organised sport before 1850 was a curious amalgam of more informal
and violent pre-industrial games with some beginnings of commercialised
and bureaucratic sport. There is no better illustration of the transitional
character of sport in the 1830s and 1840s than an informal race-meeting-
cum-sports day at the Petersham course on 17 January 1846 which was
reported in *Bell's Life in Sydney* on 25 January. The report of this minor
meeting hinted that races were organised by owners and punters on the
spot. The program began with two horse-races, each involving just two
starters. After Mr Aiton's pony Tommy raced George Evans's Skewbald
for £20, Mr King's Rob Roy raced J. Little's Alderman for £3.

Possibly because no more equine contests were forthcoming, there
was a foot-race for a small stake between N. Dillon and an unnamed
'native boy' over 1 mile, with the latter receiving a start of 20 yards:

> They went off at a good pace, the style of running being excellent. Dillon,
> however, who had been rather deeply quaffing 'the flowing bowl' during the
> morning, soon became overpowered, and after rolling to and fro for several
> yards, fell severely into the small drain which marks the boundary. The
> native, who had still kept his head, finished the race at almost the same pace
> he took up at starting.

After that there were 'jumping in sacks, and other amusements' which
Bell's Life noted were 'scarcely admissible into the columns of a sporting
periodical'. Organised sport, in the opinion of this journalist, had
degenerated into a local carnival.[43]

Formal and informal sport existed side by side for much of the nineteenth century, as shown by the custom of a 'muff' match which took
place at the Adelaide Oval in the 1873–74 season. At the conclusion of
a match between the British and colonial-born to select the South Australian side to play England, a scratch match took place. A 'muff' match
(for cricket duffers) provided incompetent but enthusiastic cricketers to
play on the Oval for the enjoyment of the spectators. The *Register*
report suggested that these ordinary cricketers enjoyed their moment in
the limelight:

> The grape (wine) and the juniper (gin) were thirstily sought after by the
> parched participants, several of whom slept the night on the ground. One
> over-indulged gentleman fell out of his gig in the early hours of the morning
> and crushed his top hat. Another cooled himself off by accepting a bet to
> swim the river.[44]

All forms of sport, both informal and formal, were characterised by
violence of various kinds: disputes, unruly behaviour, cheating, and

cruelty to animals and other humans.[45] Much of sport was frequently brutal and coarse. The game laws were far less restrictive in Australia than in Britain and all kinds of hunting—kangaroos, dingoes, emus, deer, foxes—were popular. Many of the first illustrations of Australian sport featured men riding and shooting.

An interesting incident took place at the Sandy Course, the 'first Randwick', in 1835, when 'the races seemed little more than a distraction from the main intent of "the mob", which was to get drunk at the booths and gamble their wages on pea-and-thimble games'. Two intoxicated women were seriously injured when they wandered into the path of galloping horses.[46] Clearly there was limited demarcation between performers and spectators.

Much of Australian sport of the time was informal and often went unreported. From 1829 there were occasional brief references to games of football. The first such report, which appeared in the *Monitor* of 25 July 1829, stated that 'the privates in the barracks are in the habit of amusing themselves with a game of football'. It is likely that this was an informal scratch match. From scattered reports in the 1840s it appears that working men played occasionally in Melbourne on public holidays according to a variety of rules. Football, however, was not organised as a serious sport until the 1850s.[47]

Heroes of sport in this era were self-made and self-appointed, none being more famous than William Francis King (1807–73), known as the 'The Flying Pieman'. After arriving in Sydney in 1829 King emerged as a well-known pedestrian and colourfully bedecked itinerant character who became famous for bizarre feats such as his race against the Sydney to Windsor coach; another contest against the Brisbane to Ipswich coach carrying a heavy pole; and his walk from Campbelltown to Sydney carrying a 70 lb (32 kg) dog between midnight and 9 a.m. King, who worked for a time as a barman, was undoubtedly a product of the lively public house culture where his challenges were planned and the odds laid. When he undertook to walk 1000 quarter-miles in 1000 quarter-hours the event began at the Fitzroy Hotel, West Maitland. Although he wagered on himself, King does not appear to have profited from his feats. He later became a famous Sydney street character and pie-seller, well known for his rambling proclamations, and died a pauper.[48]

Australian sport before 1850 was a curious amalgam. It consisted in part of informal, unregulated and sometimes boisterous customs which were allied with public house culture or local carnivals. There were also the tentative beginnings of more formal sporting clubs and institutions, such as the Melbourne Cricket Club, which was to play an important role in the spread of organised sport in later decades. It was also highly derivative in that Australians looked to Britain almost exclusively for models in sport, as in everything else. Club constitutions were copied almost word by word from British precept. British sport also provided the standard and the inspiration for would-be sportspeople. One of the leading Sydney cricketers of the 1840s, John Rickards, was referred to as the Australian Lillywhite and another, William Still, was called the Australian Pilch. Lillywhite and Pilch were two of the leading British cricketers of this era.

Although sport achieved wide social acceptance in Australia before 1850, organised sport lagged well behind the first great modern sporting nation, Britain. The development of a sporting culture was restricted by insufficient resources and infrastructure, a lack of regular time for leisure, a small population and limited development of the economy. Other than its climate and unlimited physical resources—land, rivers, beaches—Australia was an unlikely sporting paradise.

3
CITY GAMES

Australia, from the 1850s, provided an ideal environment—economic, social and physical—for the creation of a sporting nation. The discovery of gold in the 1850s brought great wealth and a rapidly expanding population and stimulated the development of a more sophisticated urban society with enough money to spend on sport. Improvements in technology, communications and transportation and the rise of the mass media also laid the basis for a more organised culture of sport.

While some of the conditions conducive to the growth of sport in Australia were similar to those of other industrialising societies, Australia had some particular advantages. Australia was more urban than equivalent societies and developed a prosperous and influential working class which played a part in setting political and sporting agendas. The country had abundant land and sport occupied strategic space in many cities and country towns. The warm climate and abundant open space, which favoured outdoor recreation, were conducive to the development of sport. More than any other form of culture, sport became the social cement which bound together the many new communities that formed Australian society (see ch. 6).

In tracing this development several questions arise. Why did sport occupy such strategic space in the Australian environment? Why did sport play such an important role in community formation? Did a distinctive culture of Australian sport emerge or was Australian sport merely a variant of Anglo-Celtic sporting culture?

AN URBAN SOCIETY

One key to the prominence of sport in Australia is the urban nature of Australian society and the conditions which caused this. By the end of the nineteenth century Australia had become one of the most highly urbanised societies in the world, more so than equivalent recently settled countries such as Argentina, Canada and New Zealand, and very much more so than of the United States. The rapid influx in population caused by the gold rushes (342 000 immigrants came to Australia in the 1850s) meant that many people needed to be housed quickly, and the cities provided the opportunity for this in a way that country life could not.

The most spectacular growth in the 1850s was in Melbourne, with the colony of Victoria producing one-third of the world's gold in the 1850s. Sydney had impressive growth from the 1860s and other cities had bursts of development: Adelaide grew fastest in the 1870s, Brisbane in the 1880s and Perth in the 1890s and 1900s. The percentage of Australians living in towns of 2500 or more increased from 30 per cent in 1828 to 55 per cent by 1911. This figure was higher than Argentina (50 per cent), New Zealand (49 per cent), United States (46 per cent) and Canada (37 per cent).[1] The immigrants were mainly Anglo-Celtic and came from a variety of social backgrounds.

The gold rushes created great wealth which could be spent on public works and a more impressive culture of sport. Besides ornate town halls, churches, schools and universities, banks and shops, there were billiard rooms, gymnasiums, racetracks and ovals and, later in the century, tennis courts, golf links and swimming pools.

Real incomes, which increased substantially though sometimes erratically—about 10 per cent per decade—provided consumers with a greater amount of capital.[2] The gold rushes also created a shortage of labour which was conducive to the formation of trade unions, higher wages and better work conditions. Australian workers were generally better fed, housed and clothed than their European counterparts.

Australia became what historians have referred to as a 'working-man's paradise' during the era of the Long Boom from the 1860s. While some Sydney social historians[3] have questioned the extent of this 'paradise'—noting that prosperous Sydney also had its slums and poverty—there was undoubtedly a general improvement for the majority in terms of employment and wages earned.

Along with improved work conditions, there was a greater amount of time to devote to leisure. The biggest change was the coming of the Saturday half holiday, which was introduced gradually, providing sport with a regular weekly slot. By the end of the century Saturday afternoon had become a holiday for most government officers, bank employees, mercantile clerks and teachers, and for many skilled tradesmen and shop assistants, though 'perhaps half of the men and most women' still worked on Saturday afternoon.[4] There was also time for sporting competition for tradespeople on Wednesday afternoon with the early closing of shops. By the 1870s the South Australian Cricket Association was organising fixtures on both Wednesday and Saturday afternoons.[5]

Changing regimens of time arose from a perceived need for more punctuality and synchronisation in the cities, where time was regarded as 'a more finite resource to be divided, measured and conserved'. This more rational management of time carried over into leisure. From the late nineteenth century sports began to specify set periods of play.[6] There was also a change in the character of work. Over the past century there had been a progressive decline of work which involved hard physical labour, and industrial machines 'eased work and thereby created [more] leisure'.[7]

Sport was influenced by the changing character of work. The eight-hour day was celebrated by a procession and sports day in Brisbane from 1865. By the 1890s a large procession of trade unions marched from the top of Queen Street to the Exhibition Grounds where events such as the 1 mile Eight-Hour amateur championship of Queensland were contested.[8] Informal sports were also features of annual union and firm picnics.

Improvements in transportation and communications and the growth of mass media created the possibility of a more sophisticated sporting culture. The laying of intercolonial cables in the 1850s and international cables in the 1860s enabled news to be spread more quickly. Cheaper newsprint, improved sporting illustration, photography, telephones and electric light greatly added to the appeal of sport (see ch. 10). Mass education and improved literacy rates expanded the print media audience for sport.

The gold rushes and the influx of migrants helped to create what art historian Bernard Smith has referred to as a more 'freewheeling, egalitarian and somewhat brash society'. In the gold rush era 'a spirit of energy and bustle prevailed which did much in the end to provide Australian life with a new fund of resource and an independence far finer than, though in many ways related to, the dull-spirited and sub-literate modes of resistance inherited from the "founding fathers" of New South Wales and Van Diemen's Land'.[9] S. T. Gill, the first artist to express a distinctly Australian attitude to life, provided form for a more distinctive popular culture (see ch. 10). While Australian sport continued to draw substantially on Anglo-Celtic models, sport was more adapted to the Australian social, economic and physical environment. Australian sport from the 1850s began to develop some of its own traditions.

URBAN CULTURE

The growth of city culture transformed the context in which sport operated. Urban society required a larger number of professional and white-collar workers: lawyers, doctors, architects, along with bankers, retailers and an army of clerks to service government and private sector offices. There was also an increased number of tradesmen, artisans and factory workers.

Australia, too, began in a modest way and on a small scale to develop some of its own industries: foundries, timber mills, quarries, brickyards, bakeries and breweries, furniture and clothing workshops and, later in the century, woollen mills. From the 1850s sporting equipment was manufactured locally. Henry Upton Alcock (1823–1912) was an Irish cabinet-maker who migrated to Melbourne in 1853 and set up a billiard-table manufacturing business in Fitzroy. Using local and Tasmanian timber, local slate and imported English cloth, he built tables of exceptional quality, some of which were exported. Alcock's work helped to stimulate the growth of the sport of billiards: his tables found their way into local clubs, private homes, public houses and billiard saloons.

New employment opportunities also emerged rather more slowly for women. Later in the century they were employed as schoolteachers, typists, telephonists, nurses and factory workers, though many others continued to work in private domestic service. Although women were admitted to some tertiary study from 1881, opportunities for women in the professions were limited.

The needs of a more complex society were met by a network of tertiary and secondary institutions. The universities of Sydney and Melbourne were opened in 1851. There was also an expansion of private schools (modelled on the great British public schools) for boys from the 1850s. Victoria led the way with four new public schools: Scotch (1851), Geelong Grammar (1855), Xavier's (1855) and Melbourne Grammar (1858). A network of government high schools was established by the early twentieth century. Private schools for girls were slower to develop, but from the 1880s there were several such schools for girls in all cities. After the Ladies' College was opened in Melbourne in February 1875, various churches established private schools in the 1880s and 1890s.[10]

Local and city government was also extended. Adelaide was incorporated and had an elected council in 1840, Sydney and Melbourne in 1842, Hobart in 1852, Perth in 1858 and Brisbane in 1859. Equally important was the growth of suburban and rural local government institutions. Following the Municipalities Act of 1858 in New South Wales, local communities were provided with the option of petitioning for the creation of municipalities or shires, and by the 1860s there was a substantial network of local government institutions throughout this colony. Although local councils played a fairly minor role at first—focusing on bread-and-butter issues such as the maintenance of roads and essential services—they came to take an important part in leisure facilities later in the century. Councils established parks and built ovals and other recreational facilities, and were important in maintaining and allocating resources to local sporting facilities, deciding who would have access, and under what terms, to their facilities. Every council built its own town hall, providing a venue for indoor sports such as table tennis and various ball games, and recreations such as dances.

As cities grew and suburbs were created there was greater residential segregation. The well-to-do created their enclaves in the more salubrious sections of the city, while the workers and the poor were concentrated in less attractive areas. Work and transport also defined the new residential dormitories. Working-class suburbs sprang up around factories and other places of employment.

The growth of cheaper mass transport enhanced suburban identities. A train station, together with a municipal council, provided a focal point for a community. Many of the first suburban ovals were located close to a railway station to make it easy for people from neighbouring suburbs to attend weekly club games.

URBAN SPACE

In North America the rise of cities altered the character of sport, which was slotted into a changing urban space.[11] The city was transformed from a walking city (1820–70) to an industrial radial city (1870–1960) to a suburbanised metropolis (1945–80). The walking city was a small and compact unit, with settled areas no more than 2 miles from the centre of town: vacant lots and quiet streets were plentiful and the country was nearby. Sporting groups shared open land and commons with other groups and individuals.

In the industrial radial city there was a much more highly specialised use of city land for commercial, residential and industrial purposes: more segregated suburbs (slums and well-to-do areas) and improved public transport. In the final phase, that of the suburbanised metropolis, there was a middle-class migration to suburbs and the expansion of racial ghettos in the inner city. The changes from one type of city to another led to new definitions of sporting space. In the walking city there were plenty of unofficial public playgrounds. As cities became more populated much of the public land was swallowed up. The cost of urban land dictated a more specialised use of sporting space.

After 1870, more sport took place on semi-public or private land. Semi-public space consisted of either privately owned land (such as a gymnasium) or land leased from some government authority (such as a cricket ground), both of which were accessible to the public for a fee. Access to private sporting institutions (such as a golf club) was restricted to members.

With the growth of sporting culture all manner of sports buildings, appealing to specialist audiences, were created in urban Australia. Harriett Dick and Alice Moon, who helped to popularise callisthenics, opened the Melbourne Ladies' Gymnasium in 1879. Besides the many outdoor enclosed swimming-baths, the Sydney Bathing Company opened the 'Natatorium', an indoor swimming-pool, in Sydney in 1888. The Breakfast Creek Sports Ground was built in Brisbane in the late 1880s.

City games in Australia in many ways developed along similar lines to North America. Sydney was at first a walking city with plenty of open public space for sport. As the city grew from the 1850s recreational space became more restricted. After sport was removed from the multi-purpose Hyde Park in 1856—which became public gardens—the city cricketers and footballers had to search elsewhere for appropriate space. The Moore Park area, on the fringe of the city, was developed as an alternative space for sport in the 1860s and 1870s.

There was, at least in the 1850s, far more open space and parklands available in the less densely settled towns of Melbourne, Adelaide and Perth. There was plenty of open land in the vicinity of Melbourne Grammar School, which began playing football in 1858—there was a choice of wastelands near St Kilda Road or the government reserve which ran along the St Kilda seafront. The celebrated football game between Melbourne Grammar and Scotch College in the same year was played on parkland convenient to the city.[12]

The geography of suburban sport in all the capital cities was shaped by subdivisions and land development. Sir John Young (1827–1907), the architect of Australian lawn bowls, was a wealthy landowner and developer who constructed a green on his own property, Kentville, in what was to become the Sydney suburb of Annandale, in 1876. When Young subdivided his Annandale estate, helping to establish the suburb, he used his green to help sell real estate as would-be purchasers were taken to Kentville to enjoy a few 'ends'. The first bowls intercolonial, between Victoria and New South Wales, was played at Young's home green.

Developers such as the prominent Thomas Saywell enhanced their investments by including sporting and recreational facilities in new developments such as that at New Brighton, Sydney. Saywell built a tramway from Rockdale Station to the beach, erected a hotel, opened swimming-baths and established a racecourse. He was able to offer an attractive package to the public which included a combined rail, tram, race and baths ticket.[13]

With the increasing value of urban land many sports were relocated on land unsuitable for other developments: wasteland, swampland, and land left over from industry. Sydney's major sporting complex at Moore Park was located on land which was part sandhills and part swamp and regarded as less suitable for residential development. Before it was converted into a sporting complex, Moore Park was used from the 1850s as a place to dump rubbish.[14] A number of Sydney inner-city ovals and parks, such as Henson and Arlington Ovals, were located on the sites of former brickpits.

Some of the premier golf courses, laid out in the 1880s and 1890s, were located on marginal and less-developed land. Many of Melbourne's best known courses were located in the sand-belt area. Others, such as The Lakes in Sydney, took advantage of unused land intersected by water. Royal Sydney was laid out initially in 'an area in the Bondi sandhills'.[15]

The issue of appropriate sporting space generated considerable public debate and even controversy. Sports administrators, politicians and the public were involved in many important issues about sport and urban land. Which sport was to gain which land and under what conditions? Were local or colonial authorities to contribute directly or even indirectly to the maintenance of expensive sporting facilities? Was the land to be governed by a trust?

There were also debates in Australia after 1870 about the declining green space in expanding cities as land was swallowed up for housing and industry. Public reserves which existed in Melbourne in 1851 remained unfenced and virtually undeveloped, and subject to alienation at any time.[16] During the 1870s urban reformers and suburban residents lobbied to persuade the authorities to create more green space. Creating parks was part of the Victorian movement for rational recreation: reformers believed that a well-laid out park, where nature was ordered and where band music was played in a rotunda, provided healthy recreation and helped civilise those who strolled through.[17]

Parks and even gardens included recreational and specialist sporting space, such as ovals. Public croquet lawns were located in the Launceston Public Gardens (1871) and the Brisbane Botanical Gardens (1879). The creation of a public park generated debate about what parts of it would be devoted to recreation—gardens to perambulate, bandstands for outdoor concerts—and what part should be devoted more exclusively to sport, notably the oval.

The creation of national parks and reserves outside the city, which reflected changing community attitudes towards unused land, had a longer impact on sport. Sydney's National Park (1879) was the forerunner of many such reserves. Victoria's first national park was established at Tower Hill, Port Fairy, in 1892, though it had been a temporary reserve since 1866. The establishment of many other national sports helped popularise bushwalking clubs in the first decades of the twentieth century. One of the first such clubs, the Melbourne Amateur Walking and Touring Club, was established in 1894.[18]

However, urban sporting space in Australia differed from that in North America in several ways. Water space remained more public in Australia: control of ocean beaches, and to a lesser extent rivers and harbours, was vested in the maritime authorities. The Australian beach was never privatised and later became a focal point for recreation and sport.

Australian cities developed along two main lines. Sydney, along with the other former convict settlements of Brisbane and Hobart, developed as densely settled, haphazardly planned walking cities, like typical pre-industrial cities. Melbourne by contrast, along with Adelaide and Perth, was developed along more novel lines—dubbed 'New Urban Frontier' cities—which were popular in North America. Cities of this type avoided urban congestion by spreading outwards 'through the replication of suburbs of single-family houses'.[19]

There were a number of important differences between walking cities and those of the New Urban Frontier type. The latter were dependent on the development of an effective public transport system. They also encouraged earlier suburbanisation, both for the middle and working classes, from an earlier stage than the walking cities. Finally, because the urban core was far less densely settled, urban space was less at a premium. The availability of suitable and convenient space for sport has had a profound impact on the nature and character of sporting institutions.

DIVERGENT SPORTING CULTURES

One of the continuing debates in Australian sporting history is over the greatly divergent sporting city traditions, particularly the differences between Sydney and Melbourne.[20] The sporting culture of Melbourne has long appeared stronger than Sydney's. Melbourne has the premier horse-race in the country and the largest sports stadiums. Sport also seemed to take root much earlier there: Melbourne had an important cricket club by 1838, which later became dominant, whereas Sydney never developed an equivalent authority; Melbourne had its leading racecourse at Flemington by 1840, whereas Randwick was not formally developed until 1860; organised football in Melbourne dated from the late 1850s, whereas Sydney interclub football began from the mid-1860s. And Melbourne's sports spectators are legendary for their passionate following of sport.

There have been many theories for these divergent traditions. A popular Sydney myth is that Melbourne is such a dull city that many flock to sporting events because of the paucity of alternative entertainment. Others have suggested that Melbourne has had a tradition of capable sports administrators. Others again have stressed the timing of settlement: sport was slower to develop in the penal settlement of Sydney than in the freer settlement of Melbourne. A related view suggests that Melbourne got the jump on Sydney in the 1850s because it developed a larger network of public schools, where sport was cultivated. Yet another view has placed emphasis on the greater wealth of Melbourne in the 1850s, its golden decade.

While all these theories explain the earlier take-off of sport in Melbourne they do not adequately explain the long-term differences. The more promising explanations relate to geography and town planning. Melbourne has plenty of flat ground, whereas much of central Sydney is hilly. It is also far more difficult to travel from one suburb to another in Sydney because the immediate hinterland is intersected by rivers, coves and bays. With plenty of flat space available in Melbourne, carving out recreational space was less of a problem than it was in Sydney. Geography is obviously one factor in Melbourne's sporting prominence, particularly its ability to attract large crowds. The Melbourne Cricket

Ground is at the hub of Melbourne's transport network, whereas the Sydney Cricket Ground is far less accessible.

But geography by itself does not provide a complete explanation for the different patterns of land use and sporting traditions of the two cities. Flat land was available in Sydney for sport in the Moore Park area, but in the 1860s it was considered by the cricketers to be too far from the city. This occurred partly because Sydney was still largely a walking city with less developed public transport than Melbourne.

Town planning considerations of walking cities versus the New Urban Frontier type are the most likely explanations for the divergent sporting cultures of these cities. Having adequate and convenient space for sport has always been a vital factor in the growth of any particular sport. Melbourne's strong sporting culture has emerged because it is more visible and accessible. Sport can also take on greater meaning in an elaborate cathedral of sport than in a more humble setting. Town planners in Melbourne, almost from its inception, have catered for and nurtured the sporting passion.

THE EXPANSION OF SPORT

The changes to sport in the 1850s were impressive. Before 1850 sporting crowds of up to 10 000 were exceptional, but by 1 October 1859 a crowd of over 59 000, taking advantage of the newly created rail system, was reported at Flemington Racecourse. By the start of the 1880s the Melbourne Cup attracted crowds of more than 100 000.

The 1850s was the decade which marked the 'end of the primitive years for Victorian horseracing': stakes and fields were larger and horseracing was organised on a more professional footing. The spirit of speculation, which had been fuelled by the gold rushes, was soon reflected in the larger number of consumers and entrepreneurs taking part in the sport of racing.[21]

Sporting events took place more regularly from the 1850s. Competitions were created that meant regular weekly play (increasingly on Saturdays). Seasons of play were more closely demarcated. Annual events, carnivals and premierships were being created and regular intercolonial competition was established. Sport was transformed from mere local competition to intercolonial and, from the 1860s, to international competition. The beginning of regular intercolonial and international contests created the need for bureaucracies to govern sports and to organise wider competitions.

Sport also attracted a wider range of patrons and promoters. With the growth of secondary and tertiary education, many schoolteachers, clerics and doctors believed that sport could play a positive role in promoting desirable social goals (see ch. 4). Politicians, too, discovered that backing sport and local sporting clubs could enhance their local power base (see ch. 7). Entrepreneurs and advertisers (see ch. 11) also attempted to profit from this burgeoning sporting culture.

Table 2 summarises the many changes in sport in this era. New games, such as Australian football ('Aussie rules'), were invented. Other sports, such as cricket and horse-racing, became more organised and commercialised. Some sports were codified for the first time, while others developed more elaborate rules and orthodoxies. The rise of sports media expanded the range of sporting ideology.

The first sports to flourish in Australia were the professional sports where making money and gambling on sport were accepted as normal activities and sport itself was viewed largely as entertainment. Gambling sports, such as sculling and horse-racing, were some of the first to boom in the 1850s. Amateur sport developed rather later. Although there were some people from the 1850s who believed that sport could achieve moral uplift, the rise of amateurism was partly a reaction to the established strength of professional sport (see ch. 4).

Horse-racing Horse-racing was also one of the first popular sports in the country and there was an infrastructure of clubs and courses by the 1850s. Melbourne's Flemington course was established by 1840 and Sydney's Australian Jockey Club (AJC) was formed in 1842. Race-meetings and bureaucracies emerged at an early point in the history of the other colonies.

Horse-racing boomed in gold-rich Victoria, which became the focal point of Australian racing in the 1850s. Two rival race clubs, the Victoria Turf Club (1852) and the Victoria Jockey Club (1856), staged lavish meetings at Flemington, which attracted large crowds by the late 1850s. The size of the stakes and the number of starters increased dramatically during the decade. The rich 2 mile handicap, the Melbourne Cup, was introduced by the Victoria Turf Club in 1861 and soon became the country's most famous horse-race. American writer Mark Twain had no doubt that the Cup was the country's 'national day', overshadowing all other holidays.[22]

The Melbourne Cup has long been part of popular culture, and the populace participates in office sweepstakes and other festivities. There are a number of reasons for the elevated status of the Melbourne Cup. The race was founded at the time of the Victorian gold boom and was an attempt to demonstrate that Melbourne was an important and cultured city. Although the first race was a 'relatively insignificant event', the Victoria Racing Committee (VRC) saw the possibility of enhancing its status through the promotion of the Cup, and later augmented the prize-money. The creation of a public half holiday in 1866 added to the popularity of Cup Day. The race also became popular because of its relative unpredictability due to handicapping—which gave 'an opportunity for spirited betting'.[23]

Clubs and courses emerged in other colonies. Sydney's first permanent course was established at Randwick in 1860. The South Australian

Table 2: Changes in Australian sport 1850–1914

	1850s
1850s	Rise of professional sculling
1851	First intercolonial cricket match (Victoria v. Tasmania)
1852	Western Australian Turf Club founded
1856	*Tom Brown's Schooldays* by Thomas Hughes published
	Victorian Yacht Club founded
1857	Beginnings of croquet
1858	Tattersall's Club, Sydney, established
1859	First 'rules' of Australian football

	1860s
1860	Opening of new Randwick Racecourse
1861	Melbourne Cup first run
1862	First English cricket tour of Australia
1864	Adelaide Amateur Club founded
	Adelaide Cup created
1865	First interclub rugby games in Sydney
1867	Marquis of Queensberry rules in boxing

	1870s
1871	Foundation of Rugby Football Union
	Tasmanian Racing Club founded
1874	First rules of hockey
	Southern Rugby Union formed
1874–77	Lawn tennis established
1876	Ned Trickett, sculler, Australia's first world champion
1877	Test cricket begins
	Victorian Football Association ('Aussie rules') established
1878	Sydney Cricket Ground established
	Stawell Gift first run
	King's Cup (rowing) first raced
	Melbourne Bicycle Club formed
	Lawn tennis club founded at Melbourne Cricket Club
1879	Melbourne Ladies' Gymnasium opened

	1880s
1880	Melbourne Cup draws a crowd of 100 000
	NSW Bowls Association formed—the first in the world
1882	Ashes tradition started in cricket
	NSW Rugby team tours New Zealand
	Queensland Rugby Union established
	Australian Golf Club founded
	NSW Amateur Swimming Association founded

1883	Tasmanian cricket team toured New Zealand
1884	New Zealand rugby team toured NSW
1885	Melbourne Golf Club obtains the 'Royal' prefix
1886	Hockey Association founded
	Women play club cricket in Sydney
1887	Amateur Athletic Association of NSW founded
1888	Queensland Lawn Tennis Association founded
	Harness-racing events held at Eagle Farm, Brisbane

1890s

1890s	Cycling craze
1894	Melbourne Amateur Walking and Touring Club founded
1896	Edwin Flack wins two gold medals at the Olympics
1897	Victorian Football League established
1898	Queensland Amateur Swimming Association founded

1900s

1902	Restrictive surf-bathing laws challenged
1905	Board of Control for Cricket (in Australia) set up
1906	Australian Football Council ('Aussie rules') established
1907	NSW Surf Bathing Association established
	Split between Rugby Union and League in Sydney
1908	Kangaroo tour of Great Britain
	Bondi Surf Lifesaving Club formed
1912	Fanny Durack wins a gold medal at the 1912 Olympics

Jockey Club created a rich Adelaide Cup in 1864 at the Thebarton race-course. The Western Australian Turf Club was founded in 1852, the Queensland Turf Club in 1863 and the Tasmanian Racing Club in 1871.

During the later decades of the century there was a boom in horse-racing, and a vast network of public, private and pony tracks were set up in each city. Suburban courses were established in Melbourne, for instance, at Caulfield (1859) and Moonee Valley (1883) and there were numerous other private and pony tracks. Around the turn of the century metropolitan punters were able to attend meetings at four or five separate racecourses a week and two different race-meetings on a Saturday. The creation of harness-racing events at Brisbane's Eagle Farm in 1888 and Sydney's Harold Park in 1890 added to punting options.

By the end of the century there was a backlash against unrestricted growth in the number of race-meetings and in betting activity, and the beginnings of stricter control by governments and senior racing clubs such as the AJC and the VRC. The clubs campaigned against pony and unregistered racing and succeeded in gaining greater control of race dates, registered meetings and the use of paid stewards.

Professional spectator sports   Professional sculling gained wide public attention from the 1850s, with scullers performing for large stakes and attracting large crowds of up to 30 000 on the banks of rivers such as the Parramatta. Sculling was related to work because many men made their living by rowing passengers across the wide coastal rivers of New South Wales or by ferrying people to the ships in harbours. World champion Henry Searle acquired his skill on the Clarence River rowing 7 miles daily ferrying his siblings to school. Another world champion sculler, George Towns, used to row regularly on the Hunter River conveying a boatload of farm produce. Making money out of sport appealed to scullers, who came from working-class backgrounds as blacksmiths, quarrymen or timber-fellers. The scullers were backed by entrepreneurs, notably publicans (see ch. 11). Much money was wagered on this sport: when Henry Searle defeated O'Connor for a £500 stake it was estimated that £30 000 was won on wagers.[24]

While visits from British professionals helped raise standards, Australia produced a succession of world-class scullers from the 1850s, including Elias Laycock and Richard Green; the latter was the first to compete overseas in 1863. His protégé, Ned Trickett, who won the World Championship on the Thames on 27 June 1876, was Australia's first world champion in any sport. Although the news took three weeks to reach Sydney—by mail steamer to Port Adelaide and then by telegraph—'throngs of people waited by the telegraph office for the result'.[25] Such was the interest in Trickett's deeds that many stayed up overnight to hear the result of this event conveyed on the newly laid international cable. He was fêted on his return to the country.

Australia was a dominating force in world sculling from 1876 to 1907: Australians held the world professional sculling championship for twenty-two of thirty-one years. There was a huge outpouring of grief and a crowd more than 100 000 to witness the funeral of world champion Henry Searle when he died at the age of 23. Searle, who claimed this title on the Thames on 9 September 1889, died from typhoid later that year.[26]

There is no one reason why big money deserted professional sculling and why the line of champions dried up, why the crowds went elsewhere and the sport died after 1907. Professional sculling suffered because it lacked a central organising body and contests were irregular and spasmodic. This working-class sport also had stiffer competition by the turn of the century, partly from a variety of other sports. Sculling was, as well, not an ideal spectator sport, with crowds spread along a riverbank. Greater profits could be achieved through more gate-money sports. There was also a 'lingering doubt' in the minds of some about whether races were conducted legitimately, and the rise of amateur rowing, and amateurism in general, also posed a threat.[27]

Professional sculling was one of a number of sports which flourished spectacularly for a brief time only to disappear, temporarily or permanently. They suffered from having a support base that was too narrow. More privileged sports such as horse-racing, cricket and football have always had wider and more secure support: from politicians, educationists, doctors, clerics and the media.

The sport of boxing was similar to professional sculling in that it has experienced regular fluctuations in public support. Boxing was one of Australia's oldest sports: clashes between the native-born and immigrants enlivened many contests; the clash between native-born George Hough and Englishman Isaac Reed at Middle Head in 1847 was watched by thousands. Prize-fighting also flourished on the goldfields where diggers paid to watch contests. Working-class prize-fighters managed by bookmakers, publicans, graziers and professional men were prominent until the sport suffered the first of its many declines in the 1870s.

The prize-ring was killed by increased official surveillance, greater police efficiency, and scandals such as the death of prize-fighter Alec Agar in Sydney in 1884 and the gaoling of his African-American opponent.[28] Efforts to improve the image of the sport through the new Marquis of Queensberry Rules, the use of gloves and the establishment of gymnasiums, run by champion Larry Foley, helped the sport gain more acceptance during the 1890s.

Boxing boomed in the decades immediately before World War I. Large crowds attended fights such as the epic battle in 1908 between Jack Johnson and Tommy Burns (see chs 9 and 10). Les Darcy became the idol of the working class and a hero of Irish-Australians, who viewed him as an anti-conscription symbol (see ch. 9). Sporting entrepreneurs such as Hugh D. McIntosh and John Wren profited from the boxing boom (see ch. 11). Boxing has had subsequent high points but mostly it has struggled to maintain its mass appeal. Like sculling, it has had too few powerful friends in high places.

Requiring limited facilities, pedestrianism was a popular sport before 1850, but professional running expanded in the gold-mining days. 'Gifts' originated in this era: miners ran handicap races for a purse or even a nugget donated by a mine-owner or a publican. In due course each gold-mining settlement formed its athletics club with its particular regulations.[29]

The Stawell Gift, one of the richest professional sprints in the world, evolved from a Miners' Carnival, originally in October, but established as an annual Easter event from 1878. Australia had an impressive professional running circuit by the 1870s and 1880s when there were 100 runners in Sydney and Melbourne who made a living out of the sport, while large crowds watched races, the stakes were substantial and the betting considerable. The big money in professional running also attracted many of the leading runners from overseas. Australia produced a number of world champion professional sprinters, including Arthur Postle, John Donaldson and Charlie Samuels in the late nineteenth and early twentieth centuries.

Sydney's Sir Joseph Banks Hotel at Botany was a focal point for professional running in the 1880s and it developed the first professional track in Australia—cinders separated by grass lines and ringed by gaslights. The usual prize-money was £300 and was sometimes as large as £500. The large crowds included bookmakers, who did a brisk trade. This boom in professional running ended by the 1890s when some of the runners ran dead (running slower to improve a handicap) and brought the sport into disrepute.

Cricket   While the sport was not a professional one in the sense that sculling was, there was some initial tolerance of gambling. It was normal practice in the 1830s and 1840s for games to be played for a stake and, even though stakes declined in the 1850s, gambling was a part of cricket for the next few decades. The sporting press regularly published the odds for intercolonials in the 1850s. The first contest between New South Wales and Victoria at Melbourne could have been played for a stake but the visitors chose to play for honour instead.

The game expanded in the 1860s with the tours by English teams in 1861–62 and 1863–64. The first English teams were made up entirely of professionals, and it was the professionals rather than amateurs who did most to promote the game. The important role of professionals in developing cricket, both in England and Australia, has been neglected and even denigrated by amateur administrators and historians.[30] Although the third English team to Australia (1873–74) was captained by an amateur, W. G. Grace, he was a 'disguised' professional in that he had demanded £1500 to undertake the tour. What has become known as the first Test was played between an Australian XI and Lillywhite's professional XI in 1877. An Aboriginal team toured Britain in 1868 (see ch. 9).

Profiting from the game was a central factor in tours to England, which were organised on a regular basis from 1878. Players on the first tour organised themselves into a joint stock company and for their individual investment of £50 they received a handsome tour dividend of over £700. Such was the success of this tour and later ventures that it took some time for the colonial cricket associations, and eventually the Australian Board of Control, to establish full control of the finances and the administration of the game. Cricket boomed in the later part of century with the rise of Test cricket, regular tours, Sheffield Shield and district competition. But the growth of the sport was stymied on some occasions (notably in the 1880s) by conflict between colonial associations and between players and administrators (see ch. 7).[31]

Football   The rapid growth of various football codes, the emergence of a distinctive Australian game, and the strange geography of football in Australia are some of the issues which have attracted much recent attention. While Australian football became dominant in Victoria, South and Western Australia and Tasmania, rugby was preferred in New

South Wales and Queensland. Rugby in these two colonies split in 1907 between a more professional code, rugby league, and a more amateur code, rugby union. Soccer emerged as a pretender from the 1880s but struggled to attain the status of a major sport and for a long time was confined to pockets of influence—on the coalfields, in factories and among particular ethnic groups (see ch. 9).

When football appeared in Australia as an organised game there were no organised codes as such: British traditions of football were still in a state of flux. Those colonists who were interested in football were familiar with particular variants of rules; some had played a game at Eton, others at Harrow and yet others at Rugby, and possibly most had a hazy knowledge of the rules. Without any agreed code there was a need in all the colonies to devise some common football game.

From the 1850s to the 1870s individual colonies had the opportunity to devise their own codes. This period of experimentation with rules was important because Australian football did not emerge in 1858 (a popular myth) or with the first rules (1859) but, as Geoffrey Blainey has shown, progressively over several decades.[32] It also took rugby more than a decade from 1865 to establish its dominance in Sydney and to ward off the challenges from other football pretenders.[33] Queensland too flirted with Australian football before casting its lot finally in the rugby camp in the 1880s.[34]

There were various reasons why football developed at different times from place to place. A key factor was the British schooling of a handful of individuals in each colony who developed football. The seven men who formulated the first rules of Australian football, and who were all members of the Melbourne Cricket Club, came from a variety of British public schools, and they consciously explored the rules of Eton, Harrow, Rugby and Winchester before arriving at their own compromise. Only four of the seven were present at the meeting to decide the 1859 rules and two of them, J. B. Thompson and W. J. Hammersley, were influenced by the Cambridge Rules of 1848, which was one of the first attempts to devise a standard code of football amenable to all. The Australian game may have borrowed more from English practice than has hitherto been acknowledged.[35]

A second reason relates to the differing sporting culture from city to city. Organised football emerged at an earlier stage in Melbourne and Adelaide than it did in Sydney and Brisbane and, in a sense, Melbourne was freer to devise its own rules. Interschool games in Melbourne dated from 1858 and the first rules of Australian football from 1859. The first rugby clubs and interclub competition in Sydney did not occur until 1865. Gold-rich Melbourne experienced a more rapid growth than Sydney and had an abundance of suitable parkland for football. Sydney footballers had continuing problems to find space for football.[36]

Intercolonial rivalry was undoubtedly a third reason why Sydney eventually chose rugby rather than Australian football. The grandiose

name chosen by the first Sydney rugby association, Southern Rugby
Football Union (1874)—implying that the Sydney association was the
southern hemisphere offshoot of the British body—was an attempt to
upstage the existing Victorian football organisation, which played
according to the Melbourne rules.[37]

Class may have been another factor in the development of Australian
football. While the Victorian game was based on rugby it was 'modified
as an off-season pastime for middle-class cricketers' who could not
afford to come to work with 'blackened eyes and hacked shins'.[38] While
this explanation may be appropriate for Melbourne, it does not fully
explain why another group of middle-class sportsmen in Sydney decided
to persist with rugby. Doubt has been cast on one element of Blainey's
explanation that a different code developed there in part because of a
succession of dry winters leading to harder grounds in Melbourne.[39]

Aquatic sports   For much of the nineteenth century Australia blindly
followed British aquatic practice and culture and from 1833 New South
Wales had laws which prohibited daylight surf bathing. Piers were
constructed on some ocean beaches, such as Sydney's Coogee Beach,
before it was realised that such a structure was inappropriate in the
larger Australian surf. Bathing machines appeared on a number of
beaches from the 1860s. British notions of sun, sand and health dictated
that most people who went to the beach were swathed from head to toe,
hatted and protected by a parasol or an umbrella. Imported notions
dictated that recreation should be beside, rather than in, the sea.[40]

Swimming and bathing had long been popular (see ch. 2). In the
second half of the century many swimming-pools were created in rivers,
bays, harbours, the ocean and even indoors. Although much of
swimming was initially recreational, and amounted to bathing,
competitive swimming emerged from an early stage and in 1861 the
New South Wales champion, Joseph Bennett, defeated the Victorian
champion, Stevens, over 200 yards at St Kilda. The reward for the
Champion's Cup of Victoria was a prize of £30.

Competitive swimming boomed in later decades and many clubs
were established for men and later for women. Australia was, around
the turn of the century, at the forefront of world swimming and by 1905
Australians held all the world records for recognised men's events. By
1912, Fanny Durack had established herself as the women's world
champion and record-holder.

With the boom in swimming at the end of the nineteenth century
many were able to make a living out of the sport. These included baths
proprietors such as Alex Wylie, father of Mina, swimming teachers and
coaches. One of the more famous teachers was 'Professor' Frederick
Cavill, who taught at the Lavender Bay Baths from the 1880s and whose
six sons all became swimming champions. Organisers whetted the
public appetite with trick and novelty swimming, diving feats and

swimming carnivals. Annette Kellermann made a name for herself both as a champion and record-breaking swimmer but also as an entertainer, promoted as the 'Diving Venus' (see ch. 5).

Australia has contributed to world sport with the various branches of surfing. From the late nineteenth century some Australians, who were dissatisfied with British notions of bathing propriety, began to promote surf bathing (see ch. 9). The archaic laws prohibiting daylight bathing were challenged successfully at Many Beach by 1902, when local residents gained the support for their campaign from William Gocher, editor of the *Manly Daily*. From that time there was a great boom in surf culture, and the associated practice of sun-tanning. After a Surf-Life Saving Club was formed at Bondi in 1908, there were similar institutions at many other beaches.[41]

Billiards, golf, tennis, lawn bowls, cycling and motor sports   Billiards was a popular sport almost from the start of European settlement. Publicans were the main sponsors of the sport before 1850 and billiards became an almost exclusively male pastime, linked with gambling and drinking. With the local manufacture of billiard tables from the 1850s (see p. 37) the sport diversified its social base. Billiard tables were located in private homes and in exclusive clubs such as the Melbourne Cricket Club, although the sport continued to be played by working men in billiard halls and hotels.

To boost the sport and sales, manufacturer Henry Alcock organised professional contests during the 1860s when exhibitions were staged at Melbourne's Theatre Royal. Star players such as Fred Lindrum had emerged by the 1880s when the first professional national championships were staged. The money-making potential of the sport was further realised when a number of salons were opened on the Western Australian goldfields in the 1890s and featured members of the Lindrum family.

While golf was played spasmodically from the 1820s, it was not until the 1880s and 1890s that some of the great golf clubs of the country were established, with the Australian Club (1882) being the first. Many of the first founders and players were Scottish (see ch. 9). Golf began, unlike most of the other sports discussed, as an exclusive and amateur sport founded by people of high social status. Over half of the members of the Brisbane Golf Club, for instance, which was founded in 1896, also belonged to the exclusive Queensland Club.[42] Royal Sydney Golf Club, founded in 1893, very much reflected the views of establishment Sydney. The club was also a place where 'the like-minded might socialise' and a convenient venue for social and commercial networking.[43] The democratisation of the game, which was associated with the rise of public courses where ordinary golfers could pay as they played, took place later.

Lawn tennis, which appeared in Australia in the 1870s and 1880s, was regarded as a gentle sport suitable for élite social intercourse; tennis courts were laid out in the gardens of the wealthy where the game was a prominent part of the social round of entertainment. More a social than a competitive sport, it was regarded initially as suitable for both men and women (see ch. 5) and incorporated mixed competition from its early years. Although tennis championships were played from the 1880s, tennis did not become a more competitive and democratic sport until the twentieth century.

Lawn bowls is one of the more intriguing sports in Australia in that it has undergone a number of incarnations: from an occasional public-house sport, to a sport for gentlemen in the 1880s, and then in the twentieth century to a mass sport for men and women, primarily of mature age. Australia is also the leading bowls nation and New South Wales leads the other States in numbers of participants. The NSW Bowls Association, founded in 1880, was the first of its kind in the world. Australia has more participants in this sport than any other country, accounting for 43 per cent of the world lawn-bowling population.[44]

Modern lawn bowls dates from the 1880s when it was promoted as providing a civilised and gentle relaxation for gentlemen. The initial club fees restricted the clientele which was largely white, male and middle-class. Bowls did not become more democratic and popular until the twentieth century. A number of rinks were created by businesses, industries and public enterprises, which were concerned with providing workers with more healthy outdoor activity, such as the New South Railways green at Fraser Park in Marrickville.[45]

Cycling, which was both a recreation and a sport, was popular in the 1880s, when clubs were formed and races were held, but it was not until the 1890s, with the development of the pneumatic-tyre safety bicycle, that there was a craze for cycling, involving both men and women of all classes. About 200 000 bicycles were sold in Australia by 1900.

During the 1890s cycling became a mass-spectator sport and large crowds attended asphalt cycling tracks which existed on the perimeters of sporting venues including most of the major cricket grounds. Long-distance feats of endurance, pedalling around Australia, achieved considerable publicity. Major events, such as the Austral Wheel Race, dating from 1887, attracted large gates, such as the 30 000 who attended the Melbourne Cricket Ground in 1898. The cyclists raced for prize-money totalling £200. The Dunlop company profited considerably from the cycling boom (see ch. 11).

The popularity of competitive cycling declined after the 1890s. One possible reason for this, in the opinion of some, was that it increasingly acquired a bad odour and there were regular complaints of race-fixing and 'dead' or 'crook' riders after 1900. There was much criticism of the seeming complicity among riders in the Austral Wheel Race of 1901, which had attracted large wagers. The introduction of motorcycles and automobiles also diminished the status of the bicycle and created, at least in the long term, new sports. Although the first car-race in Australia was reputedly staged at Maribyrnong Gymkhana, Victoria, in 1903, the sport emerged slowly. A motorcycle-race (a motorised tricycle) was recorded at an even earlier date, taking place at the Sydney Cricket Ground on 1 January 1901, but competitive motorcycling was restricted mostly to reliability trials and hill climbs until 1914. Speedway was not invented until the early 1920s, at West Maitland in New South Wales, and Grand Prix racing did not take place until 1928 at Phillip Island in Victoria. Motorcycle and automobile clubs began to appear in the early 1900s.

The expansion of the Australian economy and population after the gold rushes was the turning-point in the fortunes of sport. By 1914 organised sport had become a very important part of the physical, social and mental landscape of most Australians, and central to an emerging Australian way of life. Elaborate sporting venues occupied prime real estate within cities and country towns, and sporting discourse was dominant in the media. The fact that the newly rich in Melbourne spent so massively on sportsgrounds is an indication of how ardently people wanted sport.

Although Australians were still very much inspired by Anglo-Celtic notions of sport, imported culture was so adapted to the Australian environment that it had become distinctively Australian. Australia developed its own games (Australian football), events (the Melbourne Cup), clubs (surf life-saving clubs), heroes and heroines, sporting language and barracking, larger and more impressive sporting grounds and scoreboards, and other forms of sporting practice.

While it is immensely difficult to compare sporting culture (and passion) from one society to another,[46] it is likely that Australia placed sport on a higher pedestal than in equivalent countries. There are historical reasons for inferring that Australia became a distinctive and even unique sporting paradise. Sport was around and a powerful force when cities, towns and suburbs took shape, and it was incorporated prominently into the built environment. Sport, more than any other form of culture—religion, ethnicity, history—appealed to many Australians as the more attractive social cement to bind new communities: local, regional, colonial and national (see ch. 6).

4
AMATEUR VERSUS
PROFESSIONAL

The first sports to flourish in Australia in the 1850s were those based on gambling and centred on the public house and regarded primarily as entertainment. As sporting culture became more prominent, profitable and powerful, it became too important to be left to publicans. Educators, clerics, politicians, doctors and entrepreneurs began to recognise that sport could play a positive role in society. The parallel ideologies of athleticism, amateurism, Muscular Christianity and Social Darwinism which emerged from this time encouraged the view that sport could build character, enhance social discipline and provide a form of rational recreation.

Amateurism became the core and enduring ideal which dominated Australian sport for over a century. With its emphasis on playing for fun rather than for pecuniary gain, the ideology of amateurism stressed the values of fair and spontaneous play, including respect for the rules and for the opposition. The apostles of amateurism regarded money as the great evil which had much potential to debase sport.

Since Australian sporting culture in the 1850s was based on less altruistic principles, the challenge for those who subscribed to amateurism was to redefine the purpose of sport and to promote amateur sporting clubs and associations. A second strategy was to expose, undercut and marginalise those who believed that money and sport could mix freely. There were also movements to 'purify' particular sports by purging their association with gambling.

The articulation of the amateur sporting ideology led to greater class segregation, and even conflict, in sport. Though the amateur versus professional debate varied from one sport to another, in Australia it was always the issue of class in sport which lay behind it. It led to separate class organisation in some sports and class conflict in others.

The tenacity of the amateur ethic raises several questions. Why did amateurism become so influential and enjoy such an extended heyday in Australia? Why did the amateur versus professional debate vary so much from sport to sport? Why did amateurism disappear so rapidly and with so little ceremony from the 1970s?

MOVEMENTS AND IDEOLOGIES TO PURIFY SPORT

Amateurism drew on various ideological strands including athleticism, Muscular Christianity and Social Darwinism. These provided the rationale for the games cult which was so influential in the expanding network of British public schools from the 1850s.[1] The ideals behind the games cult were diverse and even contradictory, for while games were promoted enthusiastically by church leaders, other devotees of athleticism held no religious beliefs at all. Core notions of athleticism were set out in two widely read novels: Thomas Hughes's *Tom Brown's Schooldays* (1857) and Charles Kingsley's *Westward Ho!* (1855). Central to athleticism was the belief that sport should serve a moral purpose: to build character and to encourage individuals to consider the interests of the team first. Sport became an integral part in the school curriculum because many believed that it enhanced discipline and fostered a sense of co-operation. Athleticism, it was widely believed, also provided valuable training for future imperial statesmen, soldiers and public servants. Considerable resources were devoted to the pursuit of athletic goals: the creation of playing-fields, the organisation of teams, and the development of associated rituals and rewards.

Athleticism and related ideologies were prominent in early colonial sporting newspapers such as *Bell's Life in Victoria and Sporting Chronicle*.[2] There was constant reiteration of the ideal of manliness, which was enhanced by involvement in approved physical activities, particularly team-games. A love of 'manly' sports was linked with the strength of the 'parent nation' and of the Anglo-Saxon peoples.[3]

The ideals associated with athleticism gained wide credence because they were backed by public schools, the church, the medical profession and the state. Many headmasters, teachers and clergymen, arriving fresh from British public schools where the games cult was prominent, enthusiastically set about making games an important part of the school curriculum. Joseph Coates (1844–96), the second master at Newington College in Sydney, was active in all aspects of school life: he was a strict disciplinarian in the classroom; he promoted the Cadet Corps on the parade ground and coached cricket and rugby on the sportsfield. Coates, who played cricket for New South Wales while teaching at Newington, was a popular figure and was said to be 'so agreeable and jolly that any visitor would hardly know him from one of the boys'.[4] Dr J. E. Bromby, headmaster at Melbourne Grammar School from 1858 to 1874, also believed in the importance of games in the curriculum and was instrumental in organising the first interschool boat-race in 1868 and a combined sports day in 1872.[5]

The ideology of athleticism was equally influential at Shore, another Sydney public school. The first five headmasters had strong sporting backgrounds and some masters were appointed as much for their sporting as their academic talents. The emphasis on sport increased public interest in the school and any effort to diminish the role of sport was opposed by the alumni. Such was the public interest in the spectacle of school sport that the Great Public School (GPS) headmasters took the important decision in 1916 to play major rugby games on Saturday rather than mid-week.[6] With the cessation of senior rugby during the war, GPS rugby attracted large crowds and unprecedented media coverage.

The games cult, largely initiated in Protestant schools, was soon taken up at élite Catholic schools.[7] Although there was some initial reluctance to encouraging athleticism at St Joseph's, Sydney—one of the French founders was even hostile to team-games—it was not long before games were as much part of the curriculum as in the other GPS schools. In due course St Joseph's became one of the most significant rugby schools in Sydney.

The church became deeply involved in sport for a variety of reasons. The Victorian preoccupation with health and purity was one factor—a healthy body was viewed as essential for the maintenance of a healthy mind: the motto *mens sana in corpore sano* ('a healthy mind in a healthy body') was often to be found attached to various institutions. The notion of Social Darwinism encouraged many clerics to believe that Christianity and Britain's imperial strength were linked, and that the 'strongest nations' were the 'fittest' to survive. Australia had many prominent Muscular Christians in the nineteenth century such as Reginald Heber Roe (1850–1926), headmaster of Brisbane Grammar School.[8] Some clerics promoted sport, as they promoted other forms of popular culture such as music, to help make the church more relevant in a rapidly changing urban environment.

Many Protestant clerics were critical of professional and gambling sports, such as prize-fighting and horse-racing, and were enthusiastic promoters of amateur sport, particularly team-games such as cricket and football. Ministers organised cricket and football teams and competitions and played in the teams themselves. The NSW Churches' Cricket Union, founded in 1902, produced many élite cricketers. The Waddy family provided a number of cricketing clerics and educationalists. Rev. Ernest Frederick (Mick) Waddy (1880–1958) played cricket for New South Wales and taught at The King's School while his elder brother, Canon Percival Stacey Waddy (1875–1937), who played first-class cricket, was headmaster at King's from 1906 to 1916. For Muscular Christians such as Percival Waddy the promotion of cricket and the Gospel went hand in hand. Cricket, he later wrote, was 'in my bones', and he promoted the game even when he became Secretary for the Promotion of the Gospel in Foreign Parts. Waddy admitted that it would have been 'bad for me to break into the Australian XI'; instead 'I put my whole enthusiasm into slogging Church work'.[9] Some clerics even played an important role in the organisation of higher-level sport: Canon E. S. Hughes (1860–1942), known as the 'sporting parson', was president of the Victorian Cricket Association from 1932 to 1942. The relationship between cricket and religion in the Victorian era was very direct and many clerics regarded the cricket field as a suitable moral classroom.[10]

Clergy and the churches were active in promoting a sports culture in the formative years of the St George area of Sydney. The Rockdale Congregationalists formed a Young Men's Institute which entered teams in the local cricket competition. Teams also participated in the district cricket competition from the Hurstville Presbyterians and St George's Church of England, and the Hurstville Methodists fielded a team to 'draw young men of the church closer together'. Rev. H. D. Kelly of St Paul's Church of England, Kogarah, who was 'a fine hitter and a grand sport', played in the St George Cricket Club. Rev. T. Holliday of Christ Church, Bexley, was known as 'the racing parson' because he had a passion for the turf and was a part-owner of a racehorse.[11] Archdeacon Evan David was a founding member of the exclusive Brisbane Golf Club and a vice-president.[12]

THE RISE OF AMATEURISM IN AUSTRALIA

Although there had been occasional events for amateurs—one of the events at the 1840 Sydney Anniversary Regatta was for gentlemen amateurs—it was not until the 1860s that separate amateur clubs and institutions appeared in a number of sports. After the formation of the Melbourne University Boat Club in 1859, an amateur rowing regatta was held in Melbourne in 1860, and by 1863 there were five amateur rowing clubs in that city. Amateur clubs also emerged in other sports as well. The Adelaide Amateur Athletic Club (1864) was the first club of its kind. H. C. A. Harrison played a prominent part in the formation of the Amateur Athletic Club, under the auspices of the Melbourne Cricket Club, in 1866.

The establishment of separate amateur institutions represented an important change because there had been no such segregation in Australian sport before this time. Although the Sydney Anniversary Regatta was one of the city's social events from its inception in 1837, it attracted people of all classes: the local watermen, the crews from visiting ships and the colonial gentry. The definition of an amateur was decidedly loose before 1850 and amateur rowers competed for money prizes at 1848 Brisbane Regatta.[13]

During the next decades there was a great expansion in the number of amateur clubs, events and institutions. By the 1880s there were colonial amateur institutions established in many sports, including the NSW Amateur Athletic Association (1887), which was the forerunner of a national association, the Amateur Athletic Union of Australasia (1897). 'Amateur' became the tag of respectability that was included in the name of colonial associations in swimming, bowls, boxing, cycling and a host of other sports. Although professional sports continued to flourish throughout the nineteenth century and even beyond, it was the amateur sports which set the sporting agendas of the country by the 1880s and 1890s.

The rise of amateurism generated a lengthy and often heated debate about the nature of sport in Australia, about the definition of an amateur (and a professional) and about appropriate codes of sporting behaviour. Much ink was spilled over these issues. There was the question of who constituted an amateur, which was largely a class issue based on occupation and social status. Equally important to many was defining a correct attitude towards money: whether an amateur should be paid for expenses and compensated for 'loss of time' from employment or because of injury. The relationship of amateurs to professional sport was a complex issue as well: there was much debate about the role of the professional in amateur sport and whether an amateur could participate in any form of professional sport.[14]

The British definition of an amateur before 1850 was a rather loose one, partly because many sports were mixed, with gentlemen and working-class players participating in the same sport. Initially the words 'amateur' and 'gentleman' were interchangeable. With the growth of a sporting culture and more class-specific sporting associations, clubs and even teams in the second half of the century, there was a greater need to define amateurism.

The problem of definition was a vexed and a continuing one for rowing authorities from the 1860s until the twentieth century. The Melbourne Regatta Committee, which controlled Victorian rowing from 1860 to 1875, produced a definition of a 'gentleman amateur' by 1861: it proscribed from competition men who had gained their livelihood on the water and who competed for money, but it did not exclude manual labourers. When the Victorian oarsmen competed against New South Wales in 1863 there was controversy because the New South Wales definition of amateur was different. The Victorians maintained that the New South Wales crew were really 'watermen, having rowed against watermen for money prizes'.[15]

Different colonial definitions of the amateur continued to be a problem in the 1870s, as suggested in the *Sydney Mail* of 12 April 1873:

> In Melbourne, all regatta committees admit a man as an amateur who does not directly or indirectly earn his living by building, letting or attending to boats or who has not rowed for a money prize, no matter whether he be a

hardworking tradesman or a University student; whereas in Sydney and Hobart Town they exclude all who earn their living by manual labour but they have no objection to their gentlemen rowing for a money prize.

The different colonial definitions of amateur status remained a problem by December 1888, when a conference was held on the subject. The question had surfaced again after the NSW Rowing Association (NSWRA) officially complained about the inclusion of two saddlers in a Victorian team which had raced in April 1888, considering them not to be 'bona fide amateurs'.[16]

The Sydney definition of an amateur was less flexible than the more pragmatic Melbourne definition, which emphasised that a man was an amateur providing he did not row for money or receive money from other athletic exercises. It was also possible, in Melbourne, to compete as an amateur in some sports but receive money prizes in others. This was anathema in Sydney, where 'professionalism was viewed as a character trait, a defect in one's personality'.[17]

The issue of what constituted an amateur continued to be debated for decades, and the existence of races for 'bona fide amateurs' from the 1860s suggested that officials were forever watchful for individuals who might slip through the net of regulations. The definition of amateur even varied from one club to another. While two of the exclusive Sydney city rowing clubs, Sydney and Mercantile, maintained a fixed definition of an amateur—someone not wishing to rub shoulders with manual workers and their ilk—the more cosmopolitan suburban clubs, such as Glebe, were more conciliatory to 'manual labour amateurs' but were unable to make much headway with the NSWRA until such amateurs were admitted in 1903.

The purity of amateur sport was a powerful and passionate belief in many quarters. John Blackman, the *Sydney Mail*'s rowing correspondent from 1884 to 1912, was 'articulate in his efforts to maintain the pristine purity of amateur rowing'. He elaborated this ideal in the *Sydney Mail* of 24 July 1897:

The ideal amateur is a person of education, refinement, leisure and means. He does not count the cost, nor does he question the gain. As a winner he is fully satisfied with the acknowledgement of his relative merit and seeks neither money nor goods with which his victory may be magnified in the eyes of others and his fame sustained in after years. He will row because he likes to and he will win because he can. The manual man, of course, cannot be judged on one or a dozen examples. He varies very much from the intelligent educated artisan down to the factory hand, and further than that, until we don't know where to stop. I am prepared to stretch the education clause a long way; it should perhaps be no bar. Refinement, that may go, so may leisure and means. We cannot give away more. He must be a man who rows for exercise and races for pleasure ... a man who does not need to row for exercise must have some impure motive for taking to the rowing, and that he will protect himself in some way against the works so doing (unnecessarily) by becoming a pot hunter ... No doubt he would get pleasure from winning;

but would pleasure alone be all that he felt he wanted? Would he 'take a bit' to go down or row his heart out to win a cap? In my opinion—which is not that of a new hand—he would not prefer the better race with the small reward. His model is not the ideal amateur as here drawn; no, it is the world-famed professional—the man of perfect skill, cunning and self assertion.

The purity of amateur sport stood out in contrast to the dross of professional sport:

> Amateur sport was good, wholesome and worthwhile, it imbued its particip-
> ants with the traits of fair play, modesty in victory, dignity in defeat and
> sportsmanship—all essential elements in the development of character. On
> the other hand, professional sport was primitive, unworthy, and dangerous,
> as it was associated with gambling, and was open to cheating, bribery and
> corruption. The professional, motivated by reward alone, could not hope to
> aspire to the ideals of the amateur.[18]

The career of Harold Hardwick (1888–1959), the 'quintessential amateur athlete', showed how harsh, rigid and unforgiving amateur officials could be in dealing with an athlete who had a brief stint as a professional. An outstanding swimmer and boxer, Hardwick reached the pinnacle of amateur success at the Festival of Empire Sports and the Olympic Games. In 1915 he became a professional boxer and fought against Les Darcy, but had retired by 1916 and joined the Sportsmen's Battalion in 1917. Participating in the Inter-Theatre of War Boxing Tournament, he was honoured as the 'Ideal Sportsman' in 1919. When Hardwick applied for readmission to amateur swimming ranks in 1921, his application was rejected.[19]

The experience of former political leader Don Chipp in the 1950s provides testimony to the continuing strength of amateurism and to the pettiness of some amateur officials:

> While still a callow youth in my mid-twenties, I fancied myself as being
> reasonably quick on my feet. I therefore decided to test my ability, and with
> the boundless conceit which accompanies our youth I decided I should set
> myself for the 100 or 200 metres at the Olympic Games. In attempting to
> register with the Victorian Amateur Athletics Association I received a rude
> shock. I was informed that because I was a professional footballer (I was
> with Fitzroy at the time) I could not be admitted as an athlete. I stoutly
> complained that I had deliberately maintained my amateur status and not
> taken any money for my games with the club. The amateur official retorted
> that that did not matter, I had taken football knickers and a football guernsey
> and therefore had lost my lily-white status; however, if I cared to fill in the
> requisite number of forms, wait a period of up to a year, the stain on my
> blemished record, could, as an act of grace, be wiped clean.[20]

There were a number of concerted campaigns by the advocates of amateurism to make sports more 'pure' and 'noble'. This involved rooting out gambling and removing any taint of professionalism and generally cleaning up sports which purported to be amateur. The campaign against gambling emerged gradually in some sports which came to define themselves as amateur. The various cricket associations were largely tolerant of gambling in sport in the 1850s and 1860s (see ch. 3).

By the 1870s there were concerted moves against gambling on cricket, and the authorities at Sydney's Albert Ground erected signs in 1871 announcing that gamblers would be ejected from the ground. The issue came to a head in 1879 when a celebrated riot occurred at the Sydney Cricket Ground—about 2000 spectators invaded the pitch and led to the abandonment of play for the day—which English captain Lord Harris believed was 'started and fomented' by bookmakers in the stand.[21] The repercussions of this riot were serious enough for colonial cricket authorities to move with more vigour to weed out gambling from cricket.

There were many other ways in which amateur-minded officials attempted to improve the moral tone of sport. The South Australian Cricket Association (SACA) was so perturbed by the 'bad language' used by 'uncouth footballers' using the pavilion of the Adelaide Oval in 1889 that it erected signs that 'no bad language be used in this room'. Nine years before this the secretary of SACA had taken the unusual step of criticising a number of the players of the South Adelaide Football Club, who used the Adelaide Oval, for 'rough' and 'unfair' play.[22]

In some instances there were rather more direct attacks on the promoters of professional sports and the sports themselves. While amateur boxing was accepted as a 'Muscular Christian' sport, some Protestant clergy singled out professional boxing for attack. By referring to it as 'prize-fighting' they implied that it was dominated by money.[23] Hostility to the sport reached its peak in wartime when the Council for Civic and Moral Advancement, which included Anglican, Presbyterian and Methodist clergyman along with some academics and other 'solid citizens', wanted Sydney Stadium closed down in 1916. One council member stated that professional boxing was a 'moral blot upon Sydney' and everyone 'was aware that the Stadium crowd contributes very few recruits in this national crisis'.[24]

The rise of amateurism totally altered the landscape and agenda of Australian sport. By 1900 a number of sports had been divided into separate amateur and professional associations. Amateurism was the dominant sports creed, supported by leading sports journals such as the *Referee* and backed by the most powerful sports officials and the sanctioned creed of public and private education.

In late nineteenth-century Australia amateurism was linked to greater class segregation in sport, which could be achieved by the high cost of entry and the blackball system. The latter, which operated in many clubs, ensured that any future members would be of like mind, social group and even religion. Twelve members of the Glebe Rowing Club, for instance, decided the prospective fate of any new member. Each of the twelve had the option of choosing a black or a white ball. It took only two balls to veto an application. The system ensured that the Glebe Rowing Club in its first decades had few Catholics and working-class members.[25]

SOME PROMINENT AMATEUR OFFICIALS

There has been too little consideration of the role of officials in shaping sporting institutions. The influence of some administrators has in some instances been immense. Whereas the playing careers of élite performers often do not extend much beyond a decade or two, some officials have dominated, and virtually run, a sport for three to five decades, acquiring a substantial power base in the process. During an extended period of office an administrator can become a powerful figure in a sport, a position enhanced by political, social and media connections. Australia has produced many such influential administrators.

Cricket had its prominent amateur-minded administrators such as Richard Driver (1829–80) and Philip Sheridan (1833–1910) in New South Wales, Ben Wardill (1842–1917) in Victoria and John Creswell (1858–1909) in South Australia. It was said by W. J. Hammersley that 'there was not much that happened in Melbourne [cricket] in which Ben did not figure'. Wardill's influence extended beyond Melbourne because he became a close friend of Sheridan.[26]

Creswell was a dominant and enterprising cricket official who was secretary of SACA from 1883 to 1909 but who was also influential in what transpired in South Australian sport as a whole. Born in Woodville, he attended St Peter's College and, after a stint in business, became secretary of SACA. He was also one of the founders of the South Australian Football Association and its first secretary. Although he was no wowser—he was secretary of the Winegrowers Association of South Australia—he was a strong advocate of 'clean' and 'fair' sport. Creswell was a powerful figure in South Australian sport as a whole because he controlled the leading sports facility of the city, the Adelaide Oval, which was used by footballers, cyclists, bowlers and many other sportspeople and because he had the ear of the important politicians of the city.[27] Cricket certainly benefited from Creswell's good connections as it required limited persuasion to secure a government holiday when an important match took place in South Australia.

Henry Colden Antill Harrison (1836–1929) has been described as the 'father' of Australian football. He was also the champion 'pedestrian' of Victoria for nine years. After retirement he became a prominent administrator, fostering these sports 'in the best traditions of Muscular Christianity'. Although he raced against professional runners, Harrison was a founder of the Melbourne Amateur Athletic Association in 1864 and was a believer in the sporting ethos of manliness, pluck and endurance.[28]

The Arnold brothers, William Munnings Montague (1851–1919) and Richard Aldous (1849–1923), were prominent Sydney rugby administrators who were also believers in the precepts of Muscular Christianity. The brothers were influential in the rise and consolidation of rugby in Sydney, playing a part in forming the Southern Rugby Football Union (1874) and in the split in rugby from 1907. Richard Arnold was also a founder of the Sydney Amateur Athletic Association in 1872 and joined the Volunteer Artillery as a gunner in 1868.

Richard Coombes (1858–1935) was a dominant figure in many amateur sports for nearly half a century. Born in England, educated at Hampton Grammar School, he was active in many sports as a youth: as a harrier, sculler, walker and cyclist. Shortly after his arrival in Australia he helped found a number of athletic associations including the NSW Amateur Athletic Association (1887), of which he was president from 1893 to 1935, and the Amateur Athletic Union of Australasia (1897), where he was inaugural president. Before that he managed an Australian athletics team to New Zealand (1889) and arranged the first Australasian championships in Melbourne (1892). Coombes earned himself the title of the 'Father of Amateur Athletics in Australia'. He was also one of the founders of the Australian Olympic Committee in 1895 and a member of the International Olympic Committee for twenty-seven years and was involved in many other sporting organisations: walking, harriers, rifle-shooting and coursing. Coombes was an influential figure because he was also a prominent Sydney journalist, joining the staff of the *Referee* in 1890 and becoming associate editor from 1919 to 1933. He was a lifelong imperialist and an apostle of amateur sport.[29] Coombes was described as

> a redoubtable figure, in his prime the most powerful and persuasive sports administrator in the country. He became known as the Grand Old Man of Amateur Sport. Always rather gaunt, he had a dignified slightly aloof demeanour and an English accent he refused to submerge. It was once written of him that 'in spite of every temptation, including a job as a jackeroo ... he remained an Englishman'. He was driven by a passion for sport and for organisation, a strong sense of nationalism, loyalty to the British Empire and a devotion to the Olympic ideal. Sometimes these last three sat oddly together.[30]

Ernest Samuel Marks OBE (1871–1947) was another imposing amateur-minded official whose influence spanned many sports. Like Coombes he was influential in State and national athletic associations and the Olympic and British Empire Games organisations. He was also associated with many other sports including swimming, rugby union, boxing, wrestling, billiards and coursing and was the founder of the Manly Surf Club. Marks was well placed to advance his vision of sport: he was an alderman on the Sydney City Council and Lord Mayor in 1930 and was for some years an MLA. He was largely responsible for the construction of the Sydney Athletic Field, which came to bear his name.[31]

Lawrence Arthur Adamson (1860–1932), British born and independently wealthy, attended Rugby School and Oxford University. After migrating to Australia in 1887 he became senior resident master at Wesley

College, Melbourne, where he was a passionate supporter of team-games, which he saw as a means of producing the Christian gentleman and the well-rounded individual. Adamson elevated athleticism at the school—which he hoped would become the 'Rugby in the Antipodes'—by introducing many elements of the Rugby system: the award of colours, codes of privilege and sporting songs, many of which he wrote himself.[32]

Headmaster of Wesley from 1902 to 1932, Adamson was a dominant figure in Melbourne educational circles. He was a powerful advocate of amateurism who had a puritanical attitude towards professional sport, referring on one occasion to the 'curse of large gate money' sport. He was also a fervent imperialist who believed that all sport should be allied to military work. Adamson revived the cadet corps at the school and celebrated Empire Day in fine style. He was prominent in many sporting associations: he was president of the Victorian Amateur Athletic Association in 1901–5, first president of the Australian Board of Control for Cricket in 1906, and chairman of the Victorian Branch of the Royal Life Saving Society.[33]

Adamson's achievement was to inject 'sentiment' at Wesley, to create a school spirit with sport as a focal point, and the success of his endeavour was influential elsewhere. Although there were voices raised against what some saw as the extravagant emphasis on the cult of athleticism, enrolments at the school increased, pupils, parents and old boys as a whole approved, and the school achieved much favourable publicity. There were many other headmasters who promoted the games cult in Australia including Henry Girdlestone, St Peter's College, Adelaide; John Bracebridge Wilson, Geelong Grammar; Albert Bythesea Weigall, Sydney Grammar; and Alexander Morrison, Scotch College, Melbourne.

THE RISE OF AMATEUR SPORTS

Individual sports dealt variously with the question of amateurism and conflict between amateur and professional. Some sports set up parallel amateur and professional organisations, and others contained elements of both ideologies, while the amateur–professional debate was a cause of dissension in yet other sports and led to splits. The following case studies suggest the varied responses to the amateur challenge.

Rowing   Professional sculling was one of the first sports to boom in Australia in the 1850s and was one of the more popular sports of the late nineteenth century, producing a succession of world champion scullers (see ch. 3). Amateur rowing grew rather more slowly and took some time to emerge out of the shadow of the professional sport.

The first amateur rowing regatta was organised at Melbourne in 1860. The moving spirit behind this regatta and the amateur rowing movement was Martin Howy Irving, the son of a famous Scots evangelical, who had won the Balliol College and Oxford University sculls in 1852 and was appointed professor of classics at Melbourne University in 1856. Before organising the 1860 regatta Irving formed the Melbourne University Boat Club in September 1859. By the 1860s there was a network of amateur clubs in Melbourne, and amateur clubs and associations were established by the next decade in other colonies. Probably because of the strength of professional sculling, the Melbourne Regatta Committee wasted no time producing a definition of a 'gentleman amateur' by 1861. Rather than settling the issue, however, the debate about the proper definition of an 'amateur' rower proved vexatious for five decades. Great care was taken to ensure that the sport was segregated carefully between amateur and professional performers, clubs and competitions (see above).

Athletics Professional athletics, like rowing, had an established following long before amateur athletics appeared. Running, walking and even throwing weights for money, which dated from the convict era, developed a sizeable following in the second half of the nineteenth century. Many popular gifts had been established from the 1850s, before amateur competition and institutions emerged. Professional athletics grew in popularity, perhaps reaching its pinnacle by the 1880s and 1890s.[34]

Amateur athletics developed rather more slowly. The first amateur club was the Adelaide Amateur Athletic Club, founded in 1864 by a group of the 'colonial gentry'. The purpose of the club was to raise the tone of athletics, which was advocated as 'healthy, manly and moral'. The proponents of amateur athletics argued increasingly that professional athletics was tainted by money, which led to sharp practices such as mismeasuring distances, running dead, or not trying against local champions after receiving appearance money.[35]

Although some amateur clubs were formed in the 1860s, it was not until the 1880s that amateur associations began to challenge the professional foothold on athletics. The NSW Amateur Athletic Association (NSWAAA) was established in 1887 and a similar organisation was formed in Victoria in 1891. The Amateur Athletic Union of Australasia came into existence in 1897.[36]

The distinction between amateur and professional was far from clear in athletics for some decades. There were occasions even in the 1880s when amateurs and professionals competed in the same program, but only under certain conditions such as no public betting. The definition of who was acceptable in amateur competition also vexed the minds of amateur athletics officials: a 'large part' of council and executive meetings of the NSWAAA was taken up considering applications of athletes 'who had strayed into the paths of professionalism and wished to be accepted back into the fold'.[37]

Amateur athletics had one long-term advantage over the professional branch of the sport—its control of school athletics. Three schools were present at the foundation meeting of the NSWAAA in 1887. All the leading schools became affiliates of this body in due course and a fertile nursery for amateur athletics. The Public Schools AAA affiliated in 1889 and the AA of the GPS in 1892.[38]

Cricket   Cricket evolved with relative ease from a gambling-based sport to one run by amateurs. While commercialism and professionalism produced some strains within the sport, particularly from 1878 to 1912, a major split was avoided. The transition from a pub-based and gambling sport of the 1830s and 1840s to Association-run cricket by the mid-century was relatively smooth. By the 1850s the organisation of cricket had become too large and complicated for individual publican promoters, and the sport required a new cadre of organisers. The new administrators of cricket were not at first hostile to publicans: most of the cricket associations had met and conducted their business in hotels.

The larger issue which divided the Australian cricket world from 1878 to 1912 concerned the issue of payment to players and who was to run the game. The issue surfaced in 1878 when players banded together in a joint stock company organising what proved to be a highly successful overseas tour: a £50 investment returned over £700. The success of overseas tours created problems for colonial administrators: the absence of star players for extended periods diminished the domestic cricket program and reduced the revenue of colonial associations.

It took more than three decades for administrators to gain control of domestic and international cricket. A central reason was that there was much rivalry between one colonial association and another and the first national cricket authority, the Australasian Cricket Council, was something of a paper tiger.[39]

The question of amateur versus professional cricket did not loom large in Australia as it did in England. While the 1878 tourists were by and large treated as amateurs, there was increasing debate in England during subsequent tours concerning whether these 'gate money cricketers', or 'commercials' as they were called in some quarters, were entitled to be called amateurs. There was less controversy about the professional in Australian cricket because Australia only had a handful of professional cricketers at any one time, whereas England had substantial numbers of them. Economics and geography were the main reasons that Australia lacked a corps of professionals: there was neither enough money in the game, nor enough regular intercolonial competition, to sustain such a group, and the cost of travel also limited the growth of a professional cadre.

Cricket administrators were able to take a much more pragmatic stance in the amateur versus professional debate. Since professionals were the exception to the rule, they could be accommodated more easily than in England. The elaborate rituals which separated the English amateur and professional—such as separate dressing-rooms, gates to the oval and dining arrangements—were not replicated in Australia.

Football codes   While cricket was able to contain the ideological differences and even the class tensions within the sport, the football codes were unable to prevent divisions. The major football codes in Melbourne and Sydney split into amateur and professional wings which were replicated in other cities. Eight of the stronger clubs broke away from the Victorian Football Association (VFA) in 1896 to form the more professional and commercial Victorian Football League (VFL) in 1897. The approach of the two associations to sport was quite different. While the more amateur-inclined VFA suspended play during World War I, the VFL continued its competition throughout this period.

The split in Sydney football was far more dramatic and acrimonious, and amounted to a 'rugby war' in that the sport was split along class lines, the more amateur code of rugby union and the more professional rugby league. The split in Victorian football by comparison was less damaging because the more professionally inclined VFL attracted clubs from both middle-class and working-class suburbs. The rugby war occurred in Sydney because the sport was booming in the first decade of the century and had become a mass-spectator sport. The problem for rugby was that it was run by a conservative establishment—middle-class, amateur and public school—who were totally unsympathetic to the views of many working-class footballers who increasingly flocked to the game.[40] The rugby establishment generated player discontent because of its unwillingness to compensate players for lost wages and to provide adequate payment for injuries incurred during play.

The intransigence of rugby officials encouraged an association of professional footballers to emerge in 1907. The new code was not an immediate success, and the 1908 Kangaroo tour to Britain proved a financial disaster. The professional code of rugby league would not have survived without the backing of hotelier and sporting entrepreneur Sir James Joynton Smith (see ch. 11). It also benefited from its adoption by Catholic schools (see ch. 7).

The rugby split transformed the geography of Sydney football. Rugby union became the code of the middle-class suburbs of Sydney, with its greatest strength to the north of the harbour and some pockets to the south, such as Randwick, while rugby league was more popular initially in the inner-city working-class suburbs.

It is interesting to speculate why rugby officials did not attempt to heal the wounds of 1907 and to reassert control over Sydney football. It appears that the conservative rugby establishment was so wedded to amateur ideals that they had no real interest in retrieving a large part of their football empire.[41]

There is no simple answer to the question of why cricket officials were able to contain class tensions within their sport whereas football administrators were not. The most likely explanation is that while cricket's popularity rose steadily throughout the nineteenth century, rugby's transformation from an élite to a mass-spectator sport took place in the matter of a decade or two, in the 1890s and the 1900s. Cricket officials had rather more time to resolve some of the strains within their sport.

Golf and lawn tennis   Golf and lawn tennis began as pristine amateur sports. They did not become prominent in Australia until the 1880s, by which time the ideals of amateurism had been well developed. The founders of both these sports, who came from socially superior groups, were able to create the type of organisations unencumbered by any previous practices.

The first golf clubs in Australia date from the 1880s and 1890s: the Australian Golf Club at Moore Park in 1882 followed by Royal Melbourne (1891), Royal Adelaide (1892), Royal Sydney (1893) and Brisbane (1896). The membership of the Brisbane Golf Club came from the élite of Brisbane society, with over half also belonging to the exclusive and aristocratic Brisbane Club.[42] Costs of membership, equipment and the blackball system ensured that club membership were confined to establishment Brisbane.

One of the characteristics of golf at this time was the 'servile' status of professionals. While the golf professionals 'taught and played with the members ... supplied and repaired golfing equipment, and their opinions on golfing matters were canvassed and respected', the professionals were required to know their place. 'They had restricted use of the clubhouse and facilities' and enjoyed 'familiarity with the members' only on the course proper. The 'unbridgeable' social gap between the professionals and their superiors was 'reflected in the absence of Mr for the paid men'.[43]

Below the élite clubs there was a network of lesser private clubs in the suburbs and country areas with lower fees and less selective membership. Yet another tier in the hierarchy of golf emerged with the creation of public courses where individual players simply paid to play. The first public course in Brisbane was not established until 1931.

Lawn tennis, like golf, began as an exclusive and decidedly amateur game. Initially, social tennis was rather more prominent than competitive tennis. When lawn tennis reached Australia in the mid-1870s it was taken up by the wealthy, who 'rigged nets in their city gardens or in the grounds of their country estates and invited long skirted ladies and men in cummerbunds, white shirts, and formal ties to tennis parties'. Tennis clubs such as Geelong were focal points for 'WASP' men 'of the Brahmin-class—people of wealth, social standing, political and economic power'.[44]

Tennis officials did not have to deal with the issues of professionalism and commercialism for many decades because it was not until the 1920s that the first hints of professionalism crept into the game: tennis-players then became agents of ball manufacturers, earned money writing for the press or became coaches.[45] The late development of conflict over professionalism—the open tennis issue of the 1950s and 1960s—may have made the crisis a more traumatic and disruptive one because the officials who ran the game had a deep commitment to amateurism.

THE STRENGTH OF THE AUSTRALIAN AMATEUR TRADITION

The Oxford Companion to Australian Sport comments on the strength of amateurism and the suspicion of the professional in Australia:

> While it is not surprising that Australia inherited the amateur ideology from Victorian England, it is perplexing that Australia has been so slow to follow even England down the path to professional sport, and has maintained a kind of schizophrenia about the excesses and attractions of the North American professional sports of football, basketball, and hockey. Even more, it is a curious paradox that, as John Daly, Australian Olympic coach and sports historian, has argued, although Australians have seemed to regard winning as their national sport, it is only fairly recently that they have been prepared to recognise the financial consequences of the commitment necessary to achieve sporting excellence.[46]

Another writer notes that the 'suspicion of the professional sportsman has a long history in Australia'. While the paid sportsman was linked, pejoratively, with 'theatricals', competition was deemed honest in amateur sport.[47]

There have been unique elements in Australian attitudes towards amateurism and professionalism. There has been a greater suspicion and far less acceptance of professionalism in sport than in North America and even in Britain, and a corresponding deeper commitment to amateur ideals in Australia. This is rather surprising because those reforming movements to 'civilise' sport, including amateurism, got off to a later start in Australia than Britain.[48]

There are a number of possible explanations for the long sway of amateurism in Australia. Its relatively late arrival may partly account for the strength and stridency of the amateur attempt to purify and elevate sport. Those who believed that sport should serve some moral purpose had to battle long and hard against already well-established notions of sport as entertainment based on drink and gambling.

As mentioned earlier, there were relatively few restraints on drinking and gambling in Australia for much of the nineteenth century as temperance and Sabbatarian lobbies and groups such as the RSPCA emerged much later in Australia than in Britain. The militant and even strident tone of Australian wowser groups in the 1880s and 1890s may have been due to their belated opposition to seemingly entrenched attitudes and traditions.[49]

There is another possible explanation for this stridency. The Australian middle class, which emerged in the late nineteenth century, had a strong sense of cultural uncertainty, the product of a convict heritage and a society marked with great social mobility. It advanced values like temperance, Sabbatarianism and amateurism with such vociferousness in order to assert its status. Class distinctions in sport were more easily accepted in Britain, where there was an entrenched class system, than in Australia where social structure was more fluid. This might explain why the British sporting establishment was quite comfortable with the notion of a professional, because the class differences between the gentleman amateur and the working-class professional were more obvious and definite. In Australia, by contrast, there was less certainty about such social distinctions and consequently a more fervent attempt to delineate them; debate about the appropriate definition of a professional and an amateur in the late nineteenth century was an aspect of this delineation. This may be why various colonial rowing groups diverged on their notion of the 'gentleman amateur'.

Many of the more significant amateur officials at the turn of the century were fervent imperialists and Anglophiles—Anglo-Australian gentlemen—who attempted to cling to their upper-class British heritage in a difficult environment in which alternative ideologies were emerging. Possibly, too, the cultural cringe mentality of the many Anglo-Australian officials who ran Australian sports at this time may have been a factor. They desperately wanted to prove that Australian sport was even more moral than British sport itself.

AMATEURISM IN THE TWENTIETH CENTURY

By the beginning of the twentieth century there was therefore a stark contrast between two competing ideologies of sport, the amateur and the professional. Nowhere was the contrast more evident than at the time of World War I when the amateur ideologues believed that all forms of organised sport should cease and that sportsmen should be encouraged to enlist for the 'Great Game', war service. Those who believed that sport was more a question of entertainment favoured the continuation of sport during war.[50]

At the time of World War I amateurism was the dominant sporting creed of the country and remained so until the latter part of the twentieth century. Amateurism permeated most sports, including new sports such as surfing. It was the ideology which was most touted in the newspapers, applauded by officials and politicians, and inculcated in schools. It was the unquestioned ideology of many of the more popular sports—cricket and most codes of football, tennis, golf, swimming and surfing, and the Olympic movement.

Without strong social backing, the financial support of the powerful, and continuing media exposure, many of the professional sports, such as sculling, cycling and boxing, struggled from time to time to maintain public support. The aristocratic associations of horse-racing made it the one gambling sport regarded by most people, other than the wowser fringe, as respectable. Because gambling was such an established part of its culture it was one sport which was not touched by the amateur versus professional debate. Other professional sports, such as rugby league, along with motor and motorcycle-racing, carved out their own particular niche of social support.

One of the intriguing questions about Australian sport is why the spell of amateurism lasted so long, well into the second half of the twentieth century. A possible answer is that highly placed and long-serving men such as L. A. Adamson and E. S. Marks inculcated the creed so effectively that its central tenets were not questioned for decades afterwards. This was why the progressive dismemberment of amateurism proved so difficult, and even traumatic, in some sports such as tennis and cricket in the 1950s and 1970s (see chs 7 and 11).[51]

Australian sport, for the best part of a century, was influenced by British class-based ideologies. Those who promoted these ideologies believed that sport should serve a moral purpose of creating individual character and team co-operation. The apostles of amateurism were well placed to set the main sporting agendas of the country.

Although amateurism was the dominant ideology for a century, not all Australians accepted the notion that sport and money should not mix. This issue caused strains in some sports and splits in others. Money was more freely accepted in a minority of sports including horse-racing and sports that were regarded as more working-class, such as boxing, sculling and pedestrianism.

It is intriguing to speculate why amateurism, which was promoted so enthusiastically for so long in Australia, disappeared so quickly and with so little ceremony in the 1970s. There has been such a rapid transformation in sporting culture in the television era that there has been limited debate about the more pragmatic and commercial values which have come to dominate. In this time there has been a dramatic shift away from British-inherited ideologies, which derived inspiration in part from the gentleman amateur, to a more American capitalist or globalist model (see chs 7 and 9).

5
GENDER

Sport plays a central role in growing up male in Australia. By implication it has some corresponding negative significance for growing up female.

> Sport occupies a central place in the lives and in the social development of boys, promoting in them a sense of power, forcefulness, mastery, and skill. These are part of a constellation of qualities which sociologist Bob Connell has identified as hegemonic masculinity. Today boys are still taught in a quite straightforward way that sport is a significant part of manliness ... Girls are introduced to the same skills, but in a negative manner as something which they cannot do well.[1]

Sport has shaped male culture in what most men regard as a positive sense, but has contributed to female culture in a less attractive fashion. Sport has shaped male attitudes towards their bodies and how they communicate with other males. It has long been a central part of male discourse. Sport has been a powerful influence on the formative ages of adolescence when boys are encouraged to participate by peers, school authorities, parents and the media, and it is one of chief means of socialisation, helping to inculcate the values of individual ambition and assertiveness within the framework of co-operative and team effort. Norma Grieve, a Melbourne psychologist, noted that sport for boys is 'not just play ... it's training, an arena for masculinity'.[2] Sporting culture provides many attractive role models for young boys.

The bonding of males through sport has been so strong that the culture of sport has excluded women. Grieve added that 'in our culture, footballs and cricket balls have a large label on them which says MALE'.[3] While many females participate both in female and in male sports cultures—following and attending male team-sports for instance—there are some others who 'hate' sport because they are defined as second-class citizens within the male culture of sport. Women can be excluded from discussion about sport on the assumption that they don't know anything about it. One writer has argued that sport has contributed to the oppression of women in that has been a focal point for the mobilisation of bias against women.[4]

Sport is far less important for girls in the critical years of adolescence. While many girls participate in sport at this time, there are fewer incentives to become involved and to treat sporting achievement seriously. Sport is merely one of the areas of female socialisation, along with the arts, music, ballet and domestic activities. Lacking encouragement from peers and adults, adolescent girls drop out from sport at a higher rate than boys.

Some forms of male sporting culture draw on a rough masculinity which further alienates women from sport. Besides the celebration of violence and aggressive masculinity, there are some more extreme forms of male sporting culture which are unashamedly misogynist. A study of rugby clubs and soccer hooliganism has analysed similar cultures in British society.[5]

Many questions about sport and gender in Australia can be raised. Why did sport become even more male after 1850? Who constructed and created this culture? Why did women have limited access to the games revolution? To what extent did sporting culture oppress women? The historical analysis of the construction of gender through sport is an important area for further analysis because the construction of gender has changed considerably over the past two centuries and male and female roles continue to be redefined.

There is the broader issue of whether sport can be reformed. Some feminists have regarded sport as so hopelessly riddled by masculine culture that it is beyond redemption. Others in recent times have concluded that sport is such a powerful and popular institution that the task of reforming it, by exposing and stripping away gender-restricting ideologies, cannot be avoided.

CONSTRUCTIONS OF GENDER

Sport in Australia before 1850 was almost entirely associated with male culture and male space. The traditional associations of sport with gambling and drinking were part of the reason; others were the links with violence and disorderly conduct. The sports clubs which appeared in the colonies were also extensions of workplace allegiances or drinking and dining clubs in public houses. Sporting gender constructions also drew on pre-industrial notions associating sport more with men than women.

From the 1850s, however, there was a redefinition of the Australian male and female and a greater articulation of specific gender ideologies. During this period there were radically new definitions of male, female, adult, child, homosexual and heterosexual. Redefinition was a product of a variety of factors: changed work, leisure and living conditions in emerging urban and industrial society, the expansion of education, higher rates of literacy, the rise of professions and the development of the mass media and the advertising industry.

Redefinitions of gender and age categories occurred in many areas. There were changes in the law: greater legal specifications about what constituted a child and adult, a compulsory age for education and age limits concerning work and the age of consent, which were raised progressively throughout the second half of the nineteenth century. The new concept of adolescence was a product of extended education and prompted much discussion of the particular problems of this age group. Many programs of physical education and recreation, organised by churches and voluntary groups, the 'Y', the Boys' Brigade, the Boy Scouts and Girl Guides, targeted adolescents.[6]

The rise of the mass media enabled ideologies of masculinity and femininity to be more sharply focused and more widely disseminated. Photo journalism and mass advertising enabled specific ideal body types to be promoted. Ideal body types—muscular men and pencil-slim females—were promoted to sell cigarettes and other items of mass consumption.[7]

There is no better illustration of how urban and industrial society sharpened the gender distinctions than the growth of children's literature in Britain which was influential in Australia.[8] Before 1850 this market was a comparatively small one and books were published in Britain for children in general. However, with the expansion of a youth market after 1850 there was a greater market segmentation, with more specific literary genres for boys and girls: a host of books flowed off the presses by authors such as Thomas Hughes, Capt. Marryat, Capt. Mayne Reid, W. H. Kingston and R. M. Ballantyne, and magazines appeared such as *Chatterbox and The Boy's Own Annual*. The genre of the adventure book disseminated the concept of the Victorian boy who was assertive and ambitious. While boy heroes performed remarkable feats around the Empire, the equivalent books and annuals for girls, by Charlotte Yonge and other authors, were far less colourful and exciting. The ideal for girls was a non-assertive and compliant femininity.

North American historian Steven Riess has suggested that masculinity was redefined in the changed urban and industrial environment of North America and that sport was a central element in it.[9] Redefinition was in part a reaction to new types of living and work situations, but it was also based on fears that the city was an unhealthy environment, both morally and physically. Some pointed to the temptations for the urban workforce, in the form of bars, brothels and brawling. Others believed that the sedentary life of the office workers would lead to physical weakness and even effeminacy.

Some moral improvers viewed sport as a means of countering these tendencies. The evangelical Young Men's Christian Association (YMCA), which began in England in 1844, was brought to America in 1851 'to assist farm youth adjust to urban life in a moral environment'.[10] By the 1870s the 'Y' provided young men of New York with sports facilities such as gymnasiums and bowling alleys and the culture that went with these.

Similar fears of degeneration in the urban environment were expressed in Australia. The idealisation of the bush and the myth of the rugged bushman formed a rich vein in Australian writing and drew attention to what was viewed as the unwholesome character of city life. J. P. Thomson published an article, 'The Geographical Conditions of City Life', in Australia in the late nineteenth century where he argued that urban life, which led to mental and physical degeneration, could be countered by the antidote of recreation:

> Whatever may be said to the contrary, there can be no reasonable doubt that mental and physical degeneration is promoted by the influence of urban life ... there is practically no third generation in the average tenement of large cities.
>
> In every civilised part of the world, but more especially in enervating regions, recreation is essential to health. It is in the city, where the pressure of business life is more severe, that the condition of the toiler requires improving and fostering.[11]

Some believed that a perceived prevalence of nervous disease was a symptom of the 'coming national decadence' which was caused by the concentration of 'brain-workers' in urban society and would result in the degeneration of the Australian 'type', a variant of the Anglo-Australian 'race'.[12] Other social commentators focused on the problems of urban youth, on the larrikins who had emerged as a problem for city planners by the 1870s.

Many considered that by providing more sport and recreation this range of urban problems could be diminished. From the 1870s there were efforts to create parks in cities and suburbs, to provide some green space where city-dwellers could 'breathe' and pursue various forms of recreation to counter the harmful effects of work and the urban environment.[13] Gymnasiums, swimming-pools and other recreational facilities were established to improve the physical health of the urban dweller.

MASCULINITY

Feminist historian Marilyn Lake has pointed out that as 'the history of womanhood has now been much studied' there is a need to investigate the social constructions of 'masculinity'. Gender history, investigating both notions of femininity and masculinity and the contests 'between men and women' over culture, has rich possibilities. Drawing on material produced by the cultural literati, Lake argued that there developed a separatist model of masculinity which was championed by the *Bulletin* in the late nineteenth century which encouraged 'masculine camaraderie' and the separate male 'pleasures' of drinking, smoking and gambling. This culture diminished in the twentieth century when misogynists were in retreat, 'Domestic Man' was more prominent and Australian culture had been 'feminized' to a degree.[14]

Studies of the masculinity of the more ordinary male, deeply immersed in sporting culture, have been made in recent times. Bob Connell has also drawn attention to the impact of sport on growing up male in Australia: 'These anxieties have a great deal to do with the physical definition of oneself as male. The cults of physicality, and especially of sport ... give clear ideal definitions of how a male body should look and work ...'[15] Peter West has investigated the role of sport for boys growing up in the Sydney suburb of Penrith. Some of the key themes which emerged from interviews were that 'many boys tried to excel in sport to please their fathers and gain intimacy with them; boys looked for a way out of isolation into popularity, sometimes through sport; boys struggled with fears of inadequacy about their bodies and found refuge in a sport which allowed them to excel'.[16]

The notions of 'manly' sports and 'manliness' were much discussed in nineteenth-century Australia. Manliness was not a new concept in that it drew on many pre-industrial nuances evolving from the ideals of the country gentleman, the soldier, the explorer, the imperial statesman and many other models. The term cropped up quite often in the colonial press from the 1830s.[17] However, the term 'manly' was used then in a more general and even loose sense referring to the positive qualities seen as arising from participation in vigorous outdoor sports. 'Manly' also applied to sports which took place in largely male space, around the public house.

From the 1850s manliness took on much wider significance and became a much-touted concept. It was redefined mostly by many middle-class reformers who wished to use sport to create a more disciplined and moral society. Manliness was given many wider meanings in that it drew on the ideals of athleticism, Muscular Christianity and Social Darwinism which were being popularised in the 1850s through the writings of Charles Kingsley and Thomas Hughes (see ch. 4).

Sport contributed significantly to the making of the Australian male, far more than has been recognised by Australian historians, who have emphasised constructions such as the bushman, bushranger and soldier. Historians such as Russel Ward, author of *The Australian Legend*, have given too much attention to rural myths and not enough to urban legends, including sporting ones.

Sporting conceptions were an important element of the debate on whether Anglo-Saxons could thrive in an alien environment. From the 1830s many colonial apologists argued that the colonial-born male, known as the 'cornstalk', was taller and stronger than his British-born counterpart. Others even advocated that colonials were more 'masculine' and 'virile' because they occupied more frontier and rural areas—they were less exposed to the deleterious effects of city life.[18] Working-class scullers, who emerged from the 1850s, were admired for their muscularity, vigour and physical strength and it was a matter of public interest to publish lithographs and later photographs of star performers in athletic pose. The press also recorded precise physical dimensions (weight, height, the size of chest, calf and biceps) of the athletic body. Sports readers were informed that world-champion sculler of the 1880s Bill Beach, a Dapto blacksmith, was 5 feet 9 1/2 inches tall (177 cm), with a 42 inch (107 cm) chest, 15 1/2 inch (39 cm) biceps, 16 inch (41 cm) calf and he weighed 170 lbs (77 kg). The success of the colonial-born scullers was hailed as proof positive that the Australian 'type' was physically robust.

While some Australian constructs of masculinity were similar to those which developed in the northern hemisphere—which had changed from 'lean and lithe to mesomorphic' by the 1890s[19]—there were some unique Australian conceptions such as the lifesaver, who became the ideal 'national type' by the 1930s. The 'sun-bronzed' lifesaver was a variant of previous ideals: 'masculinity, the cult of mateship, the military associations, the hedonism and wholesomeness' of outdoor life. Unlike the drover and the digger, the lifesaver was identified with the city, which was where organised sport flourished, and was admired for his voluntary sacrifice in the interests of community service.[20]

The anti-authoritarian and laconic larrikin was another Australian 'type' which became incorporated into Australian sporting constructs. Maree Murray has explored notions of masculinity in rugby league biographies published in the 1980s and early 1990s. She concluded that the easy-going larrikin, violent and decidedly heterosexual, was prominent in these books, which were 'conservative, pernicious and rapacious'.[21]

Variant codes of masculinity developed from sport to sport and State to State. A long-standing tradition of 'rough' masculinity was one reason why women were largely excluded from the culture of rugby league until the 1980s. In Melbourne, by contrast, it has long been 'respectable for women to be as fanatical footballers as the men'[22] and as a result more women have attended football matches than in Sydney. One possible explanation for this disparity was that while Australian football attracted support from all sections of society—which helped modify notions of rough masculinity—Sydney rugby league was more largely a working-class game until it was transformed in the 1980s (see ch. 11).

SPORT AND BODIES

Sport has also been important in promoting actual body shapes. While painting and lithography played an important role in the enhancement and elevation of sport, photography was, and still is, an immensely powerful visual method of representing the ideals, aesthetics and values of a particular sport.

Photography helped to spawn a new sporting cult, that of body-building, when strongman Eugen Sandow introduced a 'public display of athletic muscularity' at the Chicago World Fair in 1892. Sandow, who performed for ten weeks at the fair, entered a glass booth and performed a series of muscular poses to music. Although Sandow drew on many existing forms—the tradition of the strongman at local fairs, vaudeville and classical poses which dated from ancient Greece—it was photography and the backing of promoter Florenz Ziegfeld that helped to create a new and powerful sporting cult which was spread far and wide through body-building magazines.[23]

The power of the artistic and photographic image was recognised almost immediately. When the 'great white hope', Tommy Burns, fought against the African-American Jack Johnson in Sydney in 1908, artist Norman Lindsay's cartoon captured Australian 'ambivalence born of fear, hate, sexual myths, and admiration that many Australians felt towards the black races'—most particularly to a man viewed as a 'bad nigger'—and portrayed Johnson as 'magnificent evil'.[24] Body-builders, boxers and athletes developed poses—and appeared with as limited clothing as possible, usually only trunks—to emphasise their muscularity. Physicality, and even sexuality, was central to many sporting photographs, such as the c.1900 rear full-length nude picture of black boxer Peter Jackson, who was born a West Indian but fought as an Australian. Such photographs were a common practice at the time. After the European body-builder Eugen Sandow visited Australia *Athletic Queensland* published a photograph in 1900 of the muscular torso which could be achieved by Sandow's 'combined developer', a wall exerciser, chest expander, dumb-bells and a heavy weight-lifting apparatus.[25]

There was less display of near-naked bodies and hedonism in the more middle-class conceptions of the Australian male in the rugby code in the 1870s and 1880s, which were dominated by public school notions of masculinity.[26] School team photographs, on the other hand, were carefully staged to reflect ranking, uniformity of dress and a common pose (such as arms folded) to stress the unity of the team. The influence of sport on body shapes was recognised and even debated at the time. A cartoon, captioned 'Muscular Development of the Future', which appeared in the Queensland newspaper *Figaro* of 24 May 1884, satirised the result of athleticism—the rower with exaggerated legs and the boxer with an oversized torso and arms.

There was a world of difference from near-naked muscular male bodies of the late nineteenth century and the female athletic figure, which was clothed and disguised, hidden by hats, swathed in long dresses and encumbered by corsets. The development of an ideal female sporting body took much longer to emerge and had to wait for some decades until dress reform. With one or two notable exceptions—such as Annette Kellermann who appeared in vaudeville as the 'Australian Mermaid' and 'Diving Venus' in the early twentieth century and helped to popularise a briefer one-piece swimming-costume—notions of ideal women's sporting bodies were far less developed than men's.

The rise of the mass advertising industry from the 1890s also created a greater market for 'sporting bodies'. In some areas, notably that of cigarette-smoking and drinking, advertisers targeted an almost exclusively male audience. Female and male bodies were an important part of the campaign aimed at playing on male emotions, phobias and fantasies. Some advertisers featured excessively slender females and women in 'cheesecake' poses. Others featured sporting males profiting notably from the popularity of sport with female audiences. By the twentieth century advertisers sought new outlets to sell products through association with the sporting body. 'Pub art', which became popular from the 1920s, promoted brands of beer with the male body, often a footballer, as an icon in action. The ideal male body was exaggerated in artistic representation, with oversized muscles, huge forearms and strong and definite jaw lines.

By the first decades of the twentieth century, however, women began to participate in a wider range of sports and to wear more rational dress with more display of the body, and there developed the beginning of a discourse on the female sporting body. The sports of swimming and surfing were influential in the 'production of the ideal middle-class body—slim, tanned, athletic and self-disciplined', assisting in the transformation of 'repressive bodily regimens' to more 'disciplined permissiveness'.[27]

Advertisers were at the forefront of capitalising on females, who now swam in sleeveless bathers or played tennis or cricket in a costume which reached to the knee or even above it. While women were encouraged by the 1920s and 1930s to develop a trim and toned sporting body with a hint of some muscular development, there was considerable emphasis on what the sporting woman should avoid—unsightly hair, complexion worries and, above all, unwelcome body odour. The female athlete was encouraged to buy a new range of toiletries to deal with odour, hair-removing cream to remove body hair and other products to protect her complexion. The product Odorno was advertised in the 1920s to check body odour: 'the tennis season—warm weather, strenuous exercise, light clothing—special care is needed to keep underarms dainty—to prevent unsightly perspiration stains, disagreeable odour'.[28]

While there was admiration for the male sporting body as a whole, there was only qualified acceptance of an equivalent female sporting body. The construction of an ideal feminine sporting physique proceeded slowly and often awkwardly because it did not fit well with contemporary feminine beauty myths, which stressed that women should be delicate, dainty and graceful. There has been a continuing tension during the past century between the demands of sport and beauty on the female body. While toned and developed muscles were welcomed on men and regarded as a sign of good health and vitality, they were something which sportswomen needed to guard against. It was a matter of comment for one journalist that there was no sign of 'ropes' or 'muscles' on the body of Australia's first champion Olympic swimmer, Fanny Durack.[29] Since that time, the onus has been on women sporting participants to prove that they have not lost their 'femininity'.

The physicality, and even the apparent sexuality, of some depictions of male bodies—of Peter Jackson and Jack Johnson—raises the question of sport and sexuality. In a very thoughtful piece entitled 'Sport and Eros' Allen Guttmann has argued that this question has been a taboo subject for sports historians and has even been something of an embarrassment for those who normally affirm the joy of sports. Guttmann points out the interesting paradox that while 'YMCA workers, physical educators, and coaches have propagated the modern myth that a heated contest and a cold shower diminish or divert adolescent sexuality, clerical critics of sports since the days of St. Augustine have maintained the opposite'.[30]

Guttmann says that while sport was seen by many, including Freud, as 'replacing sexual pleasure' and pushing sexual activity back upon its autoerotic components, the 'spectator's admiration for athletes and their performances is to some degree tinged if not positively steeped in erotic impulses' and the 'pleasure that athletes experience may have roots in these same mysterious impulses'. He suggested that it is better to 'test these possibilities than prudishly to deny them'.

There are a number of important issues about sport and sexuality which need to be considered. The discussion on sport and sexuality to this point has been superficial, if not prurient. The only question of seeming interest is whether sexual activity before sport enhances or detracts from performance. Jim McKay has suggested that there are many wider issues:

> Moreover, in sport, boys encounter a subculture riddled with an ambiguous array of heterosexual, homosexual, homophobic and misogynist values. Many males are also oppressed physically, emotionally and sexually by sport and those who reject its macho aura are often ostracised or stigmatised by males and females. Male dancers and figure skaters are frequently subjected to ridicule and rumours about their manliness from both males and females. As any male athlete will verify, the most insulting accusation a coach can make about a player's inferior performance is to say that he 'played like a sheila' or a 'poofter'.[31]

Throughout the nineteenth century sporting messages were ambiguous. While the ideology of manliness emphasised sexual repression to some extent—subjugation of individual ambition for the team—the emphasis on virility and individual aggression also encouraged hedonism. While youth sport was seen by some schoolmasters and clerics as a means of suppressing youthful sexual activity, sport for others was linked with sexual expression and even licence. North America had its 'bachelor subculture' for single males, who frequented bars, brothels and billiard rooms.[32] There has always been an interesting, but largely unexplored, link between sport and pornography. 'Sport and sexual innuendo' were the staple themes of *Dead Bird*, a Sydney weekly which existed briefly in the 1880s, before it was subsumed into the *Referee*, which concentrated on a more serious treatment of sport.[33]

There has also been limited discussion of important issues such as sexual stereotyping and even harassment and vilification in sport. There is a hidden history of sport which has largely occurred in locker rooms and bars. There has, for instance, been a long history of criticism of women who dared take up 'male' team-sports as closet males, or 'butch' women. While there has been very limited interest in the sexual activities and partners of males off the field, there has been much discussion (largely off the record) of these matters about sportswomen. A media remark, in the 1930s, that English cricketer Betty Archdale's hair was cropped close in the style of a boy must have been enough to set some male tongues wagging. On the eve of the 1951 Australian tour to England the Melbourne *Sporting Globe* of 5 April 1951 published the following banner headlines: 'Women Cricketers for England', 'Average 26 Years' 'Only One Married'. The one married player, it informed its readers, was 'Dot Laughton, of South Australia, whose husband is a Government servant'. Such is the strength of this perception that the onus has always been on women, according to Ann Mitchell, former president of the Australian Women's Cricket Council, to prove their 'femininity' and to disprove the 'butch' image. Mitchell noted that one of the reasons why Australian women opted for culottes rather than trousers was to counter this stereotype and present a more acceptable feminine image.[34] Other women's sports, such as hockey and tennis, have also on occasions been labelled lesbian sports.

The Denise Annetts affair was seized on by the media in January 1994 because it gave substance to the popular perception that women's cricket was dominated by lesbians. When Annetts, a world-record batter and a heterosexual, was omitted from the Australian cricket team to tour New Zealand in December 1993, she explored her situation with the NSW Anti-Discrimination Board, alleging that she had been dropped from the national team because of her sexuality. There are grounds for believing that the media sensationalised this incident in that few journalists appeared interested in probing the precise reasons for her non-selection and the particular grievances of Annetts. It is ironic that women's cricket, which had battled for media attention for decades, secured so much (adverse) publicity at this time. Homosexuality in male sports, by comparison, has never rated as a media issue. Former Australian hockey captain Sharon Buchanan suggested that on a proportional basis there were just as many homosexuals in male football as in women's hockey, but 'because football is such a macho sport, gays hide their homosexuality'. Football coach Roy Masters added that 'men are uncomfortable about discussing homosexuality in their sport' yet are eager to talk about lesbianism in women's sport and 'many display a blatant degree of voyeurism with lesbianism'.[35]

Because the issue of gays in sport has either been ignored or sensationalised, there has been limited discussion of gay male or lesbian sporting teams or of a likely greater gay representation in some sports.[36] Undoubtedly some sports are more homophobic than others. It is also possible that some lesbian women may be attracted to a sport such as cricket or football, which has been viewed as manly, while some gay men may prefer a sport such as netball, which is regarded as feminine. Whatever the reason, one former netball official reported that there was a very strong gay involvement in men's netball in Melbourne.[37]

FEMININITY

While sport played a very important role in the construction of masculinity, it was of limited influence in defining femininity in nineteenth-century Australia. There was far less sporting culture available for girls and women since there were other areas for the definition of femininity. If sport provided what most men regarded as positive cultural and body images, its impact on women was more limited and even negative.

Sport has constrained female physical expression. Until recently women have been discouraged from involvement in many forms of sport. Participation in sport for women has not been on equal terms with men: sport has underlined women's subordinate and subsidiary position, whether it be in associate membership, lesser prize-money and access to sporting facilities, inferior sporting status or minimal media coverage.

Women were late starters and missed out on most aspects of the games revolution which took place in Australia from the 1850s. This occurred in part because women's access to public space, public institutions, education and employment opportunities was restricted. The slow emergence of educational opportunity for women was probably the most crucial disadvantage because schools provided respectability and legitimacy for sport.

Various studies have pointed out how the medical profession in particular and the media actively discouraged women from participation in any vigorous physical activity. Doctors popularised the theory of 'finite energy' or vitalism. British Professor Henry Maudsley stated that too much physical and even mental exercise would dissipate energies required for reproduction: 'Nature is a strict accountant and if you demand of her in one direction more than she is prepared to lay out, she balances the account by making a deduction elsewhere.' Doctors were indirectly responsible for what Stephanie Twin referred to as a mid-century 'cult of ill health' in which women proved their femininity by 'invalidism'.[38] Australia had its own doctors, such as Walter Balls-Headley of Victoria, who were influential in promoting similar views. Balls-Headley argued that girls should not be educated beyond the primary level in that it 'not only placed them in physical peril, it also put them in competition with men—it desexed them'.[39]

Even as late as 1911 British Dr Mary Scharleib warned of the dire consequences of too much sport:

> Doctors and schoolmistresses observe that excessive devotion to athletics and gymnastics tends to produce what may perhaps be called the 'neuter' type of girl. Her figure, instead of developing to full feminine grace, remains childish or at most tends to resemble that of a full-grown lad, she is flat-chested, with a badly developed bust, her hips are narrow, and in too many instances there is a corresponding failure in function. When these girls marry, they often fail to become mothers ... they are less well-fitted for the duties of maternity than our are more feminine sisters.[40]

Women who played in team-sports were frequently seen as unattractive. Hockey for women, it was suggested in 1913, 'produces angularities, hardens sinews, abnormally develops certain parts of the body, causes abrasions, and at times disfigurement. It thus destroys the symmetry of mould and beauty of form, produces large feet and coarse hands'.

Women participated in a very limited range of sport in the nineteenth century. They were restricted to sports which were considered 'ladylike' and were not physically taxing. Drill, which was considered the lightest and safest of exercises, and callisthenics, which emphasised rhythm and grace, were some of the first sports to gain acceptance. Tennis, which was played as a social rather than a competitive game, also gained acceptance. The segregated sport of swimming had the advantage of being considered beneficial for health.

There were greater opportunities for some women in higher education from the 1880s, when a network of women's private schools appeared which encouraged sport. A growing body of evidence suggests that many women were keen to pull down some of the sporting barriers and to participate in the games revolution; in Australia, as in the northern hemisphere, 'by no means all women paid close attention to medical cautions about overuse and overstrain in sport and exercise'.[41] Many of the principals of the newly established public schools for girls took the view in the 1880s and 1890s that girls should be permitted to enjoy a wider range of physical activity because, apart from anything else, it would make them stronger and more robust mothers. By the 1880s and 1890s there were many vigorous debates about the medical ideology of vitalism and many school principals and even prominent nursing administrators like Frances Gillam Holden (1843–1924) questioned the narrow and orthodox interpretation of Maudsley and Balls-Headley.[42]

There was also the practical issue that a more diverse and progressive program of sport could increase school enrolments. Some prominent educationists, such as T. Broadribb, an inspector-general of schools and head of the Education Department in Victoria, was not impressed by medical rhetoric and restrictive clothing like the corset. In *A Manual of Health and Temperance*, first published in 1891, he argued that 'girls, as well as boys, should have a share in such amusements as running, rowing, and driving a hoop', for it was 'a mistake to restrict them to dancing, tennis, croquet and the skipping rope'.[43]

Sport for women emerged first in independent Protestant schools rather than the government or Catholic systems of Australia. One explanation of this is that independent schools as commercial ventures needed to entice students by the attractiveness of their curriculum, which would have included a broader program of physical education, drawing on the latest overseas techniques such as the Swedish Ling system of gymnastics. Teachers recruited from abroad were keen to develop alternatives to the monotonous drill offered at most government schools. The Methodist schools, unwilling to include dance in the curriculum, looked to physical education and games instead.[44]

From the 1870s sport and recreation became part of the curriculum of the denominational schools. An article on sport in Victorian private schools for 'young ladies' sees these developments as the construction of a female version of athleticism: the Misses Morris of Melbourne Girls' Grammar School considered the 'masculine' traits of 'loyalty, courtesy, modesty, compassion' inculcated through athleticism as 'worth introducing to women'.[45]

While there was undoubtedly some overlap from the male to the female curriculum—sport was seen as useful for discipline and health—there is argument about the view that the emerging female sporting ideal was a watered-down version of athleticism, an ideal modified for women. While boys were encouraged to participate in sport to prepare for future careers, such as the public service or the army, the rationale for sport for girls was primarily as preparation for motherhood.[46]

Costume was another important way in which women's sport was circumscribed and controlled politically. The fashion pages and the media went to great lengths to stress 'the need to remain feminine in appearance while indulging in sports'. Women had to perform in uniforms which were tailored to satisfy the moral scruples of the majority rather than to assist in physical performance. There has been much more controversy about women's costume than about men's attire. There have been widespread public debates about the bloomers in cycling, the one-piece costume in swimming, the culotte (box-pleated skirt) versus trousers in cricket, and acceptable dress in many other sports.

There are some interesting questions about the relationship between feminist movements and sporting dress reform at the turn of the century. To what extent was sporting reform part of the feminist program? Did feminism contribute to the reform of sporting institutions and dress? Were women who participated in sporting reform also active in feminist movements?

There was undoubtedly some overlap between feminism and the issue of women's sport. Miss Evelyn Dickinson at the University of Sydney cycled, wore rational dress, believed in political equality and, it was rumoured, she also smoked.[47] She was the founder of the Sydney University Women's Boat Club in 1897—one of the first bodies which bore the name 'women' rather than 'ladies'. Vida Goldstein, who founded the Women's Federal Political Association in 1903 to support her own candidacy for the Senate later that year, was the first president of the Victorian Ladies' Cricket Association, which was established in 1905. Prominent Sydney feminist Rose Scott was president of the NSW Ladies' Swimming Association. Jessie Street was a more recent activist who promoted women's rights through sport at the University of Sydney.[48] This overlap occurred in other societies such as Britain: H. G. Wells's Anna Veronica was a symbol of the 'New Woman' in that she rode a bicycle, wore trousers and was arrested for suffragette activities.[49]

While it is true that some prominent women were involved in both the reform of women's sport and feminism, it not so easy to determine whether sports reform contributed anything substantial to movements for women's rights or whether it was an important plank of the feminist platform. Or, did the successful movement for more rational dress in women's sport occur because of pressure from within sport or because of external factors, changing fashions and social attitudes? It is likely that sport reflected rather than caused changes in women's rights. Female sporting administrators such as Rose Scott were rather more concerned to gain wider public acceptance for women's sport and were cautious in promoting sports reforms. Scott was opposed to mixed swimming and surf-bathing.[50]

THE RISE OF WOMEN'S SPORTS

There has been a long history of the marginalisation of women's sport in Australia. For much of the past century most women's sport has been confined to the periphery and has had to survive with limited encouragement, recognition and resources. Despite this very considerable discouragement, many women and girls have participated in a wide range of sport. The extent of their involvement in the nineteenth century has not been appreciated in the past because there has been a conspiracy of silence by which their role in sport has been played down.[51]

During the 1880s and 1890s, however, there was an increase in Australian female participation in competitive sports such as occurred in England, France and America.[52] In the Bendigo Easter Fair in the 1870s, women fought hard to play cricket despite 'obscene and insulting comments' made by male spectators and the patronising attitude of the press, which focused rather more on their costume than their cricket. The women of Bendigo viewed the game 'not as risque or as a burlesque, the way it was reported, but as a perfectly legitimate recreation and fund-raiser'.[53] They used sport to reappraise social norms and roles.

Aristocratic sports   Before the 1880s there were rather more sporting opportunities for upper-class women than for others. Élite women owned their own horses and occasionally took part in hunt clubs. In country areas some women participated in show-jumping.

Rowing and sailing were taken up by the daughters of wealthy families as the sports required both access to boats and suitable storage sheds. Lady Jane Franklin, wife of Tasmanian Governor John Franklin, actively promoted water sports and founded an annual Hobart regatta. Archery and rifle-shooting were also sports enjoyed by the more privileged. Lady Roma Bowen was an enthusiastic archer and organised archery parties at Government House, Victoria. A daughter of the South Australian Governor was the Adelaide women's champion archer in the 1860s.[54]

Callisthenics   This was one of the first acceptable sports for women. It was seen as a suitable, safe and respectable form of exercise in that it was gentle, graceful and rhythmic. Callisthenics also took place within the confines of private gymnasiums where women wore 'rational gymnastic clothes, consisting of knickerbockers worn under [a] short tunic jacket'.[55] The teaching of callisthenics became part of the curriculum of girls' schools in Sweden and Germany by 1870 and Mme Osterberg Bergman was employed in Britain in 1878 to introduce similar programs of physical education there.

The establishment of gymnasiums where callisthenics were taught represented the first occasion when resources were devoted for women's sport on a continuing basis.[56] Two English women, Harriett Elphinstone Dick and Alice Moon, migrated to Melbourne in 1876 and opened the Melbourne Ladies' Gymnasium in Collins Street in 1879 where they taught the Ling Swedish method of callisthenics. Dick, who was a long-distance swimmer and swimming instructor, also began swimming classes for women at St Kilda. Dick and Moon also organised classes in Melbourne private schools. Gymnasiums and physical culture schools were established in the other cities of Australia.

Swimming   This was the most popular and acceptable leisure activity for women of all classes in the nineteenth century, though it did not become organised as a sport until the end of the nineteenth century. As a sport swimming had a number of natural advantages. It could be easily segregated: male and female swimmers could swim in separate pools or at different times and days in common pools, beaches and rivers. Bathing at the beginning of the nineteenth century was regarded as a fashionable leisure pursuit and as the century progressed many defined swimming as healthy and useful. One of Australia's famous swimmers, Annette Kellermann, was advised to take up swimming in the 1890s to correct a weakness in her legs dating from childhood.

Women's swimming went through a number of transformations in this century, from bathing to social swimming to competitive swimming. With an expanded network of suburban and municipal baths in the 1870s and 1880s there was sufficient acceptance of swimming for women for it to become a commercial enterprise. Henry Cavill's swimming classes for women during the 1880s have already been mentioned. Even so, the issue of competitive swimming for women raised considerable controversy in the first decade of the twentieth century. There were vigorous debates about female swimming-costumes and whether competitive swimming for women should be segregated.[57]

Swimming was the first competitive sport for women to gain general acceptance. Because it was largely 'hidden', did not involve 'sweat', was associated with health and was an individual sport, it attracted less criticism.[58] Women's competitive swimming boomed from the first decade of the twentieth century, and clubs, competitions and facilities for women's swimming were greatly expanded. The success of Fanny Durack and Mina Wylie at the 1912 Olympics and the career of Annette Kellermann provided women with positive and attractive sporting role models and body shapes. Kellermann, in particular, did much to challenge some of the restrictive notions which limited women's sport. When she was arrested on a Boston beach in 1907 for wearing a brief one-piece costume, the publicity helped to relax the laws relating to women's swimwear. She competed in a number of well-publicised long-distance swimming events including a 22-mile challenge race down the Danube in 1906, and made three unsuccessful attempts to swim the English Channel.

Lawn tennis, croquet and golf   The largely individual sports of lawn tennis, croquet and golf for women became popular in the 1880s and 1890s. Tennis competitions for women dated from 1884 and there was a national golf championship for women by 1894. Although there was a competitive element to these women's sports, most female involvement was social rather than competitive. Tennis gained wide public acceptance as a 'ladylike' recreation. It was regarded as an appropriate mixed sport because many games were played on private tennis courts and represented an attractive new form of outdoor home entertainment and social intercourse, including even courting. Women played all three sports in long skirts, which must have greatly reduced their mobility but satisfied even the most morally conservative.

Sports such as tennis evolved gradually from an élite social pastime to a more competitive and vigorous spectator sport. The slow, almost imperceptible, transition was one reason why there was so little criticism of women playing tennis competitively. Tennis, golf and croquet were also individual rather than team games and trespassed less on 'male territory'. While tennis extended the boundaries of women's sport, women's tennis was 'fundamentally conservative' in that it followed rather than led changing female sporting agendas.[59]

Cycling   This was the first real mass sport for women. With the development of the cheaper pneumatic-tyre bicycle, cycling enjoyed a boom in popularity in the 1890s. Perhaps reflecting a desperation for greater access to leisure and public space, many women took part in cycling, joined clubs and even raced. The six-month tour of Mademoiselle Serpolette in 1898, 'the champion lady cyclist of the world', was a much-publicised event. The exhibition riding of the young French star provided women's sport with an attractive model.[60]

Women were an important though controversial part of the cycling craze in Australia in the 1890s. The involvement of women in this sport created debate because cycling was a much more public sport than any of the more accepted 'ladylike' sports and it provided women with a greater mobility and an increased access to public space. The central issue of debate evolved around costume and dress reform. The issue of whether women should cycle in full-length dress, which restricted their ability to cycle, or wear more rational attire, such as bloomers, was not fully resolved in the 1890s.

Team-sports   Around the turn of the century the number of women who played team-games such as hockey and cricket increased. There were some instances of women forming football teams. Team-sports appeared in schools; interschool competitions were formed along with club and State associations.

Since team-sports were regarded as 'masculine', women who took up these games were criticised and even ridiculed. While there were many jokes about fashion and matrimonial stakes in the press coverage of women's tennis and croquet, the more savage attacks were reserved for women 'who were bordering on the margin of contemporary notions of male and female behaviour'. Scorn was poured on those women who performed in bloomers or trousers and they were depicted as 'large, ugly or masculine'.[61] Women's cricket in Australia has had a long battle for acceptance. While the sport has prospered at certain times, as in the 1930s, acceptance at such times by the media and society at large has been qualified and limited.[62]

Some team-sports, such as hockey, softball and netball, have been more accepted sports for women. There are several likely reasons for this. Possibly because hockey was less developed as a male sport than were cricket and football, its territory could partly be claimed by women. However, the women's team-sports which have most prospered in the twentieth century have been modified ones in that they were derived from other games.

It is paradoxical that an imported bat-and-ball game from North America, softball, was probably the fastest-growing sport, male or female, in the 1960s and 1970s. Softball, which was introduced by North Americans in the 1940s (see ch. 9), was regarded as a suitable game for women because as a modified form of baseball it did not intrude into the territory of men. Softball grew rapidly because it was accepted by educational authorities as a desirable summer sport. Its success also reflected the drive of women to participate in a socially acceptable team-sport. Such was the strength of Australian softball that Australia defeated the United States in the final of the first International Series in Melbourne in 1965. By the 1970s there was an estimated 200 000 softball-players in Australia.

One researcher has discovered that while softball was introduced to Australia by men such as Gordon Young and Mark Gilley, their wives soon took over the organisation of the sport. Softball may even have become associated with a form of feminism: from the early 1950s regulations were passed which excluded male participation from executive positions in softball administration; when the national tournament was played in a particular State it was referred to as the 'hostess' rather than the 'host' State.[63]

In recent decades softball has been overtaken by netball as the fastest-growing team-sport, male or female, in the country. Netball, which evolved from women's basketball, grew spectacularly, especially from the 1970s: national registrations grew from 2891 (1947) to 200 000 (1977) to 359 351 (1990), making netball the fifth largest participant sport in the country. There were probably one million netball participants in the mid-1990s.

There are a number of reasons why netball, like softball, grew so rapidly. Like softball, it evolved from another sport. Australian netballers have also had a long tradition of success in international competition—in fact Australia has been the dominant country in world netball since the 1970s. Netball, again like softball, has developed as a separate sport in its own right—a sport for women run by women. The rise of netball for men and mixed netball has been a more recent phenomenon.[64]

Prominent netball administrator Margaret Pewtress has pointed to another factor in the rise of netball. It was not played on ovals or territory occupied by male sport. The game used left-over and uncontested territory—a small area of earth, asphalt or grass in schoolyards. It required minimum facilities and equipment. Because netball did not compete with male sport or attempt to justify its legitimacy in male terms, it was allowed to grow relatively unrestricted.[65] The administrators of netball developed their own distinctive sporting practices: codes, costumes and ideology.

Whatever the reasons, netball has succeeded more than any other women's sport in securing broad popular support. Keeley Devery, an Australian player and administrator, attested to netball's wholesome and feminine image:

> Of all women's sports ... it is fairly feminine ... you don't have to be butch and rough and bash people ... It has a good general and family image ... to younger players as it does to older women and mothers that are involved in the sport ... It has wide appeal ... it's not a private schoolgirl sport, as rugby is with private boys, and rowing. It's not considered to be your 'westie' sport, that you might consider say wrestling or boxing. With the various ethnic groups, it is the one sport that a lot will play ...[66]

A recent researcher on New Zealand netball argues that while women developed their own model of sport in netball in the earlier part of the century, they failed to challenge wider social restrictions. Press comments on the game were often patronising, and fund-raising for the sport emphasised domesticity. The sport changed in the 1970s when it adopted a male model of sport that emphasised intense competition and an aggressive pursuit of sponsorship.[67] While there may be some truth in this perspective, the change may also represent a move from a compliant to a more assertive femininity.

The spectacular expansion of softball and netball after World War II demonstrates that many women have been keen to participate in a wide range of sporting culture. This was one conclusion of a study of women in sport in South Australia from 1945 to 1965. 'Despite claims to the contrary, women displayed a serious and dedicated attitude to their involvement in sport' and some regarded it as 'an integral part of their lifestyle'.[68]

Sport has played an immense role in Australia in the socialisation of men and women, in discourse within and between the sexes. It has been influential in dictating attitudes towards the body and desirable body shapes, and it has also, of course, enhanced male misogyny and female oppression. Studying sport provides many insights into what it is to be male and female in Australia.

Sport has been an issue of low priority on some feminist agendas because many believed that it was a bastion of a dominant male culture incapable of reform. Some even favoured opting out of 'male' sport in the interests of developing a separate female sporting culture. Despite its gender bias, however, the mainstream sporting culture has continued to attract an increasing number of women, as spectators of (largely male) sport and as participants in their own right. Because it is such a powerful institution in gender construction it is even more important that sport should be the subject of critical scrutiny.

There are many gender issues for sports historians to tackle. There is the need to delineate ways in which the culture of sport can be made less sexist and more accessible to all Australians. There is the question of exploring how women's sports can achieve greater parity with male sports. It is also desirable to examine the many unspoken assumptions and explicit ideologies concerning gender and sexuality which have long been part of Australian sport.

6
COMMUNITY AND PLACE

The association of sport with an aggressive tribalism was an important factor in the rise of organised sport in Australia. Loyalty to the local sporting tribe, a suburban or country sporting team, was a crucial bond in many communities. Sport was a form of social cement that helped men and women identify with a particular territory (or territories), real or imagined, allowing them to empathise with its political and economic system and to identify more with its history and desired future.[1]

From the 1850s strong links were established between sport—usually in the form of particular teams and clubs—and all manner of localities: work groups, neighbourhoods, precincts, suburbs, country towns, cities, regions, colonies and the nation. Individuals often developed multiple loyalties, responding to each demand of place at different times, and at any one time giving greater preference to a particular loyalty.[2] Within particular localities community leaders and media people viewed sport as useful means of furthering community formation and expressing social ideals. The identification of sport with place was a very important reason for the rapid growth of sporting culture in the second half of the nineteenth century.

There are many important issues for the historian researching sport and locality. How important was sport, compared to other cultural factors such as religion and ethnicity, in community formation? Was sport an effective social cement in new communities? Did the use of sport to bind communities represent a form of social control? It is also worth asking why there appear to be stronger links between sport and place in some areas than others. Why, for instance, are the supporters of some clubs more passionate than others? Why does parochialism appear to be stronger in some Australian States? Why do some places develop stronger sporting traditions? Why do some sports flourish in particular regions?

While sport helped to define and unify communities, even creating a sense of nationhood,[3] it also enhanced parochialism or even tribalism, dividing one community against another. We should ask whether sport has simply extended parochialism or whether it has acted as a safety valve for social and economic tensions within society. There is the related issue of whether sport was used as a social device in suburbs or country towns to express social hierarchy, to further class divisions and to demonstrate the social system in action. Did sport help to soften social tension by reducing and even papering over class differences within a community?

Two British writers have shown that the theme of sport and place in the United Kingdom is a very rich one. Many pertinent questions can be asked about the geography of sport—'who plays what where'.[4] John Bale has suggested that while sport leaves its imprint on a culture, it also leaves its impression on the landscape and creates movement, or spatial interaction, between places. Bale and others have begun to explore both the geographical boundaries of particular British sports and the extent to which sport can be used to understand regional cultures.

SUBURBS, PRECINCTS AND THE WORKPLACE

During the second half of the nineteenth century many new communities were established in urban society. Greater affluence, an expanding population, improved transportation, new occupations and changed work situations led to new aggregations of people in neighbourhoods and suburbs, along with educational and work communities such as factories and large department stores.

The process of suburbanisation was accelerated in the second half of the nineteenth century by improvements in public transport and commercial and industrial development, all of which encouraged settlement away from the city. Land booms in the late nineteenth century, fuelled by prosperity and population increase, led to more intensive suburban development in cities and created a network of densely settled inner-city suburbs. The naming of a suburb, the creation of a suburban municipality, the establishment of a suburban railway station and post office, the opening of a factory or a large retail store did not itself create a community. Suburbs were initially artificial entities which came into existence often at the whim of a bureaucrat, or because of pressure from a local élite and from developers who talked up the virtues of a particular locality. Many of the new home-owners had very little in common.

Community identification with a neighbourhood or a suburb took time to develop. It had to be nurtured by the creation of a sense of belonging, by the articulation of community ideals and aspirations and the establishment of local networks and institutions. Many voluntary associations within suburbs—churches, political groups, and a variety of cultural groups—contributed to a sense of place. The sports club was seen as particularly appropriate for generating community spirit: it provided a visible community focus and meeting-place. Through regular competition against neighbouring communities, sports clubs provided a form of theatre. The hopes and fears of a community, its sense of worth, were reaffirmed each week by its local gladiators. Sport thus provided a focus for urban tribalism, developing notions of 'us' against 'them'. By claiming to represent a whole suburb or district, a sporting team was able to develop the myth of a united community which transcended differences of religion, class and ethnicity.

A history of the Collingwood Football Club has outlined the powerful myths of community developed at Collingwood which encouraged the community to support the football club. The author argues that the strong identification between the community and the club and the football fanaticism of Collingwood supporters can be traced to an inferiority complex of a 'suburb crippled from birth' in that it was regarded as 'the lowest among the lowly inner suburbs' of Melbourne. It was established on a flat unsuitable for residential development, poorly drained and sewered, where many of the impoverished dwellers existed in dismal dwellings. They were the victims of greedy and largely unchecked developers and of pollution from many noxious industries.[5]

Central to a sense of pride in Collingwood was a deep resentment against those who lived in neighbouring suburbs such as Fitzroy, which saw themselves as superior. With its sizeable Catholic, Irish and working-class population there was also hostility to the more middle-class and Protestant suburbs of Melbourne. To defeat the silvertails of Melbourne, for instance, was a source of great community satisfaction. The establishment of a sports arena at Collingwood, Victoria Park, and a football team which played in the senior Melbourne competition from 1892 provided the means of raising the dignity of the suburb.

Prominent politicians, businessmen and other community leaders backed the club and exploited local parochialism. There was local resentment in the 1880s against Fitzroy butchers who were slaughtering cattle in the Reilly Street Drain in Collingwood. In response to resident petitions, the Collingwood Council decreed that locals must only 'kill for Collingwood'. This theme emerged at a large public meeting to endorse the creation of the new football club in 1892. John Hancock, local MLA and organiser of the boot-workers, predicted a premiership because 'the very name of Collingwood would strike terror into the hearts of opposing players'. 'Footballers, like butchers, were licensed to "kill for Collingwood".'[6]

The nexus between club and community was a particularly close one. The players in the football team lived and worked in the suburb. The community turned out in large numbers to support its team and to celebrate its first premiership in 1896. The team also had the backing

of its local politicians and businessmen. Such was the community backing for the football club that Collingwood became the largest sporting
club in the country. David Williamson's play *The Club* has explored
the continuing importance of this institution in the twentieth century.

Richmond was another inner-city Melbourne suburb where a strong
link developed between the football club and the community. While the
suburb's initial years were more promising than Collingwood—it attracted some of Melbourne's élite to its higher land initially—Richmond
had become a working-class suburb by the turn of the century with the
development of the less attractive wide river flat. Janet McCalman, in
her portrait of public and private life there, suggested how important
were the Richmond Tigers for the whole community, particularly after
they won their first premiership in 1920. By then 'Tiger fever' had
become a 'tribal loyalty' and 'a victory brought a moment of triumph
over the feelings of social inferiority'. Football was Richmond's 'most
enduring social cement'. Schoolmasters in both state and church schools
believed it was their moral duty to produce tough, skilled and fearless
recruits for the Tigers. The team were more than 'paid professional
agents of communal pride—they were "our boys", family'. A unique
feature of Australian football in Melbourne was that it became respectable for women to be as fanatical as men in their support for the Tigers
(see ch. 5).[7]

The strong links between clubs, local power-holders and community
existed elsewhere. George Parsons has argued that there was a strong
subcultural 'rump' in Sydney's St George district—'the mass of Irish
Catholics, mostly poor and largely isolated from middle-class society'—
which strongly identified with the rugby league club when it entered
the Sydney competition in 1921. Schools such as Marist Brothers,
Kogarah, provided a constant stream of players and supporters. While
the non-Catholic working class of the area also supported the club, it
was the Catholic rump which provided the core support. The success of
the club meant a great deal to its supporters: for the father of George
Parsons—a railway cleaner, 'occupationally immobile, alienated, bitterly
opposed to the bourgeoisie'—a victory for St George was both a
'personal triumph' and a 'class victory'. More often than not St George
supporters were staunch members of the Australian Labor Party (ALP)
and a number of club administrators were active in ALP branches.[8]

Close ties between rugby league and the ALP were also evident at
Newtown. During the timber-workers' strike of 1929 the Rugby League
Club Committee 'became involved in the collective activities of the
Enmore ALP branch, providing money to the Enmore Ladies Relief
Depot who in turn gave assistance to the families of timber workers'.
Newtown also fostered links with workers from local industries: the
woollen mills and the brickpits. Three of its 1914 side worked in the
brickpits. Men who worked in the woollen mills received free passes to
games in 1909.[9]

Sport also played an important role in the St George area when it underwent development after the opening of the Hurstville railway line in 1884, which led to a rapid influx of new home-owners. Speculators, who profited from rapid subdivision, had scant regard for drainage, street construction and the provision of community infrastructure. The Council, churches, schools and various cultural institutions struggled at first to develop a local sense of community.

Recreational activity, and organised sport in particular, was seen by many prominent community leaders as the way 'to improve the quality of the community and establish a set of desirable social values'. Local member (Sir) Joseph Carruthers (1856–1932) had a bowling green installed at his home which was used both by his guests and by the public. Henry Kinsela, a land speculator and businessman, had a race-track established and a wicket laid out at his estate, Kinsel Grove. William Judd, a Congregationalist, made land available near his home for church cricket and football.[10] All three were keen to promote sports such as cricket and football in the St George district and to encourage the formation of teams to represent the area in metropolitan competition.

Sport served a number of purposes in the St George district. It enhanced the power of dominant individuals who took on the role of patrons and providers. It was seen as the means of creating a St George identity and promoting it to the outside world. Sport also cut across class and religion. While some patrons, such as Carruthers, were rather more keen to promote anti-gambling sports, horse-racing was Henry Kinsela's main interest.

The value of linking a sporting club with a district was widely recognised by the late nineteenth century. Before the 1890s many Sydney football and cricket clubs were not district-based. The Wallaroo Football Club was essentially a network of friends with public school graduates prominent. This was also true of the most powerful cricket clubs of Sydney: Albert and Warwick in the 1850s and Carlton and Belvidere in later decades.

Concerned by the dominance of Carlton and Belvidere, and the perceived problem of more international cricket, the NSW Cricket Association (NSWCA) sought to deal with the problem of declining public interest in Sydney club cricket in the 1880s when crowds numbered only a few hundred. There was also the challenge for those who ran Sydney cricket to relate the game to the changing geography of Sydney. From 1871 to 1891 the population of Sydney trebled, and with the land boom of the 1880s there was a spectacular exodus to outer suburbs.[11]

The association reorganised club cricket along district or electorate lines from the 1893–94 season, thus facilitating the spread of cricket to newly established ovals and parks in suburban Sydney. The move to organise cricket on the basis of locality was strongly supported by the *Daily Mirror* of 30 September 1892. The paper welcomed electorate cricket because 'it is no use telling our readers over and over again that our cricket clubs represent no one, and nothing and nowhere and consequently they have no following'. The creation of eight district clubs proved a spectacular success: crowds of 10 000 watched electorate teams. Linking a club with a suburb proved so successful that it was copied elsewhere. The South Australian Cricket Association, noting that the introduction of district or electorate clubs in Sydney had led to 'a greater interest in the game', decided during the 1896–97 season to restructure Adelaide cricket along similar lines.[12] Electorate cricket was also introduced to Brisbane in 1897 and electorate tennis was started in Sydney in 1907.

Sydney rugby also moved to a district-based competition in 1900. Before this time, the senior competition consisted of a mixture of teams: district teams such as Randwick, Marrickville, Parramatta and Sydney; non-district teams such as Wallaroo, Pirate and Buccaneer; and the University of Sydney. There was a great deal of public enthusiasm for the concept of district rugby. At many well-attended public meetings it was argued that district competition would increase spectator interest because local players would appear on their own grounds. It would also even out and enhance the competition. In 1900 the senior competition consisted of seven district clubs and the University of Sydney.[13]

Suburban-based sport had emerged as a powerful force by the turn of the century. Ovals, which were frequently located close to railway stations, made team-sport more accessible to the general public. Although many club traditions were constructed by local power-holders and by the media, they were fashioned out of the popular culture of each suburb. Team traditions would not have become popular without the active participation of the local community. The rabbit emblem of the South Sydney Rabbitohs predated the formation of the club in 1908. One story suggests that some members of the old South Sydney Rugby Union Club hawked rabbits around the streets, calling out 'Rabbitoh!'[14] The rabbit, with its associations of the Depression, became a potent symbol of one Sydney's underprivileged suburbs.

Although suburban loyalties had diminished in intensity by the last decades of the twentieth century, the successful fight to save the Footscray AFL in 1989 indicated that the sense of community generated by the club was still strong. When the AFL decreed that Footscray would be merged with Fitzroy, the community 'fought back' and the popular groundswell of response 'defied all expectations'. What saved the club from merger and oblivion was a realisation of its importance as both a social and a sporting institution. It was seen as providing 'role models for youth in a depressed social and economic climate' and a sense of 'pride, identification and bonding for local residents'.[15]

Below the level of the suburb sport established important links with neighbourhoods and work communities. From the time that the miners from the Minmi colliery in the Hunter Valley formed a soccer club in 1884, the Minmi Rangers, there have been many soccer clubs (and other teams) emanating from coal-mines, factories and workshops. Company teams often borrowed the name of the company and took part in business or wider competitions.[16]

While the initiative for such a team may have come from the workers themselves, the success of many factory football teams had much to do with the support of employers, who provided equipment and time off for employees, and even established ovals. Many prominent manufacturers such as Lever Brothers, W. D. & H. O. Wills, Pelaco, Metters, along with retail giants such as Anthony Hordern and Farmers, patronised work sport on a substantial scale, particularly in the first three decades of the twentieth century.

Work sport was a form of paternalism. Sport was sponsored because it was believed that it reduced tensions between management and labour and led to greater productivity. It was a barely disguised form of social control. Work sports declined by the end of the 1930s because many employers began to question whether the investment of substantial capital on sport gained them increased productivity.[17]

Sport also became the focal point of new urban subcultural groups not necessarily based on a particular suburb. Royal Sydney Golf Club, founded in 1893 in Sydney's eastern suburbs, became a meeting-place for Establishment Sydney. The club was 'not quite so much a golf club as a pillar of Sydney society' as it attracted many of the leading professional and commercial men of the city.[18] Even though it became a club policy to discourage members doing business at Royal Sydney, networking took place among businessmen. A club like Royal Sydney provided exactly the same group solidarity and tribalism as Collingwood Football Club.

COUNTRY TOWNS

With improved transport many new communities were created in rural areas after 1850.[19] These included country towns, large outback stations—which often amounted to self-contained villages—and industrial settlements such as mining communities.

Numerous commentators have suggested that sporting institutions were established at the birth of many a country town. E. C. Buley, an observer of nineteenth-century Australia, noted that when a new town was created the immediate concern of the founders was to mark out the site of the cemetery and the next was to plan a racecourse.[20] The *Australian and New Zealand Gazette* commented in the 1850s that 'one of the first requirements which a newly laid out township seems to feel in Australia is a racecourse and a cricket ground'.[21]

John O'Hara has explored the important role played by the Clarence River Jockey Club in the early years of Grafton, a northern New South Wales town. Organising the Jockey Club provided the means by which socially prominent individuals could assert their status and leadership claims. The establishment of an annual race carnival provided a community festival involving all sections of Grafton society. A race carnival had the advantage of affirming social hierarchy—among those who raced and the crowd—yet at the same time advancing the myth of a community. An annual race carnival was also an occasion to boost the image of the town concerning other communities and to stimulate local business.[22]

Race-meetings held from 1846 at Gawler, a town 25 miles from Adelaide, served a similar purpose. Meetings attracted the best horses from the colony and were attended by most of the town population, which included many prominent Adelaide citizens. There were other occasions, such as a rural fête in 1859, when an entire community assembled. Dancing, football, cricket and archery were part of this local festival which was supported by local businessmen, who closed their shops, and farmers, who gave their hands a holiday.[23]

Football competition between one Riverina town and another provided a focal point for community interest. The growth of sport in this region was linked with expansion of the wheat industry and improved transport. Although much of the Riverina region fell within New South Wales, the region adopted Victorian football initially because of its close economic ties with Melbourne. An extended railway network led to an expanded wheat trade and greater prosperity for many rural towns. Football, too, followed the railway and benefited from it. Railway travel added to the atmosphere of intertown competition, making it a gala occasion. Mail trains, or even special trains, were filled to capacity with the team and hundreds of supporters who left their town in the early morning, not to return till late at night or even the next day.[24] An intertown football match could provide a focus for sporting and social activities. Before the Wagga versus Albury match of 1883, which took place on a racecourse, there was a coursing match. So important were the railways to intertown competition that railway timetables were consulted at the time of the competition draw.

Football thus became the 'means of social cohesion, team identification and town loyalty'. Country football teams 'cut across class, religious and economic barriers to unify people'.[25] Although football in the Riverina was at first played by men in professional, business and clerical employment, by the turn of the century football clubs attracted a broad cross-section of local society: white- and blue-collar workers and players from both town and country.

Country tennis also provided a focal point for broader social interaction in outback Australia. This description of the organisation of a tennis party, before World War I, vividly evokes the relaxed and informal ways of rural society, the camaraderie which isolation fostered, and the real appreciation of the game:

> 'It is a fine day, let's have a game of tennis,' says Bill Williams of Onkaparinka Station, 'who can we get? There's you and Mary can play well

enough, but we want six. Ring up Balubri and see if Wilson can ride across. He can easily do the eight miles by three o'clock. Then the McPhillamy girls can possibly get across from the 'Overflow'. Get Mary to ring them up—we'll send the car if they will—it's only a twenty mile run ... and they know nothing of a backhand ... have no other stroke, but the recollection of a successful passing stroke, or a fine smash, or a fluke volley, will stay in the memory for quite a while, and will come back in many a strenuous burst of speed in rounding up a steer, or bringing in a mob of sheep ... and the sequel of such a pleasant interlude, naturally ... is that all stay to tea and spend a pleasant evening in song and perchance to dance, and ring up over the 'wire fence bush telegraphs' that they are going to stay all night at Onkaparinka and come home in the morning.[26]

Country cricket in South Australia in the nineteenth century was often a social event. One of the inducements to city teams to travel for up to a day for a match was to offer 'good hospitality'. Although the journey from Adelaide to Gawler by horse occupied half a day, the outings were 'jolly affairs': 'they would play cricket all day and sup at night and in the early hours of the morning be hoisted into the six-horse bus'.[27]

There were other forms of sport, involving whole rural communities, at the annual agricultural show. The show was primarily a display of farm stock and produce of the district aimed to improve the quality of local produce. Country shows, which attracted a range of travelling entertainers and showmen, were an offshoot of the European pre-industrial fair which provided fun and entertainment for all. While there were some imported customs, such as chasing the greasy pig, Australian shows developed their own sporting contests, which included wood-chopping, sheaf-tossing and sheep-shearing. Each district show developed its idiosyncratic traditions and events including rolling-pin throwing, rabbit-skinning contests and tractor ballet.[28] Campdrafting, for instance, was a sport developed in northern New South Wales, probably dating from the Tenterfield Show of 1885. The sport involved the selection (or drafting) of a beast from a herd held in an area known as a camp. The mounted rider then had the task of driving the chosen beast around a pegged course.

Geoffrey Blainey has written that many rural sports were work contests. Large crowds attended ploughing matches in country areas, while woodchopping was common in timber-milling districts and hammer-and-tap contests and shovelling contests were popular on the mining fields. Sport as work declined in the twentieth century when it became more a compartment of leisure.[29]

Sheep-shearing contests developed out of the demands of the grazier to have his shearing completed promptly 'to meet the market, beat the weather, save feed or ease a possible water shortage'. Great rivalry emerged between teams of shearers, who competed to get the patronage of one or another grazier. Contests emerged between teams and individuals, who raced against the clock. Since shearers were paid on piece-work rates, faster work also meant more money.[30]

Many Australians of the 1890s, Blainey suggests, would have regarded Jacky Howe (1855–1922) as the greatest athlete in the country. Born on the Downs in Queensland, Howe revolutionised shearing by his legendary feats. In an era when the average number of sheep shorn by a shearer was about 100, he created new records including the shearing of 321 merinos in a work day using plain blade-shears. Howe was larger than life and became a folk hero: he stood 5 feet 10 inches (178 cm), weighed 15 stone (95.3 kg) and had a chest measurement of 50 inches (127 cm), biceps of 17 inches (43 cm) and thighs of 27 inches (69 cm). He belonged to an élite band of shearers known as 'dreadnoughts', who could achieve the 300 mark in a day. His reward was that he provided the name for the Jackie Howe singlet.[31]

Woodchopping was one sport which transcended its country show context to become a more organised sport. Tasmania was a focal point for the sport, with prize-money of $2000 for a tournament at Latrobe in 1891. The United Australian Axeman's Association emerged shortly afterwards. A Tasmanian, David Foster, won the first world championship in 1979, but although he had collected 105 world titles a decade later there was limited recognition, and money, outside his own State. His success, however, did help him achieve employment: he became a public relations officer with Associated Pulp and Paper Mills. The greatest recognition for axemen occurred in their long-standing participation in the Sydney Royal Easter Show, the premier competition in the country.

Boxing tents at country shows represented the first rung on the ladder of success for many a boxer. The most famous tent show was run by Jimmy Sharman Senior (1892–1965) who became a colourful and successful boxing showman, the 'Barnum & Bailey' of Australian boxing, known for his trademark cry 'Who'll take a Glove?' One of thirteen children and born into a poor family, Sharman discovered at an early age that tent boxing was far more lucrative than work on the family dairy farm. From about 1912 he established Jimmy Sharman's Boxing Troupe, pitching his tent at agricultural shows around the country and dominating tent boxing for decades. Many prominent boxers began or ended their careers in his tent including George Barnes, Teddy Green, George Cook, Billy Grime, Jackie Green, Jack Hassen, Harry Mack, Mickey Miller and Tom Uren. Jimmy Sharman Junior carried on his father's troupe until 1971.[32] Travelling boxing tents such as Sharman's provided a connection between the country and the city.

Jimmy Sharman Senior was a shrewd entrepreneur who maintained good relations with the staid and respectable management of the Agricultural Society. He also exploited racial feeling in rural society as no Sharman bill failed to include some Aborigines, whose appearances in country towns enhanced local interest. He also imported African-American and Samoan fighters, but there was 'no colour discrimination in Sharman's tent' as such, for 'black fought black, white fought white, and white fought black'.[33]

While some sports were designed to enhance a sense of community in country towns, other forms of sport were self-consciously exclusive and class-specific. The ideal of the gentleman-squatter was particularly strong in rural Queensland, and a conspicuous number of settlers, who viewed Queensland at the last outpost of the gentlemanly ideal, set about replicating the lifestyle of the English gentry.

Hunt clubs represented attempts to underline the élite status of gentlemen (and in some instances women) and to create a greater distance between them and their society. The extent to which some people tried to emulate British sporting ideals in unlikely places suggests how important this activity was. Some gentlemen met on 17 January 1888 to form the Charters Towers Hunt Club in this mining town. The subscription fee was high: 5s per quarter. It was agreed, in addition, that members should procure a uniform of a 'scarlet coat, top boots or gaiters and breeches'. When the first hunt was held two weeks later five kangaroos, three kangaroo rats and one dingo were shot.[34]

Polo, with its aristocratic and imperial associations, provided another means of emulating the culture of the English gentry. While many of the first clubs were established in cities—polo was first played in Melbourne in 1875—the appeal of this sport was to the 'country squire' rather than to the city gentry. Victorian polo has been dominated by the graduates of Geelong Grammar, a favoured school for wealthy rural families.[35] In Queensland polo became particularly popular on the Darling Downs and in the south-west corner of the State.

There was probably more female sporting participation in the country than the city, because so much of the former involved the horse and many women were adept riders. The Alexander sisters were expert rough-riders and the best jackeroos at Dunmore Station near Dalby, Queensland. The sisters became famous in the Kogan district in the nineteenth century and were known as the 'Kogan Girls' because of their expertise as bushwomen.[36] Women featured in many equestrian competitions, such as show-jumping, and participated with men in hunt clubs. By the twentieth century there was even more female involvement in sports such as rough-riding. Violet Skuthorpe, whose father had pioneered buckjumping in Australia, became rough-riding champion in 1942 when only 20.[37]

Although the first Australian rodeo was held at Gayndah, Queensland, in 1897, the sport did not become popular until much later: the Australian Roughriders' Association was not founded until 1945. Whereas the participants of the more élite sports attempted to emulate British ideals, those who were drawn to rodeo, with its 'cowboys' and 'cowgirls', looked to the rougher notions of the American frontier (see ch. 9).

One feature of country towns was that 'class divisions' were 'more stark' and 'conflicts more open'. There was a greater possibility that ethnic, religious and class differences could be disguised in cities—where one urban enclave was separated from another—than there was in smaller rural societies. While there were a number of occasions when sport involved a whole country town, and may have appeared to be egalitarian, social hierarchy was reaffirmed in reality. Race-meetings were 'social occasions' organised by the leading citizens, who took pride of place at the event. Country shows, similarly, reinforced social divisions as well: there was a place for everyone, whether it was sitting down to dinner with the committee or taking a glove in the boxing tent. Sport thus perpetuated and reinforced the social order because it was used to promote the myth of community.[38]

Sporting institutions in country towns have also been a flashpoint in relations between the white and black communities. Existing on the margins of country towns, Aborigines were not accepted as part of the sporting community. Race has emerged as a problem in a number of country towns; a race riot took place, for example, between Kanakas and Europeans at a race-meeting at Mackay in 1883 (see ch. 8). During the 1960s 'Freedom Rides' led by Charles Perkins drew attention to the fact that Aborigines were denied access to sporting facilities such as the swimming-baths. There are also continuing tensions in many country towns in team-sports where black teams play in predominantly white competitions or where the majority of players in a particular competition are black but the organisers and officials are white (see ch. 8).

MINING AND FRONTIER AREAS

Sport on the frontier tended to be more democratic and egalitarian. From 1851, the time of the first gold rush in Victoria, new communities were peopled by a motley crew of diggers from various social backgrounds. Conditions on the fields were rough and ready, the social structure was fluid but decidedly masculine, and there were relatively few social constraints on leisure pursuits.

Apart from the public house, there were no structures for sport on the goldfields, and gambling and drinking were prominent leisure activities for a population which had plenty of money to spend but few other opportunities for leisure. Although Victoria did not replicate the glittering gambling saloons of the Californian goldfields—the Victorian government took early steps to maintain order on their diggings—the Victorian mining town of Beechworth had three hotels, McCarrick's, the Bella Union and the Star, where sums of between £50 and £100 could change hands each night at the card tables.[39]

The sports which prevailed, such as boxing and pedestrianism, required very limited equipment. S. T. Gill's painting of McLaren's boxing saloon, Main Road, Ballarat (1854) conveys the primitive character of this sport and its gambling and drinking context (see ch. 10). Many of the professional running 'gifts' emerged from of the goldfields (see ch. 3).

Some of the Queensland goldfields were established in 'rough and difficult terrain' and conditions in these new settlements were extremely primitive. After gold was discovered at Charters Towers in 1871, the population swelled to 10 000 by 1877. As on other goldfields, drinking was a favourite recreation and in its boom years the town boasted from seventy to ninety public houses. Blood sports such as cock-fighting, dog-fighting and ratting flourished in the first years of settlement. There was also an emphasis on sports which needed little organisation, such as boxing and goat-racing. The preferred sports, boxing, rugby and wrestling, epitomised frontier values of strength, physical endurance and toughness.[40]

In due course even the relatively heterogeneous frontier mining towns developed a social hierarchy which was reflected in sporting institutions. The Charters Towers Jockey Club (founded 1877), which organised horse-racing there, 'was primarily controlled by the elite'. The workers had their own racing events, such as the Miners' Union Races, and even the Irish-Australians held a separate race-meeting. It is likely that social divisions were not as rigid as in other country towns; the Towers Jockey Club was not an exclusive social institution since some non-élite members gained positions of control.[41]

There was considerable variety in the society and sports from one mining town to another. A sizeable number of Cornish and Welsh miners, from 1844 onwards, emigrated to Australia to work at the copper-mining towns of Kapunda and Burra in South Australia. The Cornish migrants brought a love of wrestling and cock-fighting, which became prominent sports in the town.[42]

The Northern Territory was very much a frontier in the nineteenth century and the organisation of Territory horse-racing reflected its polyglot and fluid society. Punters of all 'size, shape and colour' attended and the owners were 'scarcely different'. The patrons at a Territory racecourse in the nineteenth century were 'a weird mob at the best of times' and included many eccentrics among their ranks.[43] Paddy Cahill, a consistently successful owner-jockey at the Palmerston Cup meetings of the late nineteenth century, was a buffalo-shooter who was immortalised by Banjo Paterson in the *Bulletin*: 'He is popularly reported to pursue the infuriated buffalo at full gallop, standing on his saddle, and dressed in a towel and diamond ring, and yelling like a wild Indian.'[44]

Racing in the Territory frequently degenerated into chaos and pandemonium; there were fights on the ground and many sore heads the next day because 'numerous meetings were formulated in grog, and ended, with grog'.[45] The chance of this occurring was enhanced by the ready availability of alcohol, the curious variety of racing events, and the 'rough-and-ready attitude of organizers'. The novelist Xavier Herbert has captured some of the atmosphere of licence which characterised the Territory racetrack:

Bushies and Townies came to mingle in circumstances that enabled them to speak to themselves as Northerners, to join in ways comprehensible to all, the excitement of the race track, the bonhomie of the booze, the fraternal cavorting on the dance floor after the clod-hopping of their forebears ...

The spirit prevailing during the Races, from the moment the mob poured itself out of the trains (such being the way the alcoholic detrainments were described) on the Wednesday afternoon to that when, by those responsible for getting them home again, they were poured back on, was surely as near to Carnival, in its true sense of behaviour with riotous excess, as was possible in a community predominantly Anglo-Celtic.[46]

The Bong Bong Picnic Races represent a more recent, though rather different, example of a race-meeting as carnival. During the 1970s and 1980s this small country race-meeting in New South Wales became a focal point for a counter-cultural festival which attracted hordes of young people, mainly from Sydney. The unusual feature of this event was that the racegoers and the revellers were segregated from each other: the racegoers occupied the flat area by the course whereas the revellers were confined to the hill inside the racetrack. Most of the spectators had very little interest in the races but took part in counter-cultural theatre which continued well into the night.

Sport in the early days of some Queensland country towns was equally rough and ready. There were limited facilities for sport in many towns, such as Ayr where the main street doubled as the racetrack and the adjacent hotel verandah served as the grandstand. At the time when Roma was formed the main preoccupations were 'racing, fighting and drinking'. Crowds gathered and bets were laid for any type of fight: between individuals, stray dogs or even a domestic dispute.[47]

NATION, STATE AND REGION

W. F. Mandle, in a seminal article, has argued that sport, and cricket in particular, contributed to the emergence of Australian nationalism. Australia had its own cricket team, known as the Australian XI, from the late 1870s. Its success against the motherland provided 'a symbol of what national co-operation could achieve—the best example of Federation yet'.[48] An article in the *Bulletin* stated that victories against the motherland did 'more to enhance the cause of Australian nationality than could ever have been achieved by miles of erudite essays and impassioned appeal'.[49] Political nationalism, Mandle implied, drew inspiration from a 'cricketing nationalism' which could be traced from the 1860s. An initial hesitant and deferential nationalism was replaced by a greater pride and self-confidence by the 1870s and 1880s when many social commentators satisfied themselves that Anglo-Saxon culture could flourish in a different environment and society.

The growth of 'cricketing nationalism', according to Mandle, helped reduce the 'the old bugbear of intercolonial rivalry' which 'vanished in the surge of victories [of the early 1880s]'.[50] Parochial rivalry between one colony and another was a powerful current in the 1850s and 1860s. One Victorian newspaper reported that it was perilous for the Victorians to visit Sydney in the 1860s as a popular cry was that 'There's a Victorian cricketer, 'eave arf a brick at him'.[51] Intercolonial cricket matches, which tapped into this strong sense of rivalry, were major social and sporting events which drew very large daily crowds of up to 15 000 spectators. The *Sydney Mail* of 26 December 1875 commented that 'the excitement in Sydney during the progress of the Intercolonial match [New South Wales versus Victoria] was intense, and even the international matches must dwindle into insignificance beside the interest which was centred in the contest'.

Undoubtedly the desire to thrash the motherland has been a powerful motivating factor in Australia for both players and spectators. Equally strong, in the twentieth century, has been the desire to challenge and even defeat the United States, because Australia has had greater cultural and economic ties with North America and diminishing links with Britain. Sport provides an attractive opportunity for a relatively small power on the world stage to have a tilt at one of the superpowers (see ch. 9).

The shoe has been on the other foot regarding Australia–New Zealand sporting rivalries, which have intensified since the 1970s. While the relationship is more one of sibling rivalry (big versus little brother rather than motherland versus offspring), it has assumed larger proportions with the closer economic and cultural ties between the two countries in recent times. For New Zealanders Australia is now the country to beat and New Zealand Test captain Martin Crowe referred to the Test cricket battles between the two countries in 1993 as 'our Ashes'. Regarding themselves as superior in both sporting and more general terms, Australians have yet to place as much store on these contests.[52]

Contact between New Zealand and Australian sport has gone through a number of cycles and has run parallel to political and economic links. Sporting and political relations between the two countries were much closer at the turn of the century when there was a possibility that New Zealand and Australia might federate. Australia and New Zealand marched under the one banner, Australasia, in the Olympic Games and played as one team in the Davis Cup. Australian football made headway in New Zealand and forty-four clubs were established in the late nineteenth century. A New Zealand Australian football team competed in a Melbourne Carnival in the first decade of the twentieth century.[53]

There has been a diminished sporting contact between the two countries for much of the twentieth century when Australia and New Zealand went their separate and independent ways in politics. This was particularly true in cricket: only one cricket Test was played between the two countries before 1973. Australian cricket officials treated New Zealand cricket in a condescending fashion, regarding it as inferior but doing little to improve the situation. Australia had more cricket contact with South Africa, the West Indies, India and Pakistan.

The growth of mass communications, however, along with economic and political change, has resulted in closer sporting ties since the 1970s and a greater awareness of each other's sporting traditions. Australian rugby league has penetrated the New Zealand media market so successfully that a New Zealand team, the Auckland Warriors, joined the Australian competition in 1995. It is ironic that as relations between the countries have become closer, Australia has become the enemy that New Zealanders love to hate. This love-hate relationship is similar to the Australian sporting relationship with the United States, where there is a fear that Australia will become swamped with American culture.

While the Mandle thesis is in many ways a persuasive one, it represents an optimistic assessment of the role of sport in creating nationality. Research by David Montefiore and Richard Stobo[54] has suggested that Mandle understated the continuing role of intercolonial rivalry, which bedevilled cricket organisation in the last decades of the twentieth century. Montefiore has described how the heady cricket victories of the early 1880s were followed by an extended 'slump' when it became clear that nationalist and imperialist sporting achievements 'remained prey to parochialism, intercolonial rivalries and class tension'.[55] While cricket may have contributed to some general sense of nationalism, there were many other examples of unfederal behaviour among the many authorities who scrambled for power at this time: the cricket associations of New South Wales, Victoria and South Australia, the Melbourne Cricket Club, the Sydney Cricket Ground Trust, and the players themselves. The lack of co-operation between these bodies was the main reason why the first national cricket authority, the Australasian Cricket Council (1892–1902) was so weak and ineffectual. It also suffered because 'it lacked the full support of its member associations'.[56]

Regional parochialism has been one of the enduring elements of Australian sport. Intercolonial and interstate rivalries have sometimes overshadowed international contests. During the 1980s the State of Origin clash between Queensland and New South Wales in rugby league has often loomed larger in the public imagination than Test matches.

Regional parochialism is particularly strong in the outlying and previously less populated States of Queensland, Western Australia and Tasmania and is mainly directed against the more powerful States. There is no greater pleasure for a 'Sandgroper' than to defeat the 'Vics', and Lang Park is famous for its parochialism, particularly its hostility to the 'Blues' (NSW). Parochialism draws on perceived sporting and wider political inequities which include selection bias, talent drain, the dominance of the most populous States in sporting administration and the greater sporting resources of the more powerful States.

Before the 1980s Queensland rugby league had experienced a continuing drain of players to the wealthier Sydney competition, with the result that Queensland was regularly thrashed by New South Wales. Queenslanders welcomed the State of Origin concept because it restored the Queensland-born to the Maroon team even if they were playing in Sydney.

Sporting parochialism also draws on a range of wider political grievances of the more 'outlying' States, those furthest from the south-eastern hub of Australia. There has long been a powerful feeling that central governments in the more populous States and cities have neglected more distant areas. A State parochialism was sufficiently strong in Western Australia in the 1930s for two-thirds of the population to vote in favour of secession from the Australian Federation. There have been moves, in more recent times, for separate States in northern New South Wales and Queensland.

Western Australia, a latecomer to Shield and international cricket, was saddled for several decades with an invidious subsidy in that it had to pay half the return fare of interstate teams from Adelaide to Perth. Western Australia was also treated at first as a junior partner in Australian cricket; it had only one board member out of thirteen—compared to New South Wales which had three—which entitled it to only one-thirteenth of Test and tour profits. When Graham McKenzie became the State's first regular Test player in 1961 he 'carried the hopes and aspirations of his State' because he had triumphed despite a cricketing system which was seen as biased against Western Australians.[57]

No one has yet established whether sport enhances parochialism or whether it is a harmless social safety valve. There is some subjective evidence that sporting regional parochialism, such as State of Origin contests, may defuse rather than exacerbate tensions between one State and another. The success of Queensland against New South Wales in the State of Origin contest since 1980 may have helped already to dissipate some past grievances. The introduction of mascots for Queensland and New South Wales—the ubiquitous but also fanciful cane toad and cockroach—suggests that some of this rivalry is light-hearted and humorous.

Rivalry exists not only between one State and another but also within States. In Tasmania there has long-standing north–south political and sporting divide. There has long been a strong anti-capital (Hobart) feeling in the northern and north-western regions with their respective focal points at Launceston and Devonport. Former northern Tasmanian footballer Bob Cheek conveyed how his coach exploited this parochial feeling when the Northern side competed against the Hobart-based Southern team:

Tasmanian [regional] parochialism in ingrained and incurable ... Hatred runs deep. From the time I pulled on a pair of boots in the North I was brainwashed. John Coughlan said at my first night's training with the NWFU team to play the TFL that Southern footballers dined on caviar at Government House before a game and went on to the ground in chauffeur-driven Rolls Royces.

'We'll get bloody spuds and a broken down bus!' he roared.

Sure it was an exaggerated build-up to beat the South—but there was never the same feeling in the TFL teams.[58]

Queensland also has a strong north–south divide which produced a movement to carve out a new State in northern Queensland in the late 1970s. There have been continuing efforts to establish separate sporting institutions for this region which bore fruit in the 1990s with the creation of more national competitions. A basketball team was formed at Townsville and the North Queensland Cowboys joined the national rugby league competition in 1995. North Queenslanders have welcomed the Cowboys because they will put the region on the map, provide greater sporting competition and an opportunity for the team to assert the superiority of this region.

The successes of the Canberra, Illawarra and Newcastle rugby league teams suggest that there are similar imperatives in the national capital and in regional cities. Bob Turner, coach of the Canberra Cannons, suggested that Canberra was a 'city without a soul' in the early 1980s and that sporting institutions such as the Cannons and the Raiders would fulfil an important community purpose. Recognising this, Turner made every effort for the team and town to complement each other.[59] The comment of American Michael Novak on Miami and its football team was equally applicable to Canberra and the steel cities of Wollongong and Newcastle. Miami became a 'different sort of city once it had the Dolphins', for a team 'is not only assembled in one place, it also represents a place'.[60]

The Canberra Raiders have been a spectacular success from the 1980s. After decades of 'apathy and, at times, embarrassment', and derision from people who lived elsewhere, Canberra was 'crying out for someone, something, to provide the community with inspiration' in the early 1980s. The Canberra 'Green Machine' helped to transform the place, making the city into something more than a place 'full of useless politicians and faceless public servants'.[61]

The expansion of the rugby league competition in the 1980s and 1990s has been rather more successful at some points than the Australian Football League in that rugby league authorities have tapped rather more into regional parochialism. They have taken rugby league to places such as Canberra where the community yearned for sporting recognition to provide a focal point for a greater sense of community. While it may have been important to establish an AFL team in Sydney, in the interests of a truly national competition, Sydney had far less social need for another sporting team than Canberra, Newcastle or Illawarra. In retrospect it would have been more prudent for the AFL to build up its national base first in Australian football States by exploiting interstate rivalry, or in regions such as Canberra or Riverina.

The evidence of whether sport unites or divides communities is mixed. Undoubtedly sport has been used effectively at times to help unite suburbs, country towns, frontier communities and even the Australian nation. It is also true that the unity achieved by national sporting triumphs—such as cricket victory of the early 1880s, the Olympic Games achievements of 1956 and the America's Cup success of 1983—represents something of an ephemeral and short-lived fillip. National pride achieved on the cricket field in 1882 did not overcome intercolonial bickering. In fact success in the 1882 Ashes Test may have intensified intercolonial rivalry because there were more resources to squabble over.

While sport unites a particular community, it is on the basis of us against them. There is a continuing debate about whether ethnically based soccer clubs are a positive or negative expression of multicultural-ism (see ch. 9). While sport may have contributed to some degree of Australian nationalism, it has also perpetuated urban, regional and State rivalries.

But while the sense of community created by sport may play a limited role in political culture, reflecting rather than changing it, there is no question that the links between sport and space have had important social and cultural ramifications. Sport has been one of the most import-ant elements of the 'social cement' which binds together all manner of communities in Australia. Sporting culture was well established and popular at the time when suburbs and country towns were founded. Sport, more than religion and other forms of culture, was able to unite communities otherwise disparate. Sport was universally popular and better able to cut across religious and class divisions. The links between sport and all manner of communities are important reasons why sport has such an elevated status in Australia.

It is likely that the rise of regional and city teams participating in national competitions is not simply the result of the television search for larger and larger audiences. It has also occurred because of changed communities and community loyalties. The suburban community— where people worked and lived—has diminished in importance as individuals became more mobile and participate in wider networks beyond their community (see ch. 10). Intersuburban rivalries now play a secondary role to regional, city and even State rivalries. Three Sydney rugby league clubs, Balmain, Canterbury and Eastern Suburbs, recognised this in 1994 when they changed their names to the Sydney Tigers, Sydney Bulldogs and Sydney City Roosters respectively. While the changed title reflected the reality that Balmain and Canterbury supporters were spread throughout the metropolitan area, it was a frank admission that a historic link was no longer important.

The passion attached to international sporting contests reflects Australia's changing cultural and economic ties with other parts of the world. With ever-diminishing links between Australia and the British motherland it is likely that sporting contests with America and near neighbours such as New Zealand will continue to assume larger proportions in the future.

7
POLITICS

The belief that 'sport and politics should not mix' has been reiterated so consistently and frequently in Australia, both by people within sport and those who comment on it, that it is still widely accepted. Yet it is a very curious assertion. It does not take very long to demonstrate that sport has always been deeply enmeshed in all manner of politics, ranging from team selection, access to preferred grounds, disputes between one sport and another, and conflicts between players and officials. There have also been continuing debates about sports boycotts and acceptable sponsorship, about the indirect and direct involvement of politics in sport.

The popular cliché about sport and politics only makes sense if it refers to a dislike of the intrusion of 'outside' politics—notably the involvement of professional politicians and government in the running of sport. Sportspeople who express the hope that sport and politics will remain separate yearn for sport to be left to put its own house in order without any pressure from professional politicians.

This attitude perpetuates two long-standing myths. While sportspeople at times bemoan the intervention of politicians and government in sport, they have often pursued and welcomed this outside involvement and support, whether in the form of direct or indirect assistance. From the beginning of organised sport in Australia there has been a close relationship between government, politicians and sports bureaucracies. Those sports which progressed and developed most were the ones which produced skilful administrators who were able to manage politics within their sport but also to effectively network with politicians, businessmen, educationists, clerics and the community itself.

There has long been a myth, which is both beguiling and powerful, that sport exists in a separate cultural box, safely removed from the difficulties which beset other cultural endeavours such as business, which has its scandals, corporate failures and white-collar crime. Most sportspeople don't want to know about the broader politics of sport; their interest is narrowly focused on issues such as selection policy. Sporting news is presented in separate compartments in newspapers and on radio and television—seemingly above criticism and detached from what happens elsewhere. The myth of sport as a separate arena, untouched by the gloom and seemingly intractable problems that surround other institutions, is perpetuated by the media. Sport is one of the cultural institutions which prosper in difficult economic times because there is continuing optimism and continuity in the sports media.

The reason so many yearn for a separate sporting realm is that 'outside' politics does not fit into the moral universe manufactured by the sports media. Sports administrators and fans alike prefer to maintain their faith in a tried and trusted sporting moral order which is a conservative one in that the focus is on the play itself. In the moral world of sport, participation is still seen by many as being fair, democratic and egalitarian, with law and order maintained through the power of umpires backed by judiciaries. There is no room in this black-and-white world for sexism, racism and class bias. While institutions appear to be breaking down (or changing rapidly) in other social spheres, sporting tradition is both a constant and a comfort to many Australians.

In contrast to this perspective, it cannot be avoided that organised sport and politics have been closely intertwined from the earliest days of European settlement. Governor Macquarie regarded the 1810 race carnival both as social diversion and a form of social control (see ch. 2). From this time sport was encouraged in many ways: through the provision of land, resources and patronage and through the allocation of public holidays on important sporting occasions. As sport became more organised and important in society, governments have become more directly involved. Sport has changed from a largely privately organised activity in the nineteenth century to a more public venture involving government investment and supervision. Since the 1970s the federal government has funded sport directly.

This and the next chapter will investigate the following questions. What is the nature of sports politics and its relationship to other forms of politics? What has been the relationship of government to sports bureaucracies? To what extent has the conservative moral universe of sport helped to perpetuate various forms of discrimination? Why has government become more directly involved in sport in the twentieth century, particularly since the 1970s?

Before World War I

From the time of European settlement of Australia many well-placed and influential people regarded it as desirable to promote a culture of sport. Sport was part of the gentlemanly ideal which was imported from

Britain. The establishment of some of the more aristocratic sports, such as hunting and horse-racing, was regarded as one way in which a civilised society could be replicated in the Antipodes.

Governors and leading citizens encouraged the emergence of sporting institutions. Governors became patrons of many sports clubs and attended important sporting events. They granted sizeable portions of land for sports bodies, providing them free or at a nominal rent. They supplied labour to help create sporting venues: twenty convicts were assigned by Governor Bourke to improve the Sandy Course (later Randwick) in the early 1830s. Military and naval personnel were encouraged to participate in sport (see ch. 2). The allocation of a public holiday for a major sporting occasion did much to swell attendances.

While government support for sport in the nineteenth century was largely indirect, and more in kind than in cash, it was not inconsiderable. Sport could not have grown as much as it did, in the second half of the nineteenth century, without government promotion. Municipal governments helped create a large number of ovals, and other facilities such as public tennis courts, golf courses and swimming-pools. Facilities essential for the establishment of senior competition were heavily subsidised by ratepayers. Creating an oval and maintaining a turf wicket, for instance, was (and still is) costly and beyond the resources of a suburban cricket or football team.

Local politicians played a part in allocating community resources to sport and in deciding which sports would get the best venues. There was often competition between sports for the most favourably located grounds. During the 1880s there were three football codes in Sydney— rugby, Australian football and soccer—which competed for public interest, to secure a foothold in educational institutions and to gain access to the best revenue-producing grounds.

Mutual interest helped develop a close nexus between sporting teams, local politicians and their communities. By allocating sufficient resources to a sports club, politicians were able to enhance their popularity. A sure way to assist re-election was for a politician to be active in the club's affairs. Politicians have long cultivated sports clubs and acted as boosters for them, and in turn clubs have welcomed the active involvement of their local representatives.

There was also a very close liaison between sports administrators and colonial (State) politicians. An Act of Parliament was passed in 1871 providing the South Australian Cricket Association with exclusive right to 12 acres of prime real estate in the North Adelaide parklands for a peppercorn rent of only £7 per year for the first seven years, and then £14 for the following seven years. An ongoing close relationship between SACA and all levels of government ensured that government cast a sympathetic eye on various proposals for the development of the Adelaide Oval. The strength of this relationship was demonstrated in 1874 when SACA had only twenty-four hours to organise a match against the visiting Englishmen. 'A quickly gazetted government half-holiday granted for the Friday afternoon' assured the success of the match.[1]

A race between Canadian Edward Hanlan and Australian Elias Laycock for the sculling 'championship of the world' at Penrith in 1884 also led to a public holiday for the people of Parramatta, Windsor, Camden and Penrith. The NSW government further subsidised the event by providing divers to remove obstructions from the river, public servants to help organise the event and police to maintain order.[2]

The creation of trusts to manage major sportsgrounds was another reason why sporting associations needed close and continuing liaison with government. When the NSW government was in the process of upgrading the Military and Civil Ground to become the major city sporting venue (later the Sydney Cricket Ground) in 1875, it was confronted by the problem that demands for the use of the ground were becoming 'numerous and conflicting'. The NSW Cricket Association had friends in high places including the Minister of Lands, Thomas Garrett—whose son was about to break into the colonial cricket side—and Richard Driver, a prominent member of parliament and solicitor for the Sydney City Council. The government settled on a trust of three to control the ground, two nominated by the NSWCA and one by the government. By the time the SCG was ready for its first match in 1877 the NSWCA regarded the ground as its own property, spent much money in developing it, and referred to it as the Association Ground. The link between the trust and the NSWCA was such a close one that over the next six years they pooled funds.

Unfortunately for the NSWCA, this favourable arrangement lasted only until 1883, for by then the NSWCA had lost control of its ground. This occurred largely because Philip Sheridan, the dominant figure on the trust, chose to act independently of the Association in that he regarded the ground as vested in the trustees. So began more than a century of conflict between the trust and the NSWCA over access and rights to the ground. There were a number of disputed areas including the relationship of cricket to the other sports, promoted by the trust in the interests of profit. Sports such as rugby, tennis and cycling were keen to gain favourable access to the premier sporting venue of the city. When trust plans for a cycling event clashed with a cricket match both parties ended up in court in 1904. There were also continuing disputes about financial arrangements, the charges levied and the extent to which the NSWCA should secure a proportion of the fees paid by members. Finally, there have been changes in the way that trustees have been appointed by governments which have progressively whittled away the influence of the NSWCA.[3]

The nadir in the relationship between the NSWCA, the trust and the State government occurred when Kerry Packer's World Series Cricket (WSC) was established and when it applied to use the SCG in 1977.

When the trust refused this application, Neville Wran's Labor government passed legislation to reconstitute the trust, which became weighted in favour of government interests. Under the new Act the government nominated twelve members, with another two elected by the members of the SCG. Legal action by the NSWCA stalled Packer's access to the SCG for a season and WSC games were played at the Showground in 1977–78. But the NSW government then passed a Bill 'stripping the NSWCA of its traditional right over the SCG' and Packer cricket was played at the SCG in the following season.[4]

The successful growth of a sport also required effective involvement in community politics, in schools and churches. A number of commentators have noted that the strong nexus between the new code of rugby league, the ALP and the Catholic Church was an important reason for the consolidation of the code in its initial years. The networking between league and church officials paid off when the code was introduced to some Catholic schools by 1913 and, by the 1920s, rugby league had established a strong foothold in Catholic primary and secondary schools in New South Wales.[5] This development provided rugby league with a future nursery of players and at the same time gave the new code greater respectability.

Soccer, by comparison, suffered because it had fewer friends in high places, being initially a minority sport confined to areas such as the coalfields and factories and particular ethnic communities, such as the Scots (see ch. 9). Soccer in the late nineteenth century had limited political clout which might have enabled it to break into the education system. With the scarcity of revenue-producing grounds in Sydney in the first decades of the twentieth century there was cutthroat competition between the various codes to secure access to grounds such as the Sydney Cricket Ground, the Sports Ground and Wentworth Park.[6]

Sports associations also looked to government for recognition. To get government support added to the authority of a governing body and offered the prospect of assistance. Such was the case with a surf-bathing umbrella organisation which emerged after the turn of the century. When the Surf Bathing Association of New South Wales (SBANSW) was formed in October 1907 it lobbied the government to grant it recognition as an official authority. The conservative and respectable character of this body ensured that its claims were successful. Government backing had immediate tangible benefits for the SBANSW. The State government appointed a Surf Bathing Committee in 1911, which was chaired by the president of the SBANSW, to examine the needs of the sport, including by-laws defining beach behaviour. The government virtually accepted all the recommendations of the committee, which advocated, among other things, improved dressing accommodation and the retention of existing by-laws against sunbathing, which the SBANSW regarded as a form of loitering on the beach. As a result the SBANSW was able to increase 'its control' over the beaches of the State.[7]

Sporting institutions, not surprisingly, became closely integrated into the local political and social landscape of cities and suburbs. The Western Australian Turf Club (WATC), founded in 1852, had become a meeting-place by the 1890s for those in the colony who had social, economic and political power—the established colonial families who were often organised by marriage into tight social networks. It was a frequent complaint in Western Australia that it was more difficult to enter the WATC than to enter parliament. To maintain its exclusive character, the club was extremely careful in the choice of members. Since horse-racing was regarded as *the* sport, the club itself 'symbolized the power of the colonial elite'. Like the Royal Golf Clubs of Sydney and Melbourne, it was a suitable venue for networking—political, commercial and social.[8]

The 'Royal' prefix was an appellation much sought after by clubs with social pretensions because both local and British authorities, including the Colonial Office, took the matter seriously as it confirmed that a club was held in 'high esteem by the authorities, both local and in London'. When the Melbourne Golf Club secured the Royal prefix in 1895, it placed Royal Melbourne at the apex of colonial golf clubs which were recognised later: Royal Sydney in 1897, Queensland in 1921, Adelaide in 1923, Hobart in 1925, Canberra in 1933 and Perth in 1937.[9] The royal distinction underlined the social gulf between privileged sports, notably horse-racing, golf and yachting, and more plebeian sports.

The politics involved in securing the royal prefix must have been intense and often baffling. The exclusive Brisbane Golf Club, which was founded in 1896, applied unsuccessfully for a Royal Charter on no less than five occasions. The reasons for its repeated failure were not made clear.[10] Members of the club, which attracted the cream of Brisbane society, must have been more than a little puzzled and even peeved when a newer club at Hamilton became the Royal Queensland Golf Club in 1921. So while every other Royal golf club in Australia bears the title of a city, Queensland has the Brisbane and Royal Queensland golf clubs.

Although the assistance of colonial governments to sport was largely indirect, many colonial governments believed that sport could serve a useful purpose and was a convenient and cheap way of bolstering the defence forces. This was particularly true of rifle clubs, which were encouraged because they served a paramilitary function: 'they fostered proficiency with a rifle, they could be regarded as reserves to the military forces.'[11] When a Queensland Rifle Association was founded in 1863 by enthusiasts from the Queensland Volunteers, the colonial government constructed rifle ranges at Victoria Park in 1877 and later at Toowong in 1887. The Governor regularly attended club presentations, which were fashionable events. The movement in Queensland was given a fillip by the 1884 Defence Act, which established a permanent military force and a militia besides the Volunteers, and made provision 'for the encouragement of rifle shooting throughout the colony'. Adult males had an incentive to join the rifle clubs because they were exempted from the draft.[12] After Federation, rifle clubs were provided with recognition and a subsidy from the new Commonwealth government, and the prestigious King's Prize was created.

AFTER WORLD WAR I

During the first half of the twentieth century governments for the most part continued to believe that sports should run themselves, raise their own funds and develop their own talent. The widely accepted amateur ethic provided no role for direct government involvement and funding of sport. Governments only intervened directly in the more professional sports where the issue of gambling required some State regulation and presented the opportunity for expanding State revenues.

When Australia first competed as a team (as Australasia) at the 1908 Olympics—Australians had competed as private individuals in earlier Games—there was no government support whatsoever. Requests for government assistance were turned down in 1908 and 1912. The responsibility for raising funds was left to individuals, their clubs and State associations.[13] One of the reasons for the emergence of what is now the Australian Olympic Committee (AOC) in 1914—known until 1990 as the Australian Olympic Federation—was to raise funds for future Olympics from the public and from business. From this time until the 1980s the size of Australian Olympic teams was determined by the effectiveness of AOC fund-raising.

During the 1920s governments began to provide a small amount of funding for major events such as the Olympics, but the amounts were token and reinforced the assumption that the bulk of the finance should be raised by the sports themselves. In 1923 the federal government made a grant of £3000 to the AOC for the 1924 Games, but it was conditional on the AOC raising £10 000 through public subscription.[14]

Australia almost did not compete in the first British Empire (now Commonwealth) Games at Hamilton, Canada, in 1930. The initial Australian response to the Canadian invitation to the Games was to decline to attend because of lack of funds. It took a Canadian subsidy of $5000 to secure an Australian presence at Hamilton. The Canadians hoped that their generous offer would be matched by additional Australian funds, but there is no evidence that more money was forthcoming. Australian government officials were rather more interested in raising funds for the 1932 Olympics than in assisting with the first British Empire Games.[15]

Governments played a more active role when the Games came to Australia, such as the 1938 British Empire Games held in Sydney, and the 1956 Olympics located in Melbourne. Acceptance of the Sydney offer to host the 1938 Games was conditional on a guarantee of £10 000 from the NSW government—the federal government did not contribute to these Games—to cover the organising committee's administrative costs. The support of the State government was made easier because the Games became linked with the State's Sesquicentenary celebrations. J. M. Dunningham, who was the minister in charge of the celebrations, was also a member of the Games organising committee. Given the limited budget for the Games, the committee made an effort to use existing facilities. Athletes ran on a makeshift grass track at the SCG. Male athletes were housed in a temporary 'village' at the nearby Showground and female participants were housed in a private hotel near Kings Cross.[16]

In many instances athletes themselves raised money so that they could attend one or other Games. The AOC was able to raise only £23 918 for the 1948 London Olympics, which funded a team of thirty-four competitors and seven officials. However, there was the possibility of a larger team if individual athletes could each raise £550. The process of individual fund-raising must have been very effective because the actual Australian contingent was seventy-seven.[17]

By the time Melbourne hosted the 1956 Olympics there was a need for greater infrastructure support from government because of the size of the Games. The Melbourne bid had the advantage in that it was headed by a former Lord Mayor of Melbourne and Olympian, Sir Frank Beaurepaire. Government helped construct facilities for the Games which included an Olympic pool costing £500 000. The total cost of building programs for the Games amounted to £2 million, which was shared by the federal and State governments and the Melbourne City Council.[18] The Victorian Housing Commission built a village for the athletes consisting of 365 houses and 841 units which after the Games became public housing. The federal government played an active role in the success of the Games. When there was the very real possibility that IOC President Avery Brundage would take the Games away from Melbourne, Prime Minister Robert Menzies became involved. Menzies recognised that the failure to put on the Games would have been politically embarrassing for Australia.

Melbourne almost lost the Games because the Organising Committee from 1949 to 1952 failed to settle on an acceptable site, with no less than seven sites considered. While the State government preferred the Showgrounds, the federal government opted for the MCG, but the MCG's Board of Directors opposed staging the Olympics there. For a brief period in 1952 it appeared that the Games would be held at Carlton Cricket Ground before the MCG Board relented and the Games were staged at the MCG.[19] It took an unprecedented three-day summit meeting, organised by Victorian Premier John Cain, to resolve the situation. The meeting was attended by Prime Minister Menzies, deputy opposition leader Arthur Calwell, all State political leaders, civic leaders and Olympic officials together with the trustees and officials of the Melbourne Cricket Club.[20] Because sports politics in the 1950s was decentralised and involved part-time amateur officials, there was ample scope for disagreement and dissension.

Voluntarism, a practice which sat comfortably with the cult of amateurism, remained an integral part of the Games. The public performed an important role in these Games besides contributing to the usual Olympic fund. Because of insufficient hotel and boarding house accommodation for visiting spectators, the Civic Committee requested Melburnians to open their homes and billet visitors. Billeting proved to be a 'popular and memorable part' of the 1956 Games and 20 000 extra 'beds' were found.[21]

Until the 1970s, however, the bulk of Olympic funds—to cover actual fares and accommodation—continued to be the responsibility of the AOC. With ever-increasing Olympic budgets the AOC had to develop more professional fund-raising campaigns to tap into corporate sponsorship. The 1976 budget target was $800 000 to send teams to Montreal and to the Winter Games at Innsbruck, Austria. The disappointing results at Montreal—when Australia won only one silver and four bronze medals—demonstrated vividly the problem of relying on public and private generosity when other national teams enjoyed substantial government funding. The Montreal Games represented a nadir in the Australian Olympic movement and helped to transform federal and State government attitudes towards the promotion of sport.

Although politicians had long been reluctant to become directly involved in the administration and funding of amateur sport, they were aware of the importance of sport as a cultural and social institution. Politicians did intervene in sport occasionally when sport needed help or was threatened by crises. The controversial Bodyline tour of 1932–33 occurred at a time of fragile Anglo-Australian relations. What was seen as the unsportsmanlike tactics of the English bowlers created bitter relations between the English and Australian teams and led to acrimonious exchanges between sports officials of the two countries which were seen as potentially damaging politically. The crisis led to formal discussions at the highest levels which involved Australian Prime Minister Joe Lyons and the Dominions Office. However, the involvement of politicians was behind closed doors, indirect and subtle; sports administrators were left to resolve the problem on their own.[22] The matter was settled when cricket officials of both countries agreed to outlaw Bodyline bowling.

Although (Sir) Robert Gordon Menzies (1894–1978), Prime Minister of Australia in 1939–41 and 1949–66, adopted a *laissez-faire* policy towards sport,[23] he was one of the first prime ministers to use sport subtly, and cricket in particular, to enhance his image as a man of the people and to express his Anglophile vision. Menzies actively associated himself with the game in numerous ways, by frequently attending Test matches and by persuading cricket authorities to add to touring schedules a charity match against a Prime Minister's XI and by offering to meet all the costs of this match.[24] This tradition was revived by another cricketing Prime Minister, Bob Hawke.

Menzies did no harm to his reputation as a cricket lover when he wrote an article, 'Cricket—An Enduring Art', which appeared in the

1963 *Wisden*. While he admitted that he was not a very good cricketer, he waxed lyrical about the game and its traditions. Anglophile that he was, Menzies valued cricket as part of Australia's rich British inheritance, for 'Great Britain and Australia are of the same blood and allegiance and history and instinctive mental processes'.[25]

His familiarity with the language of cricket also helped Menzies advance his status within the Commonwealth. Menzies even played a part in urging the Australian Board of Control to undertake a tour of the West Indies in 1954–55 since it would be of 'great diplomatic value'. Menzies had been asked by a prominent West Indian leader, Eric Williams—who was at the opposite end of the political spectrum to Menzies—to assist in setting up this tour which would represent a 'small but very important matter on the road to national dignity in the West Indies'.[26] In spite of his declared public love of sport, Menzies, like others before him, regarded sport as an area where natural talent, nurtured by amateur associations, would rise to the top as a matter of course. There was no need for governments to promote and encourage sport.

Until recently, governments took very limited responsibility for physical education and the promotion of recreation. It was left to individuals to develop initiatives. Professor Harvey Sutton (1882–1963) co-founded Health Week in the 1920s, which encouraged a healthy diet and greater physical activity. The University of Melbourne created a chair in physical education in 1937 and its initial appointee, Fritz Duras (1896–1964)—'the father of physical education' in Australia—did much to promote physical education in schools and universities. The question of physical fitness was placed higher on government agendas during wartime and the federal government passed a National Fitness Act in 1941 in response to perceived defence needs. The Act set up national fitness councils and led to an expansion of physical education in schools and universities. The scheme was probably best known for the provision of enjoyable holiday camps and outdoor activities for schoolchildren, though whether they contributed much to 'national fitness' and sport is not certain.[27] Before the 1970s the main government contribution towards sport took the form of grants to voluntary bodies: national fitness councils, the Olympic and Commonwealth Games organisations, the Royal Life Saving Society and the Surf Life Saving Association of Australia.

Although governments did not take an active part in amateur sports, they did raise some revenue from them. The expansion of gate-money crowds in the twentieth century and the rise of a sports 'industry' was too tempting to resist. An entertainment tax, which was applied to both sport and recreation, was introduced after 1918.

Governments played a more active role in gambling sports such as horse-racing, mainly because of revenue benefits. There was a perceived need for the state to regulate gambling and to monitor changing community attitudes towards its practice. While many favoured an extension of gambling facilities, there was also a concerted Protestant backlash against gambling in the late nineteenth century. The introduction of total-isators at racecourses was one of the first areas of government inter-vention. In South Australia and Queensland in 1882 the change required acts of parliament which nominated the amount that could be retained by the clubs (it varied from 5 to 10 per cent). When a Totalisator Act was passed in New South Wales in 1916 the government—which was con-cerned with revenue-raising in wartime—took 7 per cent for itself, leav-ing the clubs with only 3 per cent.

Governments introduced regular reviews of horse-racing and gam-bling to examine the structure of racing and the type of clubs and meetings involved. The issue of illegal bookmaking has been a continuing issue of debate and the subject of numerous commissions. The most famous illegal bookmaker was John Wren (1871–1953), who operated his Collingwood Tote shop, seemingly immune from police investigation, from 1893 to 1906, when anti-gambling legislation finally closed his business. The scale of operations was very substantial, with a weekly profit of £750 for Wren and a large clientele: at one point there were 1571 punters in the tote yard. The illegal bookmaking industry was resilient and well organised, continuing to flourish in the twentieth century despite the attempts of politicians to control it. The rapid expansion of telephone subscribers in the 1920s and 1930s provided the SP industry with new opportunities for growth.[28]

One of more dramatic examples of government involvement in sport was the restructuring of horse-racing in New South Wales by the McKell Labor government in 1943. This led to the closure of proprietary clubs, replacing them with a single non-proprietary authority, the Sydney Turf Club (STC). Before the war Sydney had a multiplicity of tracks and a variety of race-meetings—there were four tracks alone in the eastern suburbs with meetings on four or five weekdays and sometimes two on Saturdays. McKell, who had a keen interest in the establishment of the STC, took advantage of the wartime situation—when pony-racing had been disbanded—to alter totally the face of Sydney horse-racing by rationalising it. McKell's motives included 'a labour man's distaste for racing's profits going into the pockets of company shareholders and a dislike for the gentlemanly exclusiveness or snobbishness of the AJC'.[29] A better-organised sport also reduced the possibility of corruption.

A continuing government interest in gambling revenue altered the context in which many sports operated. Off-course betting was estab-lished in South Australia and Tasmania in the 1930s. It was seen by poli-ticians in other States as the means of curtailing the SP industry; New South Wales politician R. J. Heffron believed that government-operated off-course betting shops would 'see the end of child runners, welshing bookmakers, "standover" men, and the other evils of the present vicious system'.[30] A totalisator agency board—better known as the TAB—was introduced into Victoria in 1960; other States followed soon after. There was also the prospect of substantial revenue because SP bookmaking was a multi-million pound economy from which the government received no revenue. Government-legislated changes in gambling in more recent decades—with a wider range of off-course media coverage and gambling outlets with the sky channel and 'pub' TABs—have led to significant changes in horse-racing. It is one of the factors in a dramatic decline in on-course crowds which has adversely affected the bookmaking industry. Before the introduction of the State TABs, bookmakers accounted for 46.1 per cent of the $2.1 million turnover in legal racing gambling Australia-wide, but by 1990–91 the bookmaking share had dropped to only 23.9 per cent of the $11.3 million figure.[31]

The progressive extension of gambling facilities changed the environment for other sports as well as the gambling sports. Legislation in 1956 in New South Wales to authorise the use of poker machines in clubs, subject to state-controlled licensing, has had immense repercussions for sport in general and rugby league in particular. The growth of poker-machine gambling was spectacular and profits were large. It led to the creation of a number of opulent leagues clubs which became both the focal point and lifeline of many rugby league clubs.

GOVERNMENT PROMOTION OF SPORT FROM THE 1970S

There has been a remarkable change in government policy in the 1970s and the 1980s when federal governments became directly involved and took responsibility for the provision of sporting facilities. The ALP introduced sport into its platform in 1972, and in the Whitlam government sport figured as an arm of government policy: a Ministry of Tourism and Recreation was established. This government also began a Capital Assistance Program providing funds for sporting facilities, while a Sports Assistance Program allocated travel, coaching and administrative resources. State governments followed the federal lead by creating their own departments of sport which were variously allied to recreation, tourism, the arts and the environment.

The election of the Whitlam Labor government in 1972 marked a watershed in government involvement in sport, recreation and other forms of culture. This government became more active in leisure-planning to solve the problems of urban society, in improving the health and fitness of citizens and in supporting popular culture. A core element of the Whitlam government policy was to make sport, and the arts for that matter, more accessible to all Australians. The first Minister for Tourism and Recreation, Frank Stewart, stated that while the government wished to encourage excellence in sport, it was not the intention of the government to emulate the gold-medal 'factories' of East Germany, for 'our task lies clearly elsewhere, in meeting more basic needs, in catering for masses, not just a small elite'.[32] Matching grants to local government, to improve sport and recreational facilities, was one of the ways in which this policy was pursued.

While Liberal-National (formerly Liberal-Country Party) governments were slower to provide support for sport, recreation and the arts, it was a Coalition government which had initiated a move for greater government support for the arts in the 1960s, at first in the area of film and literature. By the end of the 1970s federal government promotion of sport, in one form or another, was gaining bipartisan support. The Fraser government minister responsible for sport, Bob Ellicott, was keen to formulate a long-term national sports development policy and was instrumental in establishing the Australian Institute of Sport (AIS) in 1981. The creation of this body reflected another shift in federal government sports policy. From the 1980s the government has been committed both to the pursuit of excellence—training and funding élite athletes who could compete successfully on the world stage—and encouraging grass-roots participation.

Although Malcolm Fraser was not known for a love of cricket, he became deeply enmeshed in cricket politics in the late 1970s at the time of the World Series Cricket (WSC) crisis. Fraser was drawn to the issue because he actively supported the cause of the media magnate Kerry Packer, at whose initiative WSC was started, and because he was worried by the impasse which had developed in one of the major sports of the country. He was concerned, in addition, with thwarting any possible tours of South Africa.[33] Cricket-loving Bob Hawke was also involved in WSC: he was approached by players before the crisis. When Prime Minister, Hawke even took the liberty of offering the position of national coach to West Indian Clive Lloyd. While this was not acceptable to the Australian Cricket Board, they did accept another Hawke initiative, to add cricket to the AIS.[34]

The dramatic change in federal and State government support for sport from the 1970s could not have taken place without the decline of amateur ideals, which became seen as increasingly irrelevant by the 1970s and 1980s. While amateurism had been alive and well in the 1950s and 1960s—when the introduction of professional tennis was widely criticised—it has largely vanished from sporting agendas in a very short time, without any real debate and without much regret. The Packer cricket crisis of 1977–79 (see ch. 11) represented a last and unsuccessful stand against greater commercialism in sport.

There are many reasons why politicians, the media and the public turned their back on amateurism, regarding the once-hallowed ideals as obsolete. During the 1970s many 'amateur' sports began to change from part-time enterprises to more professionally run businesses. With untold opportunities for sponsorship and media exposure through television, there was the possibility for sports to grow in a way they had never experienced before. There was also the negative incentive that a failure of

a sports authority to transform itself into a more smooth-running corporate and professional body would reduce the growth prospects of
that sport in a market which was becoming both more lucrative and
more competitive. It also became abundantly clear to sports administrators, the media and fans alike that the ethic of amateurism was no
longer a priority in world sport and that if Australia continued to be
guided by amateur notions it would fall behind in world competition.
Ultimately this was the most telling reason why amateurism became
seen as irrelevant.

Since the 1970s the federal government has regularly increased its
funding of sport and sports infrastructure. The AIS was one of the most
important government initiatives in sport. It created a 'splendid institute
with facilities unmatched anywhere in the world'[35]—the 'gold-medal
factory' as it became known—where the best athletes in the country
could benefit from experienced coaching and modern sports science.
The Australian Sports Commission (ASC), created three years later in
1984, was established to provide a more co-ordinated approach to
sports development in the country. Government programs and priorities
have spawned numerous other programs and priorities. The need to encourage women's sport, for instance, led to the establishment of a
separate Women's Sport Promotion Unit (later Women and Sport Unit)
within the ASC in 1989.

The establishment of a federal government sports infrastructure encouraged sporting groups to engage in more intense lobbying. The
Confederation of Australian Sport (CAS), which was formed in 1976,
was an independent grouping of sports bodies designed to express opinions on federal government deliberations and decisions on sport. The
umbrella organisation grew from an initial membership of 42 to 128
members, representing about seven million sports participants. The initial activity of the CAS was to protest against cuts in the federal sporting budget. While maintaining its role as a lobby group, it has moved into
a wide range of issues concerning sports policy and promotion. The CAS
was not as effective at first as it might have been, since it took time for
the amateur officials who headed it to master the tactics of a professional
lobby group.[36] Its activities included the development of policies, the
dissemination of information and the publication of reports, the holding
of conferences on sporting issues and the establishment of the Sport Australia Hall of Fame in 1985.

STATE GOVERNMENT POLICIES

State governments, like the federal government, have increasingly
become involved in sports policy to enhance their image and popularity,
to add to State revenue, to provide greater employment, to encourage
tourism, and even to put a State and a city on the map. John Bannon,

former Premier of South Australia, enhanced his electoral prospects when he secured the Adelaide Grand Prix shortly before he faced the voters. New South Wales and Victoria have been in competition for the equivalent motorcycle Grand Prix, which they have both staged. Former Queensland Premier Joh Bjelke-Petersen also basked in the reflected glory of what most commentators regarded as a successful Commonwealth Games in Brisbane in 1982. Various State premiers had been active in trying to get the Olympic and Commonwealth Games for their respective cities. The success of Sydney's bid to stage the 2000 Olympics appeared to provide a much-needed boost for John Fahey's NSW government.

There have been many recent instances of State premiers intervening in sport to alter sporting agendas. Neville Wran's wrangle with State cricket authorities over WSC has been replicated elsewhere. John Cain took issue with the VFL about where the Grand Final should be played—the VFL favoured Waverley but had to bow to Cain's pressure to keep the game at the MCG. The Queensland government enacted a Commonwealth Games Act 'to keep Brisbane free of Aborigines and their "friends"' at the time of the 1982 Games.[37]

State ministers of sport have also kept a keen eye on the health and welfare of sporting groups and interests. Former NSW Minister for Sport Bob Rowland-Smith, who wanted to prop up the ailing bookmaking industry, tried to extend the opportunities of bookmakers to include a role in rugby league in 1990. The move was dropped when it was opposed by rugby league authorities. When it appeared that the ailing Sydney Swans would be axed in 1992, no less than twenty-four State politicians spoke out in favour of the continuance of the AFL club in Sydney.

The NSW government's involvement in a motorcycle track at Eastern Creek has turned out to be a continuing source of embarrassment for it. In the interests of securing the world motorcycle title for Sydney, the government backed a private promoter, Bob Barnett, agreeing to 'fast-track' the project. The initial failure of the course to make a profit and the inability of the promoter to meet the shortfall in funds meant that the government had to cover the deficit since it had acted as a guarantor for Eastern Creek.

During the 1990s State governments have become involved in the needs of particular sports, helping to build facilities that are beyond the budgets of individual sports. They have increasingly viewed high-profile sport and world events such as the Olympics, Grand Prix events and World Cups as beneficial for employment, tourism and State revenue. There has been keen competition, sometimes leading to bitter recrimination, between one State and another to secure these sports festivals.

The involvement of State governments in sport since the 1970s is a rich area for research. Because of the cost and status of providing major football, the NSW government has been caught up in many continuing problems of creating suitable grounds for international and major matches. The search for a major ground for Sydney rugby in the 1980s—when international matches were staged at suburban Concord oval with a seating capacity of only 20 000—has been a continuing problem both for rugby authorities and the NSW government. The State government has also been caught up with the problems associated with the Sydney Football Stadium, particularly its inadequate shelter from rain. One of the attractions of the Sydney Olympic bid was that the government could appease football interests by providing them with a large and conveniently facility seating 100 000 at Homebush.

DEBATES AND CONTROVERSIES

Sport and foreign policy

With the growth and expansion of international tours in the twentieth century, sport and foreign-policy issues have become closely intertwined. The Australian government has been increasingly active in deciding where Australian sporting individuals and, in particular, teams visit. There has been the practical question of safety: whether it was advisable for an Australian cricket team to visit Sri Lanka in 1992, when the country was still in the throes of civil war. Then there is the broader issue of whether a tour to a particular country is in the national interest in terms of foreign policy and trade.

Before the 1970s it seemed that sporting individuals and teams were relatively 'free' to tour wherever they liked, mainly because many tours were along established routes within the Commonwealth and there was limited interest in touring countries with communist or totalitarian governments. Even so cricketers were encouraged to tour the West Indies in 1954, while table tennis players were discouraged from touring Indonesia in the 1950s. Governments at this time only intervened in sports policy subtly, indirectly and occasionally.

The question of South African sport emerged as a serious issue for sports administrators and for the Australian government from the 1970s, and the subsequent sports boycott became a major part of Australian foreign policy towards South Africa. Although Australia and South Africa had exchanged sporting tours from the first decade of the twentieth century, the long-standing South African apartheid surfaced as a controversial issue at the time of the Springbok Rugby tour of Australia in 1971. It took place against a backdrop of protests against the Vietnam War and conscription. During the tour there were disruptive public protests featuring violent clashes between pro- and anti-tour demonstrators and police, leading to hundreds of arrests. Games were played behind barbed-wire enclosures. The Queensland government declared a state of emergency and the McMahon federal government offered to transport the tourists in RAAF military aircraft for their protection. A number of prominent newspapers argued that McMahon's support for the tour and his criticism of the unions who attempted to disrupt it were based on political expediency. There is the suggestion that the tour represented a watershed event exposing the myth that sport and politics do not mix. The troubled tour also helped pave the way for the more direct involvement of politicians and government in sport.[38]

During the 1970s and 1980s there were no official rugby and cricket tours, and a sports boycott of South Africa became a long-standing policy of the Australian government, until it was relaxed in 1991. Sport was seen as a central lever to help South Africa remove its system of apartheid and relax its policies, which were regarded by various governments of the Commonwealth as institutionalised racism. It has been argued persuasively by those who support this policy that while a trade boycott was easy for South Africa to exploit—there were always countries willing to trade with South Africa—the sports boycott did hurt South Africa because there was no way that it could compete in international sport, including the Olympics.[39]

In these decades the question of sporting relations between Australia and South Africa was a heated and much-debated one. Some argued that the boycott policy should be relaxed because the South African government was trying to develop interracial sport. Others argued that it was hypocritical for the government to boycott South African sport but to tolerate sporting links with totalitarian countries or ones with a poor record in human rights. There was also the question of whether individual sportspeople should participate in South Africa and what penalty should apply to rebel tours of cricketers and rugby-players in the 1980s.

During the 1980s there was consistent evidence from polls and other sources that the majority of sports followers did not approve the continuing boycott of South African sport.[40] There was a widespread belief among sports followers that politicians were becoming too influential in deciding sporting priorities and agendas. It is ironic that this criticism of federal government policies did not lead to any significant public interest in the 'rebel' tours, such as the cricket teams led by Kim Hughes, in 1985 and 1987. Because there was negligible media coverage of these tours the 'rebel' tours were seen as a South African sporting event.

An equally divisive debate about sports boycotts took place at the time of the 1980 Moscow Olympic Games when many questioned whether the Australian government should use sport as an arm of foreign policy. The debate took place after the Soviet Union had occupied Afghanistan in December 1979 and the United States set about organising a large-scale boycott of the Games. Although the Fraser government and most of the leading dailies favoured a boycott of the Games, the community was split on the issue, with the Labor opposition arguing in favour of participation.[41]

While the federal government strongly supported the boycott, it left the decision up to the Executive of the Australian Olympic Federation, which decided, by a margin of 6:5 votes, to participate in the Games. This vote led to even more controversy in that pressure was brought to bear, from government and other sources, on officials and athletes not to take part. The situation was an odd one: while some teams and individuals competed, others did not. Equally bizarre was the decision of the federal government to pay $488 738.14 to seven teams and $36 000 to six individuals who boycotted the Games. These government 'bribes', which totalled $524 738.14, were more than the original approved allocation of $500 000 to the Australian Olympic Federation.[42]

It is unlikely that any future Australian government will allow itself to become enmeshed in a similar sporting débâcle. Since 1980 the government has taken more direct responsibility for the funding of the Australian Olympic effort, and this has led to much closer liaison with Australian Olympic authorities. The indecisiveness of 1980 occurred because the federal government was only indirectly involved in Australian Olympic participation; during the 1980s it became more directly involved in planning and funding.

Smoking

The nexus between sport and the smoking lobby has had a long history. When cigarette-smoking became popular among males in the late nineteenth century, it was acceptable and fashionable for sporting males to smoke. The smoking lobby, which targeted a male audience—in that female smoking was not at first socially acceptable—has long been involved in sports promotion and sponsorship. The Rothmans National Sports Foundation, founded in 1964, was a high-profile organisation, which employed top sportsmen such as Alan Davidson and promoting national and grass-roots sport.

The link between the smoking lobby and sport became closer in the 1970s, and particularly after 1976 when smoking advertisements were banned from television. Since that time, much of the money which might previously have gone into television advertising has gone into sports sponsorship. Most of the major sporting competitions of the country get their biggest funding from smoking companies: the Winfield Cup in rugby league, the Benson & Hedges Series in cricket and Phillip Morris in the AFL. It is ironic that while smoking advertisements have been banned from television since 1976, the brand-names of the sponsors appear regularly in sports telecasts on the fences of ovals, painted on the grass and in the actual name of contests. It was in this year that Benson & Hedges became the major sponsors of cricket, devising a package of $800 000 for the following three seasons. This was more than what was paid by W. H. & H. O. Wills (Australia) Ltd in the 1973–74 ($50 000) and 1974–75 ($100 000) seasons.[43]

The issue of smoking in sport has been a divisive one. While some governments have been keen to promote the anti-smoking campaign, notably the federal and the Victorian, others, such as New South Wales, have been far less critical of the smoking lobby. The New South Wales acceptance of smoking advertisements was one reason why it gained the Motorcycle Grand Prix from Victoria. The issue has also divided people within a sport, notably the celebrated exchanges between officials of the NSW Rugby League, with their sponsor Winfield, and the then president of the North Sydney Rugby League Club, David Hill, an ardent anti-smoking advocate. Former Test-player Greg Matthews, who took a stand against smoking in a magazine article in 1992, was fined by the Australian Cricket Board, whose major sponsor was Benson & Hedges.

While there are various arguments about the nexus between sport and smoking, it was the contention of former Minister for Sport Ros Kelly that the association between sport and smoking was detrimental in that it encouraged young people to smoke because they were influenced by sporting role models. Government initiatives to end the link between sport and smoking have already proved effective. The Rothmans National Sports Foundation closed in 1994.

Sport has long been seen as important in the business of being Australian and, with sport becoming a larger and larger enterprise in the twentieth century, professional politicians along with the big players of business and the media have vied with each other to be seen as associated with sporting culture. If Robert Menzies was the first to recognise that such an association could enhance his image, Bob Hawke developed this to an art-form in the 1980s.

As sport has moved from a part-time amateur enterprise to a professional one, big business, party politicians and corporate, media and advertising interests have become involved as a matter of course. Sport has become linked with many wider political issues. Sport is a more important element of politics than before and will continue to be so in the future. The issue of sport and politics involves some wider issues including the question of race and of Aborigines in sport.

8
ABORIGINES AND ISSUES OF RACE

Aborigines have participated more readily in sporting culture than in any other form of Australian culture. They have even been over-represented in some sports—notably boxing, some of the football codes, and pedestrianism. While being only 1 per cent of the population, Aborigines have produced thirty of the 225 boxing champions (15 per cent) in eight major Australian professional divisions over fifty years.[1] But their success in these sports has not been repeated in others. Aborigines have been grossly underrepresented in more middle-class sports such as golf, motor-racing, polo, gymnastics, swimming and yachting.

There are many questions which can be asked about Aboriginal sport. Why, and under what circumstances, did Aborigines become involved in the sporting culture of the European settlers? Why have they participated so noticeably in some sports and not in others? Has Australian sporting culture enhanced and perpetuated European paternalism and racism? Has the substantial involvement of Aborigines in sport been beneficial or detrimental to them?

It is also important to try to explore the way Aborigines themselves see sport and their involvement in 'mainstream' sporting culture. In recent times there have been some attempts to develop separate Aboriginal Games and sporting contests and to develop more Aboriginal notions of sport. There have also been attempts to use the popular theatre of sport to make the Australian population more aware of the prevalence of racism.

PATERNALISM FROM THE 1850s

Aborigines before 1850 had very little to do with sporting culture. Many Aborigines of south and eastern Australia were still engaged in ferocious and guerrilla wars of resistance in the 1840s, which resulted in the slaughter of many of them and a much lesser number of Europeans. Effective resistance was at an end in Van Diemen's Land by the 1820s and in New South Wales and Victoria by the 1840s. By that time violence and disease had decimated the Aboriginal population in these colonies. The Aboriginal pre-contact population of Port Phillip for instance, estimated at 10 000, had been reduced to only 1907 in Victoria by 1853.

Other Aborigines became part of European settlements. For some, 'coming in'—giving themselves over to white control—was the result of military exhaustion, disease and starvation. For others it was a question of curiosity. When these Aborigines became part of European society, even when they obtained casual work, they were exploited and underpaid, and existed on the margins of European society. They had limited access to sporting communities in the same way that they had few legal, economic and social rights. There was also the handicap, which has continued ever since, of restricted access to sporting facilities.

European attitudes towards Aborigines and towards their involvement in sport changed in the second half of the nineteenth century in south and eastern Australia. By the 1850s and 1860s Aborigines in Victoria, for instance, were no longer regarded as a threat to European landowners; instead they were regarded as a 'doomed race'. Those who subscribed to this popular theory saw Aborigines in less hostile and even more humanitarian terms advocating, as an *Age* editorial put it on 28 October 1858, that Europeans should help to 'smooth the pillow of a dying race'. Some at this time viewed Aborigines in paternalistic terms of sentimental romanticism, believing that they could be 'civilised'. Among other things they encouraged Aborigines to take part in sports such as boxing, cricket, horse-racing, pedestrianism and rowing.

There is considerable evidence that Aborigines participated more freely in mainstream sport in the 1850s and 1860s than later in the century. In the Moreton Bay Settlement in the late 1840s Aborigines were prominent in horse-racing, pedestrianism and rowing. 'Black boy Jimmy', a jockey, was successful in the Maiden Plate at Drayton in 1848, and there was no attempt to disguise the Aboriginality of 'Sandy', a jockey who rode at the exclusive Moreton Bay Racing Club.[2] But one writer on racing believes that there were relatively few Aboriginal jockeys and that Aborigines participated less in horse-racing than did Maoris in New Zealand, who both rode and owned racehorses.[3]

By the 1850s and 1860s there were large numbers of Aborigines playing cricket on missions and country stations. Paternalists encouraged Aboriginal cricket for a variety of reasons. Missionaries believed that cricket was a game which could 'civilise' Aborigines. Rev. Mathew Hale, who established a missionary institution at Poonindie, near Port Lincoln in South Australia in 1850, believed that games, and cricket in particular, could make Aborigines more industrious and moral. When the

1.1 Some hotels have provided attractive and even lavish venues for sport. George Hotel, St Kilda, 1900. (courtesy Melbourne Cricket Club)

3.3 It was natural to fraternise socially with team-mates. Coxed four and coach at the Glebe Rowing Club, 2 December 1894. (courtesy The King's School)

4.2 The headmaster of The King's School, Dr E. Harris, took a keen interest in the school First XV in 1892. P. S. Waddy (to his right) became a prominent muscular Christian and a later headmaster of the school. W. S. Corr, the coach, (standing right) was a strong believer that sport could promote character. Corr, a co-founder of the AAGPS, was an international referee. (courtesy The King's School)

5.1 Indian club drill at Glebe Primary School in the 1890s. Drill was an acceptable form of exercise for primary school girl students. (courtesy New South Wales Department of Education)

5.4 The muscular body of the champion athletes was much admired. Champion swimmer Barney Kieran flexed his muscles for the camera. (Mitchell Library)

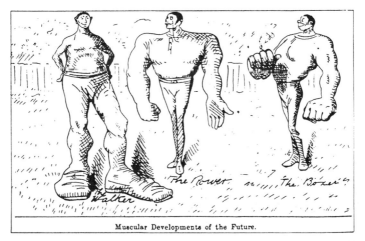

Muscular Developments of the Future.

5.5 Muscularity was a topical issue in the 1880s. The Queensland newspaper *Figaro*, of 24 May 1884, published this caricature of the future athletic body, with a large torso and a small head.

B.Chequer. H.Smith. H.Mellor(Pat.) N.Greville. S.Bremner (Belt.)

5.6 Lifesavers were male icons, depicted as heroic individuals who were intent on serving the community. Collaroy Surf Life-saving Club *c.* 1920s. (courtesy Collaroy Surf Lifesaving Club)

5.7 Girls about to start a race at the Adelaide City Baths in the 1890s appeared in a variety of costume. (Archives, Corporation of the City of Adelaide)

5.8 Women's costume restricted sporting activity. Cricket at Evandale, Tasmania, in the 1890s. (courtesy Launceston Reference Library)

5.9 When the men went to war in 1939 women took over many activities, including lifesaving, but their services were no longer required soon after the men returned from the war. The Collaroy Surf Lifesaving Club's Ladies March Past Team competing at Manly in 1947. (courtesy Collaroy Surf Lifesaving Club)

5.10 It was not necessary to have an athletic body or an attractive sporting costume to enjoy croquet, which became largely a sport for women of mature years. Marrickville Ladies' Croquet Team *c.* 1930s. (courtesy Marrickville Local Studies Collection)

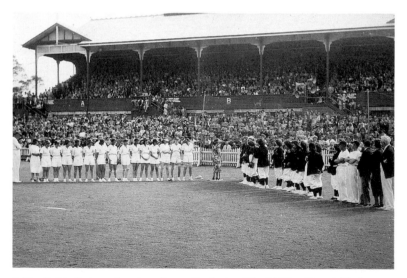

5.11 Softball, introduced to Australia during World War II, quickly became popular. There was a sizeable crowd at the St Kilda Oval to watch a Test between Australia and New Zealand in 1949. (courtesy Australian Softball Federation)

6.2 'Cor, he doesn't support a football team!' It was considered unmanly not to support football in the 1880s. There are definite hints of anti-intellectualism and homophobia in this depiction of an anti-football dandy. (*Town and Country Journal*, 6 June 1885)

6.5 The passion of Melbourne fans for football was legendary. Crowds braved the worst elements. (*Daily News* photograph, collection of the Victorian Football League)

8.2 Mulga Fred, who regularly entertained the crowd at Victoria Park at half-time with his boomerang and whip, with the 1924 Collingwood Football team. Aboriginal players were rare in the Victorian Football League until well after World War II. (courtesy Richard Stremski)

9.1 Australian-born Lebanese cricket team in 1934 with Archimandrite Antonios Mobayed, priest of St Nicholas Orthodox Church in Melbourne. The St Nicholas team played in the North Suburban Cricket Competition. (courtesy Batrouney family)

9.2 The bowling alley of the Tanunda Kegel Club, Barossa Valley, in the 1890s, was laid out in 1877. This German game was played in the Barossa Valley from 1858. (courtesy Tanunda Kegel Club and John Daly)

9.3 Schuetzerfest [an annual shooting contest], Hahndorf, Adelaide Hills probably 1886. King of Shoot, M. C. Bom in centre, was awarded a prize medal which was added to the 'garland' of previously won medals. (courtesy John Daly)

9.4 American trotters gave an exhibition of trotting at Randwick in 1881, twenty years before the New South Wales Trotting Club was formed. (*Illustrated Sydney News*, 29 October 1881)

9.7 Australian-based Argentinian fans were passionate supporters of the Argentinian side in the World Cup qualifying game at the Sydney Football Stadium on 31 October 1993. (courtesy Australian Soccer Federation)

9.11 Hawaiian Duke Kahanamoku, who pioneered surfboard riding in Australia, in front of an admiring crowd at Freshwater Surf Club in 1914. (courtesy Heather Rose)

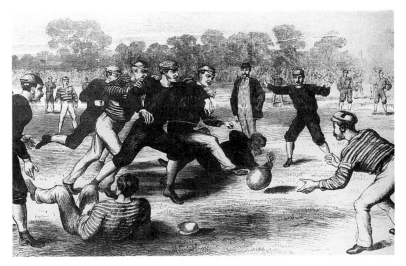

10.2 Lithograph depicting football on Moore Park, Sydney, in 1874 when the game, facilities and sports illustration were primitive. Moore Park was unenclosed, so the sizeable crowd paid no gate entry. (*Illustrated Sydney News*, 25 July 1874)

10.4 Action photography had a profound impact on sport. Although Fred Spofforth was 51 when this photo was taken, George Beldam captured the 'Demon's' classic leap, before the delivery of the ball, giving the illusion of a much younger man.

11.3 Muscular New Zealand sculling champion Richard Arnst endorsed the idea that tobacco was soothing and seductive. (The *Bulletin*, 22 October 1908)

12.1 The State of Origin match at the Sydney Football Stadium in 1991 attracted a packed and enthusiastic house in spite of drenching rain. Michael O'Connor and Ben Elias from New South Wales are to the left and Mal Meninga and Willie Carne from Queensland to the right. (courtesy Colin Whelan and Action Photographics)

12.2 Grant Kenny, champion ironman and kayaker, became a household name in the 1980s promoting Uncle Tobys. (photograph Harvie Allison)

12.3 Greyhound-racing has never achieved wide appeal but its largely working-class supporters were keenly involved in the sport. Kedron Coursing Club Meeting, Brisbane, 1 April 1940. (courtesy Ian Jobling)

12.4 Radio and Bradman helped cricket boom in the 1930s. Not everyone appreciated the national ball-to-ball descriptions from 1932–33 which took cricket into the living rooms of the country.

BRADMAN

Brisbane Cricket Ground,

FRIDAY to TUESDAY,

SHEFFIELD SHIELD

Q'ld v. South Australia

Play commences at 11.30 a.m. each day; luncheon adjournment 1.15-2 p.m.; afternoon tea, 4-4.15 p.m.; stumps, 6 p.m.

Gates open on FRIDAY, MONDAY, and TUESDAY at 11 a.m., and on Saturday at 10.30 a.m. Entrance Main Street gates. Members' entrance at Vulture Street will be open Saturday only.

ADMISSION Grandstand 3 . Outer 1 6. Children Half Price. Full catering arrangements on ground.

Pass-out checks will be issued luncheon adjournment only.

Parking area with attendant in Main Street, near Police Station 6d per car.

R. T. STEPHENS, Secretary Q.C.A.

12.5 Bradman was a powerful drawcard in the 1930s. Administrators were well aware that when Bradman batted crowds flocked to the ground.

12.6 Politicians have long been prominent at major horse-racing events, particularly the Melbourne Cup. Two prime ministers, Sir Robert Menzies and Billy Hughes, study the form.

12.7 Cathy Freeman's 'statement' at the 1994 Commonwealth Games attracted much public attention. (courtesy Australian Coaching Council)

12.8 The issue of racism in sport became a matter of public discussion by the 1990s. Aboriginal Nicky Winmar, best on the ground St Kilda Versus Collingwood 1991, responding to the taunts of a section of the crowd by pointing to his skin. (photograph John Feder, courtesy Herald-Sun Pictorial Library)

12.9 Sponsorship is prominent at the Kingdom, Sydney Entertainment Centre, and the fans, in corporate boxes, are close to the action. Sydney Kings' Damian Keogh is about to throw the ball in while Dean Uthoff sets up a screen. Sydney Kings versus Southeast Melbourne Magic in 1994. (courtesy Sydney Coca-Cola Kings)

Bishop of Adelaide visited the mission he was impressed with the play
of the Poonindie XI, regarding their cricket as 'proof of their progress
in civilization'.[4] A romantic painting, 'Boy Playing Cricket' by John
Michael Crossland (1854), conveyed this changed European perception
of Aborigines and sport. The subject, Nannultera, a pupil at Poonindie,
was neatly dressed in European costume, a civilised and athletic black.

There is a danger of reading too much into the rhetoric that games
could 'civilise' Aborigines at Poonindie. Only ten games are known to
have taken place from 1850 to 1894, and games were a fairly minor feature of life at the mission. There are grounds for believing that the success of the Aboriginal XI inflamed rather than softened local prejudice.
The brothers Adams, model workers, Christians and captains of the
Poonindie XI in the 1870s, received no special favours when they
requested government assistance and land grants.[5]

The belief in the efficacy of games to civilise was cogently expressed
by the Spanish Benedictine priest Salvado, who encouraged the formation of a very successful team at the New Norcia Mission in Western
Australia in 1879. Salvado recognised the force of the English belief
that 'Aborigines who know how to play cricket against the white teams
are more civilized than if they knew the whole Summa of St Thomas by
heart'.[6]

Station-owners had other reasons for encouraging Aborigines to participate in sport. The guilt of the land-takers may have been one reason
why some station-owners patronised Aboriginal cricket. Probably more
important was that Aborigines had become an important cog in the Victorian economy, when there was a labour shortage after many labourers
took off for the goldfields. As useful members of many station communities they were allowed to take part in some of its recreational life.[7]

Aboriginal participation in sport also occurred in the 1850s and
1860s because attitudes towards Aborigines were not as fixed and rigid
as they later became, when racism became more institutionalised. While
the legal rights of Aborigines had steadily declined from the first years
of settlement, they retained a measure of freedom of movement and
other rights. Although a Central Board for the Protection of the
Aborigines was established in Victoria in 1860, it did not become a
statutory authority until the Aboriginal Protection Act of 1869. Had
this board been constituted earlier the Aboriginal cricket team might
not have visited England in 1868.[8]

By the 1860s many Aborigines were playing cricket, and Aboriginal
teams made a name for themselves in various colonies. The Poonindie
XI competed successfully in its own locality from the 1850s and even
played against an XI from St Peter's, one of the leading public schools
of the colony, on a few occasions in the 1870s. Station cricket in Victoria became so popular that a team of Aborigines representing several
stations took on and defeated a team of Europeans near the Bringalbert
woolshed in 1865. The success of this team encouraged two local

landowners, Tom Hamilton and William Hayman, to take some of the Aborigines to Edenhope, where they played against local European teams, and then to Melbourne in 1866, which was the first step towards the 1868 English tour.

There was also some Aboriginal involvement in other colonies. Three Aborigines were members of a successful Ginninderra team in the New South Wales Riverina in the 1860s. Later in the century there were other successful teams at Deebing Creek, near Ipswich, Queensland and at New Norcia, Western Australia, where Fr Salvado encouraged a local pastoralist, H. B. Lefroy, to form and equip a team which played widely and successfully throughout the colony. Known as the 'Invincibles', they were successful in Perth cricket for a quarter of a century.

There is evidence that there was considerable 'Aboriginal enthusiasm for cricket'[9] and they played with 'apparent skills and enjoyment'.[10] There were also wider opportunities for Aborigines to fraternise with Europeans. After an Aboriginal cricket team played in a match at the MCG in December 1868—billed as 'Black and White Natives of Australia vs Players from All Parts of the World'—the Aborigines 'attended Christmas pantomimes, were presented with cricket bats on stage, and watched burlesques featuring themselves'.[11]

Aboriginal teams played in front of large crowds on the leading cricket grounds in the 1860s, including the MCG and Sydney's Albert Ground, and toured England in 1868, the first Australian cricket team to do so. Four Europeans, William Hayman, Charles Lawrence, George Smith and George W. Graham, managed the side and raised £2200 to underwrite the tour. The side was captained by Lawrence, a Sydney cricket coach and hotelier.

Many spectators undoubtedly watched the Aboriginal cricketers out of racial curiosity and to watch the associated sports carnivals when some players demonstrated their skills at weaponry, running backwards, dodging cricket balls and throwing boomerangs. The second match of the English tour against the Mote Park Club was even suspended, with the match in the balance, to allow time for a display of Aboriginal sports. The cricketers wore colourful costumes: military red shirts with diagonal blue flannel sashes, neckties, blue elastic belts, white flannels, and different-coloured caps which identified each player. While the tour was an exercise in paternalism, and there were racist assumptions about Aboriginal cricketers, it should be noted that the Aboriginal tour took place at a time when 'professional exhibition cricket' was still popular. From the 1840s there had been a tradition of 'troupes of clown cricketers' providing both sport and spectacle.[12]

Two writers on the subject have concluded that this tour cannot be dismissed as a 'mere speculation or stunt'. The team proved sufficiently popular for the scheduled ten matches to be extended to forty-seven. While reactions to the tour were mixed, the team performed creditably—fourteen wins, fourteen losses and nineteen draws—given their relative inexperience and the gruelling schedule. The receipts of £5416 more than covered the costs of £3224 and additional allowances for the tour organisers. The principal investor, Graham, received a moderate surplus rather than a financial bonanza.[13] While there was a promise that the players would receive regular wages and a bonus of £50 at the end of the tour, there is no evidence that they did.

Aboriginal success in cricket brought a grudging respect from Europeans. It also enabled them to extend 'a degree of power' in the arena of sport which enabled them to develop some of their own traditions.[14] Daniel Matthews, a missionary who established the Maloga Mission in New South Wales, wrote in the 1880s of what Aboriginal involvement in sport led to: 'they had discovered that their prowess in sport, particularly in cricket and running, gave them a passport to the white man's world, even to his respect and friendship.'[15] Matthews did not regard this experience as beneficial, believing that it encouraged greater Aboriginal drinking and gambling.

There are good reasons for arguing that Aborigines had a higher status in cricket in the 1860s and 1870s than at later times. Two 1868 tourists, Bullocky and Cuzens, played for Victoria—a match between a Victorian XI and a Tasmanian XVI in 1867 not having first-class status—while another two, Twopenny and Mullagh, played first-class cricket. The 1868 tour proved to be a 'one-off' affair which did not lead to any continuing Aboriginal involvement in cricket.

In the next 110 years there have been only another five Aboriginal first-class cricketers, and their careers in the game have been brief and in three instances controversial. Only one Aborigine, a woman, has played Test cricket for Australia: Faith Coulthard (later Thomas) played one Test for Australia in 1958. Albert Henry (1880–1909) played seven games for Queensland from 1902 to 1905; Jack Marsh (1874–1916) represented New South Wales in six games from 1900 to 1902; while Eddie Gilbert (1908–78) played twenty-three matches for Queensland from 1930 to 1936. Since then only three Aborigines have played first-class cricket: Ian King (1969–70) and Michael Mainhardt (1980–82), who played for Queensland, and Roger Brown, who represented Tasmania 1984–87.

While it is difficult to give precise reasons for declining Aboriginal involvement in cricket, it was undoubtedly related to the replacement of a benign paternalism by a more pessimistic institutionalised racism by the turn of the century. With greater segregation and less contact between Aborigines and Europeans at work, there were fewer opportunities and incentives for Aborigines to continue playing cricket.

PEDESTRIANISM AND SOCIAL DARWINISM

While Aborigines achieved prominence and even a measure of respect in cricket, it was in the more working-class sport of pedestrianism that they made a bigger impact because the sport required limited facilities and equipment. Pedestrianism emerged as a major sport in the second half of the nineteenth century and enjoyed a boom in the 1880s. New tracks were created, large crowds attended and professional athletes ran for huge stakes—such as the 700 sovereigns prize-money for the Botany Handicap in 1888. Bookmakers at the track profited, with £10 000 changing hands at this meeting.

Aborigines produced many prominent pedestrians including Charlie Samuels (1863–1912) who became a celebrated champion in the 1880s and 1890s. Originally a stockrider born at Jimbour Station, Dalby, Queensland, Samuels broke professional sprint records and became rated by many as the greatest sprinter in the world. Although he hardly ever trained, in his prime he was unbeatable from 50 to 130 yards.

Aborigines who were involved in the pedestrian boom were exposed to greater exploitation and racism than Aboriginal cricketers of the 1860s and the 1870s. Since pedestrianism was a more working-class sport, the big handicap events attracted larger promoters, bookmakers and trainers, all of whom were inspired more by mercenary than humanitarian motives. Huge amounts of money changed hands at major meetings such as when Ted Lazarus was backed to win £90 000 at the 1887 Botany Handicap but, to the relief of the bookmakers, Samuels won. Aboriginal runners had to cope both with exploitative white managers and with the sport itself which, with rudimentary organisation, encouraged severe handicapping, running stiff to get a few yards back, cheating and race-fixing.

The chequered athletic career of Charlie Samuels indicated how difficult it was for a runner to survive in the complex white world of professional running. After proving himself in Dalby, Samuels was brought to Sydney by William Robertson, a fellow stockrider from Jimbour, and won the eighth Botany handicap in 1886 in spectacular fashion. He was then managed by bookmaker Billy Lees and his associate T. M. Rose. During the 1880s Samuels defeated all comers and was admired for his courage and determination and graceful style of running. He received only a fraction of the prize-money he earned: when he won £12 500 for his backers in one race in 1890, he received only £250 plus board.[16]

When tougher handicaps began to take their toll on Samuels he ran 'stiff' in one race and, in another, received £10 to lose a handicap. It was a case, as the *Referee* of 14 August 1889 noted, that the 'backmark men' had their champion status exploited and did not have 'much encouragement to run as straight'. Living for a time at the 'black's camp' at Centennial Park and later at the Aboriginal mission at La Perouse, Samuels's life became increasingly unsettled and he was charged variously with assault and being 'drunk and disorderly'. From there it was mostly downhill: after three months at Callan Park he was sent back to Queensland at the expense of the Aborigines Protection Board, ending up at the Barambah reserve. His decline was a product of exploitation but was also due to his 'defiance and resistance to white authority'.[17]

The boom in professional running coincided with the general accept-ance of Social Darwinism, which popularised racist views that Abori-gines were an inferior race doomed to wither and disappear. By the mid-1880s the organisers of pedestrianism had incorporated racial distinctions into the sport. Aboriginal and Asian competitors were so designated on programs: 'a' after a name indicated Aboriginal; 'h.c.' denoted 'half-caste', while 'c.p.', 'coloured person', referred to an Asian athlete. Aboriginal runners also suffered because of increased media racial stereotyping which suggested that they lacked discipline and were sexually promiscuous.[18]

The rise of amateurism compounded the racial (and class) discrimina-tion of Aborigines involved in professional athletics. There was consider-able debate at the turn of the century whether an Aborigine could be an amateur. The Queensland Amateur Athletic Association (QAAA) rejected the entry of Tommy Pablo (of the Toowong Harriers) to race in an event in 1903 because as 'a full-blooded aboriginal it would be almost impossible to make him conform to the amateur definition'.[19] The associ-ation then notified the national Amateur Athletic Union Executive of their decision to exclude Aborigines from any QAAA event and asked if the Executive would concur with their decision.[20] The Australian Ama-teur Athletics Union was unwilling to endorse such an extreme position.

LEGALISED RACISM FROM THE 1890s

The Queensland Aborigines Protection and Restriction of the Sale of Opium Act of 1897, which was a product of racism and humanitarian paternalism, altered the status of Aborigines in that colony. Under the Act all persons of any Aboriginal descent were granted 'protection', which meant that they could be moved to a reserve and kept there against their will, virtually as a prisoner. They were not allowed alcohol, a vote or, at a later stage, any sexual fraternisation with Europeans. It provided the model for similar legislation in Western Australia (1905), South Australia and the Northern Territory (1911). These rigid controls remained in force until the 1960s.[21]

Racist laws emerged in colonies such as Queensland because, for some decades after 1850, the frontier there was settled more violently and slowly, leading to a continuing problem of lawlessness and violence. The confrontation occurred also because Europeans, outnumbered by Aborigines in the far North, were more fearful than elsewhere. A stated objective of the 1897 Act was to end the decimation and exploitation of Aborigines by separating them from Europeans. Frontier disorder also became a problem in Western Australia and the Northern Territory by the end of the nineteenth century.

Colin Tatz has noted that the spirit of the 1897 Act was to be 'protect-ive' but that 'the protections in practice at once became discriminations':

Stopping white grog, sexual, or opium predators from coming near Aboriginal communities resulted in their incarceration, for life, even generations, on the most remote and inaccessible reserves like Yarrabah, Palm Island, Cherbourg (Barambah), Bamaga, Woorabinda. Protection of Aboriginal morality came to mean censorship of their movement, labour, marriages, leisure, religious and cultural rituals. Protection of their income came to mean officials controlling their wages, withdrawals from compulsory savings bank accounts, their rights to enter into contracts of labour.[22]

Dr Walter Edmund Roth (1861–1933), one of the architects of the 1897 Act, helped design similar legislation for Western Australia and was appointed the first Northern Protector of Aborigines in 1898. Roth was trained initially as a physician, but developed an interest in Aboriginal anthropology and published a monograph, *Ethnological Studies among North-West Central Queensland Aborigines*, in 1897. A stated purpose of Roth's policies was to 'bring Aboriginal–white relations more securely under the rule of law', which he believed could best be achieved by the separation of the races. Roth, who viewed race relations in Social Darwinist terms, believed that the 'weaker race' could only survive if it was isolated from the 'stronger'. Contact between Aborigines and whites in any form—sporting, sexual, economic—would prove demoralising to Aborigines. Roth and others of this era were far more pessimistic about the potential of Aborigines to be 'civilised'.

Roth regarded Aboriginal participation in games of cricket with Europeans as detrimental because this contact represented a threat to the discipline and stability inculcated on the reserves. He noted on one occasion that 'seven adult [Aboriginal] malcontents had to be subsequently returned to Bowen ... [as] they had evidently been too much encouraged in competition with Europeans in the way of cricket matches, etc. and had been treated socially far above their natural station in life'. Roth proscribed Aboriginal participation in many sports gatherings in 1904, limiting competition against 'whites' in townships.[23]

Roth was not opposed to Aboriginal sport as such, provided that it was segregated and inculcated discipline. He praised the 'gymnastic exercises' which were organised at the Yarrabah Reserve, North Queensland, since this form of exercise was calculated to remove that 'appearance of indolence which is so characteristic of the savage when brought under civilised conditions'. He was also enthusiastic about the good discipline which resulted from weekly drills, which had been part of mission life since 1893.[24]

Although Aborigines could participate in some forms of sport after 1900, the majority were effectively cut off from many forms of mainstream sporting culture. Many Aborigines were relegated to remote areas of Queensland, Western Australia and the Northern Territory and were thus removed from the centres of organised sport, which were in the cities. The greater separation from the wider social and economic life also meant removal from community recreational life. While Aborigines may have been encouraged to participate in gymnastics and drill, sports facilities on most reserves were meagre. Denied many opportunities to compete against other Australians, and even the sportspeople of other countries, Aborigines had little incentive to take up sport.

The situation was different in south-east Australia. Sport was prominent on some reserves such as the tiny Cummera mission on the Murray which produced many noted athletes, such as Sir Doug Nicholls and Lynch Cooper, a world champion sprinter in the late 1920s.[25] It is likely that this occurred because Cumeroogunga was a more open reserve which encouraged Aboriginal enterprise and fostered a more confident outlook. It was founded in 1888, when a group of Aborigines left Maloga to settle on a government reserve, established a thriving village community and were soon able to compete successfully with the growers of the district.[26]

When sportsmen from missions gained permission to play in mainstream sport, they had to walk a delicate tightrope of coping with an unfamiliar white sporting world and dealing with racial prejudice, yet at the same time behaving impeccably. The brief first-class cricket career of Albert Henry showed that this was no easy task. A resident of Deebing Creek mission, the promising fast bowler needed government permission to become a resident of South Brisbane to take part in district cricket. It has been argued that the career of this fiery and erratic fast bowler, who was also a brilliant fielder, was cut short because he was involved in behaviour which was perceived by administrators as threatening. After he was constantly no-balled by a well-known umpire, Henry could not contain his anger and clashed heatedly with the umpire, which earned him a month's suspension. His later defiance of authority—he was considered guilty of 'loafing, malingering and defying authority'—led to his removal and imprisonment to Barambah before his complete exclusion and isolation at Yarrabah.[27]

WIDER ISSUES OF RACE

Australian sport developed in a wider context of racial notions, and sport played an important role in race relations within Australia. A Boxing Day race-meeting at Mackay in 1883 degenerated into a 'race riot' between whites and Islanders and resulted in an official count of two dead (unofficially many more) and many others seriously injured. The riot 'fuelled racial antagonism' in Mackay and, in the long term, provided the stimulus for legislation forbidding the recruitment of Pacific Islanders to Queensland.[28] A race-meeting provided a theatre for racial antagonism because it was an occasion when whites and Kanakas met and it was associated with heavy drinking.

Richard Broome has argued that a sporting event, the celebrated boxing contest between the African-American Jack Johnson and Cana-

dian Tommy Burns, the 'great white hope', in Sydney in 1908 was 'a
landmark in relations between black and white in Australia'.[29] The fight
attracted great public attention because it gave form to popular racial
discourse: it was portrayed as a contest between the 'brains and dedica-
tion' of Burns versus the 'brute strength and flashness' of Johnson. A
Norman Lindsay poster used to publicise the fight featured a towering
and brutish black—'magnificent evil'—facing the smaller and courage-
ous white, and 'must have evoked the deepest feelings Australians held
about the symbols of blackness and whiteness', the notion of populous
coloured races versus the numerically smaller white races.[30] Fifty
thousand spectators attended the Sydney fight, partly out of interest in
a good contest but also because of the racist desire to see the 'black
man' beaten, particularly because Johnson was regarded as a 'bad nigger'.[31] The fight was portrayed in the media as a battle between good
and evil, civilisation versus animalism, the brainy Spartan versus the
brutish braggart. It also touched on wider issues such as physical prowess and violence and the expression of sexuality in a repressed society.

Despite the defeat of the 'great white hope', there was a continuing
public fascination with the event afterwards, and large crowds viewed
the film of the contest. Part of this interest was focused on Johnson,
who seemed to epitomise the darker side of racial myths which had
their elements of fear, hate and sexual expression. The fight generated
popular debate about many issues of race, including the future of the
Anglo-Saxon 'race', the danger of the Yellow Peril and the White Australia Policy.

Racial politics has long been part of the complexion of Australian
sport and has manifested itself in various forms. There was considerable
controversy about whether a Fijian cricket team should visit Australia
in 1907–8, with prominent Cricket Board officials arguing that it would
be a breach of the White Australia policy. The tour only went ahead
when Melbourne delegate Edward Mitchell was 'so incensed by the
racist attitudes put forward' that he stated that if the board did not
support the tour, the Melbourne Cricket Club would back it.[32] The
Sydney Morning Herald of 12 December 1907 contained a lengthy
report of a Sydney match, which confirmed popular racial stereotypes
about the exotic 'fuzzy wuzzy' islanders who played cricket in bare feet.
Their appearance, rather than their cricket, was clearly the big
attraction:

> The Fijians marched on to the ground headed by their captain Prince Ratu
> Kadavu Levu and what a fearsome sight they presented. Eight of them wore
> their national costume, beads, etc., with the addition of short white trunks.
>   When the men took their places in the field there was an opportunity of
> scrutinising their dress. The skirt was the principle article of attire. It seemed
> to be made of seaweed, and as the men ran it blew out behind them, exposing
> their running shorts. Round their necks they wore another contrivance,
> apparently of seaweed, which fell to the waist and formed a loose blouse ...

Boots or shoes were tabooed. Only two men wore caps. The other members of the team were bareheaded, if such a term can be applied. There was no fear of their being sunstruck, for each man had more hair than twenty white men put together. That perhaps accounts for the absence of caps, for to fit them a cap would have to be as big as a football. In addition, they have all undergone a special greasing or oiling operation to temper the effect of the rays of the sun on the bare skin of their legs and bodies.

A couple of decades later the first West Indian tourists to Australia in 1930–31 were indignant to find the seven white team members booked into one hotel and the eleven blacks into another one. After complaints from the tourists they were booked into the same hotel.

There is also the interesting question of how discrimination restricted the first-class careers of the three bowlers Gilbert, Henry and Marsh. It has been recognised that Gilbert was one of the fastest bowlers of his time and that Marsh, in the opinion of the much-respected journalist J. C. Davis, 'could have been one of the world's greatest bowlers if he had been a white man'.[33] It has been suggested by various writers that Marsh and Gilbert were good enough to have gone further but for a 'pervasive racialism'.[34]

To gain selection, Aborigines had to be more skilled than white players, and once selected their behaviour had to be above reproach, since they could easily fall foul of both cricket and reserve authorities. While playing for Queensland Eddie Gilbert lived in the backyard of the secretary of the Queensland Cricket Association, which had come to an agreement with the Protector of Aborigines. His interstate trips were 'complicated by increasingly stringent clearance regulations and conditions' determined by State government authorities, who appear to have wished to curtail his freedom of movement and speech.[35] There is also some evidence that Marsh was a victim of the anti-throwing hysteria then prevalent. It was certainly difficult for Marsh, 'who was taken from his bush haunts and given civilised garb', to survive in what must have been the complex and baffling world of organised cricket. After being no-balled fourteen times for throwing by umpire Crockett in his first Shield match in Melbourne in 1901, Marsh became so frustrated that he 'deliberately threw three consecutive balls'. Like Henry, Marsh became typecast as a natural athlete who unfortunately was erratic and unreliable.[36]

That Henry, Marsh and Gilbert were the victims of racial discrimination can only be inferred. Bernard Whimpress has attempted to unravel the subtle operation of prejudice by exploring key indicators: selection policy, accusations of 'throwing', where Aborigines were placed in the batting order, and the evaluation of their fielding ability.[37] He argues that discrimination represented covert rather than overt racism: race was certainly an issue but it was compounded by class and even personality clashes. There is 'strong circumstantial evidence' that the New South Wales sole selector M. A. Noble colluded with the English captain A. C. MacLaren so that Marsh was left out of a vital match between England and a New South Wales country team at Bathurst. This adversely affected his chances of selection for the Fourth Test of the 1901–2 series and his chance of touring England. Whimpress believes that Noble's view may have been influenced by jealousy—Marsh could bowl a better outcurve than he could—and even a defensiveness concerning the legitimacy of his own bowling action.[38]

Racial factors were undoubtedly reasons why so few Aborigines played in any of the major football codes before World War II. Although Australian football and rugby were immensely popular by the turn of the century and rugby league grew rapidly after 1907, (Sir) Doug Nicholls (1906–88) was one of the few to play in the top ranks of football. After he was initially rejected on racial grounds at Carlton in the VFL—they said he smelled—he played instead for five years for Northcote in the VFA before transferring to Fitzroy. From early on Nicholls had discovered that 'the only way to crack the white world was to do something better than the white man'.[39]

GREATER ABORIGINAL SPORTING INVOLVEMENT FROM THE 1920S

There was an increased Aboriginal presence in sport from the 1920s when 'greater Aboriginal freedom of movement' coincided with 'rising professionalism' in sports such as boxing, football and running.[40] Boxing has long been attractive to working-class communities and impoverished ethnic groups, who have seen the sport as an escape from the poverty and racism of the ghetto. World boxing has been dominated by a succession of such minority communities: Poles, Irish, Jews, Italians, African-Americans and Latin Americans. Boxing in Australia has provided the promise for Aborigines 'to escape the usual subordinate and outcast condition assigned to them' in a European-dominated Australian society.[41]

The first Aboriginal boxing champion, Jerry Jerome (1874–1950) from Dalby, Queensland, required an exemption certificate from his employer before he could participate freely. After taking part in touring boxing tents at country shows, he came to the city to win the Australian middleweight crown in 1912. Title wins by Ron Richards and Merv 'Darky' Blandon in 1933 ushered in an era of Aboriginal champions. Lionel Rose, world bantamweight title-holder in 1968–69, the Sands brothers, George Bracken and Tony Mundine were some of the more prominent who later became household names.

Richard Broome has provided a balance sheet weighing up the positive and negative factors of Aboriginal involvement in boxing. One positive factor was that in the gymnasium, the core institution of the boxing subculture, some of the complications of the outside world were left behind as boxers who trained, sparred and talked about the sport became 'close'. It was here that many 'young Aborigines from the country felt secure and accepted'. There was even a 'camaraderie' between white and black boxers who engaged in tent boxing which amounted to an 'inter-racial mateship'.[42]

Boxing in the cities, however, was a sport controlled by Europeans, from trainers and promoters to media personnel. Relationships between some of the élite Aboriginal boxers and their managers was often close and paternalistic. While the relationship could be exploitative, there were beneficial aspects. Young Aboriginal boxers, fresh from small rural communities, needed guidance to survive the faster-paced and more complex city life. When Jack and Shirl Rennie took Lionel Rose into their home when he was only 15, they did more than attempt to profit from his considerable sporting talents. They became Rose's mentors, parents and financial advisers. Shirl Rennie, who bought a sandwich shop on behalf of Rose, tried to help Rose manage his money and to develop interests outside boxing.

There were some instances when a boxing career was beneficial both to the individual and the Aboriginal community. Boxing provided Tony Mundine, who won eight titles in the 1970s (two of them Commonwealth titles), with greater self-confidence. 'I was a bush boy', born at Baryulgil near Grafton, and 'being in Sydney and boxing opened me' so that 'I came out of my shell'.[43] Success at boxing enabled Mundine to acquire property and to play a part in Aboriginal sport and community affairs. George Bracken (b.1935), who was born at Palm Island and won the Australian lightweight title in 1955, was another success story. Bracken used his status to speak out about many sporting issues—the exploitation of Aboriginal boxers, the need for an insurance scheme and an Aboriginal sports foundation—but also on wider issues such as criticism of settlement life and missionary paternalism, race prejudice and the lack of Aboriginal education and welfare.[44]

Successful boxers provided role models for Aboriginal youth. Given the paucity of Aboriginal role models in other cultural fields, the importance of such models in sport cannot be underestimated. When the African-American boxer Muhammad Ali came to Redfern in the 1980s he was mobbed by the Aboriginal community there.

However, while Aborigines have benefited in some respects from this sport, boxing was on the whole detrimental to Aboriginal fighters. Broome's conclusion is stark and unequivocal: 'boxing has done more to reinforce the basic oppression of Aborigines than to overcome it.'[45] Tatz believed that boxing has achieved less for the Australian Aborigines than for American blacks and African fighters.[46]

While there have been some good managers, such as the Rennies, most have exploited their powerful position by raking off a substantial cut of the profits, regarding their charges as 'fighters' rather than 'people' and taking limited interest in their welfare outside the ring. Broome has concluded that 'the control exercised by managers did not help the independence or self-esteem of the boxer, nor did it aid the retention of his money' in the long run.[47]

Aborigines who were successful in boxing faced a host of cultural problems. There was the awesome problem of retaining their identity in a white-dominated sport and urban culture which denigrated Aborigines. The sport of boxing was also allied to European values such as the work ethic, individualism and the discipline of the clock. Successful boxers were tempted by the glamour of material possessions like fast cars and snappy clothes. If boxing was an escape from poverty, the cost was the 'whitening' of the successful boxers.

While many Aboriginal boxers earned large amounts of money in a very short time—Lionel Rose had career earnings of over \$350 000— few retained this money or benefited from it in the long run. Unused to handling large sums of money, many, including Rose, dissipated large amounts in short periods. The task was made more difficult because Aboriginal notions of reciprocity encouraged the successful boxers to share their wealth with their kin.

The story of Aboriginal boxers is as tragic, in the main, as the story of Aboriginal sportspeople in general. Jerry Jerome, the first champion, died in squalor at the Cherbourg reserve after his earnings were poached by hangers-on and by the Native Affairs Department. The life of Ron Richards was a disaster: besides the early death of his wife, he had to battle with poor management, police harassment and alcohol; arrested for vagrancy, he died penniless at Palm Island. Lionel Rose (b.1948), who became the first Aborigine to win a world boxing title when he defeated 'Fighting' Harada in Japan in 1968, returned to Australia to tumultuous applause. But his moment of glory was a short one and he soon dissipated his winnings. Success was followed by a rapid downhill slide to a life 'littered with indiscretions and transgressions' before he rehabilitated himself.[48]

Aborigines are not unique in this: many other working-class Australians have been equally ill prepared for the fame and fortune which are part of sporting stardom. The personal lives of sportspeople, along with entertainers, are littered with all kinds of failure and tragedy: suicide, alcoholism and poverty. Many players have found it hard to deal with the all too brief time of public adulation and the rather longer period when they are no longer centre stage. But undoubtedly the situation has been worse for Aborigines. There was a much greater gap between life in a small rural community and life in the fast lane in the city, especially for those from reserves who had all aspects of their lives controlled by paternal officials. Aborigines were also less equipped to make it in white-dominated culture and sports where there were many forms of racism.

Aborigines did taste success in the ring but it inevitably seemed to be something of a Pyrrhic victory. Boxer Henry Collins recognised the racial elements of sport and that 'racial victory' in the ring did not change the situation outside. Collins stated: 'I felt good when I knocked white blokes out. I felt good. I knew I was boss in the boxing ring. I showed my superiority.' But he added: 'they showed it outside.'[49] Collins recognised that sport was a dead end for blacks, as one study of British black sportsmen has argued.[50] Many boxed under the illusion that the ring was the only way in which their blackness would be accepted.

Aboriginal football-players became so prominent in the major codes of football by the 1980s that few may realise that this is a recent phenomenon. While there were a few Aboriginal footballers in some of the major city competitions in the 1940s and 1950s, it was not until the 1960s that Aboriginal sportsmen came to real prominence. Lionel Morgan, the Queensland winger, was the first Aborigine to represent Australia in rugby league, playing two Tests and a World Cup match in 1960. Arthur Beetson, one of the finest post-war forwards, began his distinguished career in the 1960s, becoming his country's captain in 1977. After retirement he was captain and coach of the successful Queensland State of Origin team. 'Polly' Farmer, the Geelong ruckman, made an equally impressive reputation in the VFL in the 1960s. He was an innovative player who developed the offensive potential of handball in masterly fashion.

Since the 1960s there has been an increasing Aboriginal presence particularly in rugby league and Australian football and to a lesser extent in rugby. By the 1980s Aborigines were overrepresented in many sports given their proportion of the population. As part of National Aborigines Week, an all-Aboriginal NSW Rugby League 'honour' side was selected and announced before the 1987 semi-final: eight of the fifteen named were present or future international players.[51] Mal Meninga, a South Sea Islander, captained Australia in the late 1980s and early 1990s. By the 1980s Aboriginal players had also made a mark in the more middle-class game of rugby union, with the Ella brothers becoming a dominant force. Mark Ella captained the Australian team nine times.

Behind the star footballers there were many lesser lights who played in grade football in increasing numbers from the 1960s. Forty-nine Aborigines have played for South Sydney from 1944, all bar four of whom have appeared since the 1960s.[52]

There are several reasons for a greater Aboriginal presence in football since the 1960s. Racial prejudice was the main reason why there were so few élite Aboriginal footballers before the 1940s. More liberal community attitudes towards Aborigines playing sport, and participating more in Australian society, slowly emerged from the 1960s. 'Greater mobility from country to city, improved health and living conditions, a greater sense of self-assurance, and a newly-found determination to assert Aboriginal identity' have been other factors.[53]

Tatz has suggested that Aborigines have been far more successful in rugby league because it was 'less class-conscious' than other codes and was 'perhaps' more 'generous to Aborigines', providing them with easier access and greater acceptance.[54] While it is true that Sydney clubs have been keen to recruit Aborigines, less is known about the operation of junior rugby league in country areas. Most of the players at Moree in New South Wales are Aboriginal, but the competitions are run by non-Aborigines. Racism has been reported to be a continuing problem there.[55]

While an increasing number of Aborigines have reached the football pinnacle, it is not clear whether football represents a more certain passport to improved social and economic status than boxing. Star Aboriginal footballers have been subjected to enormous social pressure. Australian football-players such as Jim Krakouer and Chris Lewis have been the objects of continuing racist abuse and media stereotyping.

If life for the star Aboriginal footballer can be difficult at times, there is some evidence that Aboriginal teams playing in junior leagues dominated and run by non-Aborigines face some additional problems. Dave Nadel in his study of the Purnim Bears Australian football team, which played in the Victorian Mt Noorat League in 1987, has argued that the team became a scapegoat for a 'wider range of negative community attitudes' towards Aborigines. Nadel believed that the decision to expel the Purnim Bears from the competition was probably 'racially based'.[56]

Sport by itself appears insufficient to create social acceptance, upward mobility and greater economic and political opportunities for Aborigines. Charles Perkins commented that sporting fame gained them 'acceptance, not as Aborigines or even as people, but merely as sports stars—everyone's heroes'.[57] Perkins, who rose to become permanent head of the Department of Aboriginal Affairs, was one of the first Aborigines to play first-grade soccer; he also was one of the first Aboriginal university graduates and led the politically important Freedom Rides in New South Wales in 1965. His rise to political prominence occurred because he had other qualifications.

The lot of Aboriginal sportswomen is a particularly invidious one, in that they suffer from 'double discrimination' for being both Aboriginal and female. While there is a long list of Aboriginal male champions from the nineteenth century, there have been few female champions who have achieved prominence, with the notable exceptions of tennis-player Evonne Goolagong (later Cawley)[58] and sprinter Cathy Freeman, who won two gold medals at the 1994 Commonwealth Games.

Daughter of a shearer and brought up in the white town of Barellan in New South Wales, where there was little discrimination, Goolagong began her tennis career by hitting tennis balls with a broom handle and then playing with a borrowed racquet. A central factor in her rise to stardom was that she was spotted as a rare talent by Sydney coach Vic Edwards when only 9 years of age. To advance her tennis Goolagong stayed with the Edwards family in school holidays before living with them permanently from the age of 13. Goolagong followed the path to international success which had been forged by male boxers such as Lionel Rose, who were taken in and developed by white sports promoters. While there were many other Aborigines who 'benefited' from white paternalism, Goolagong was an exceptional case.

There has as yet been no adequate explanation of why there have been so few prominent Aboriginal sportswomen in the past and why champions have emerged only in recent decades: for example Faith Coulthard in cricket, May Chalker in golf, Marcia Ella in netball, Dalma Smith in volleyball, Ivy Hampton in darts and Cheryl Mullet in badminton, Cathy Freeman in athletics and Rose Damaso in various sports. Undoubtedly Aboriginal women have benefited from the improving atmosphere for women's sport and the pro-active Aboriginal politics of the last two decades. And there are probably economic reasons among others for their failure to emerge in the past. It has been argued that those Aboriginal men who were involved in the economy of the country, even casual and seasonal workers, have had more access to the recreational life of the community than women have.

Marion Stell has provided some support, indirectly, for this explanation. She noted that many Aboriginal women have been strong swimmers and at Broome were used as divers for pearl-shell, but by a 'strange twist' have not been prominent in the sport of swimming. No doubt the remoteness of Broome, and its distance from the centres of organised sport, was a telling factor.[59] Lack of coaching and unfamiliarity with the culture of competition would have been other disincentives. There were also many competent Aboriginal woman stockriders in the Northern Territory, but in this frontier society there was a limited amount of organised sport.[60]

AN ABORIGINAL NOTION OF SPORT

Since the 1960s there has been considerable effort to articulate an Aboriginal notion of sport. Although this was a new development in one sense, it also drew on past understandings and approaches to sport developed by Aboriginal participants. The aim was to encourage forms of sport which are run by Aborigines and in Aboriginal interests, given that in the past there have been so few Aboriginal coaches and administrators. There has been an increasing number of separate Aboriginal sporting events, institutions and teams. A central purpose for some has been to 'purify' and to appropriate sport, which is immensely popular in Aboriginal communities, both by removing aspects of racist exploitation and by redefining sport to reflect Aboriginal values. The issues which confront Aboriginal sport—separation versus integration—are remarkably similar, and equally intractable, as those which face women's sport, where there is a continuing debate about whether mainstream sport can be reformed.

The organising in 1962 of the Yuendumu Games, known as the 'Black Olympics', is an interesting attempt to create an alternative sports carnival. This annual four-day event, which takes place at a remote settlement 300 kilometres north-west of Alice Springs, is a mixture of a sports and cultural festival organised exclusively by Aborigines. The Games include sporting contests such as Australian football, softball, basketball and athletics, along with spear- and boomerang-throwing, a corroboree and various forms of music.

While the Yuendumu Games provide a continuing focus for wider culture, they take part in a remote part of the country where sporting facilities are primitive. Many travel immense distances to participate in the Games which attract crowds of 3–5000. Although they are influential in that they articulate an alternative Aboriginal notion of sport, the Games are not reported in the media and are not part of the sporting culture of the vast majority of Australian Aborigines.

The development of a distinctive Aboriginal sporting culture has been encouraged by greater government support since the 1960s. Recognising the need to encourage Aboriginal sport and to provide improved facilities, W. C. Wentworth, the minister responsible for Aboriginal Affairs, agreed to establish the National Aboriginal Sports Foundation in 1969. The foundation, chaired initially by Doug Nicholls and including prominent Aboriginal sportspeople, had an annual budget of $50 000.

Since the 1970s there have been many changes in the funding of Aboriginal sport and the character of the funding agencies. Vicky Paraschak has investigated government policies towards Aboriginal sport in the 1970s and 1980s and has begun to document and explore the many shifts in policy and funding. One of the policies of the Sports Foundation in the 1970s was to promote annual national Aboriginal sports carnivals, but after a 1980 Darwin carnival accumulated a large deficit, the minister suspended all such funding and reduced the size and functions of the board of the National Aboriginal Sports Foundation. Three years later the minister dissolved the foundation and moved its function to the Aboriginal Development Commission. After responsibility for the Aboriginal sports program shifted to the Department of Aboriginal Affairs, an Advisory National Aboriginal Council was formed in 1986. This body, which represented thirty-two sporting communities, had an initial budget of $3.65 million for 1986–87. It too was dissolved in 1989 in anticipation of the formation of the Aboriginal and Torres Strait Islanders Commission (ATSIC). A section of ATSIC then administered the Aboriginal sports program.[61]

Paraschak has found that ATSIC and its antecedent institutions have yet to articulate long-term priorities and a clearly developed Aboriginal ideology of sport. Policy and funding have frequently been piecemeal and reactive, merely responding to the requests of various local communities. Undoubtedly, the *ad hoc* character of funding for Aboriginal sport reflects the difficult and complex problem of defining an appropriate ideology of Aboriginal sport. There are a number of practical problems, whether funding should be directed to élite and mainstream sports or to junior and recreational sports and whether there should be a more developmental focus.

There have been other continuing attempts to develop separate Aboriginal sporting institutions to encourage an appropriate Aboriginal notion of sport. There are now many separate all-Aboriginal teams, particularly in country areas, such as the Narwan football team in Armidale, which was formed in 1977 because a number of Aboriginal players did not believe they were getting a fair go in the Armidale team. During the 1980s this team won five successive premierships.[62] There has been a proliferation of sports carnivals such as basketball in Geraldton, rugby league in towns such as Moree and Walgett and the Barunga Festival in the Northern Territory. There are also separate associations and awards, such as the National Aboriginal Golf Association (1987) and the National Aboriginal Sports Awards (1986, 1988 and 1992). An increasing number of Aboriginal teams have toured overseas.

While all-Aboriginal teams provide Aborigines with a greater voice in sporting culture, most participate against non-Aboriginal teams and in leagues which are run and dominated by non-Aborigines. In some instances, as in the case of the Purnim Bears, this can extend the potential for racial discrimination.[63] Tatz has also reported some instances where Aboriginal teams have been unable to get admission into appropriate leagues. He noted that in 1986 some Aborigines in Victoria went to the Equal Opportunity Board in an attempt to secure entrance for their team in the Kyabram and District League.[64]

During 1989 and 1990 Colin Tatz visited seventy Aboriginal and Torres Strait communities to investigate whether recreation played any role in reducing and even preventing crimes of violence within Aboriginal communities. He argues that the presence of sporting facilities and competition reduced the level of criminal and delinquent behaviour: during the football season in Port Lincoln, South Australia, juvenile offending was virtually nil, whereas it soared in the off season. After visiting forty-five communities Tatz reported a 'deep sense of anger' because there was no real improvement in sporting facilities despite advances in funding, recognition, local decision-making, progress in land rights and education.[65] It appeared that while there may be an increasing number of high-profile Aboriginal athletes, Aborigines as a whole still have limited access to adequate sporting facilities.

Richard Broome's conclusions about Aboriginal boxers may have significance for Aboriginal sportsmen and women as a whole. It can be shown that in many ways sporting involvement has been more detrimental than beneficial for Aborigines and that progress and uplift through sport has been something of a mirage. Because most sporting institutions have been dominated by whites, involvement in sporting culture involves a process of 'whitening' and 'mainstreaming', exploitation, racial stereotyping and, at best, partial acceptance. However, Tatz has countered this view by suggesting that 'such respect as Australian accord Aborigines—however little it is, however grudgingly it is given—comes from their sporting prowess'.[66]

There is also the question of how important sport has been in fostering pride among Aborigines. Broome has argued that work skills—such as riding, gardening and bush mechanic skills—'fostered as much pride among Aborigines (including women) as sport, and did so from the 1840s on'.[67] Ann McGrath in *Born in the Cattle* has documented the long tradition of Aboriginal pride in bush skills.

It is also true that initial, hesitant attempts to develop separate notions of Aboriginal sport, separate leagues and teams, while important to those who take part, have not yet been taken up by the majority of Aborigines. Even though many Aborigines support separate carnivals and a smaller number attend the 'Black Olympics', most Aborigines are still very much locked into mainstream sport.

For better or worse, sport is immensely important to Aboriginal communities, who have developed their own traditions and champions within the framework of organised sport. The film *Black Magic* demonstrated that the Noongars of Western Australia have not only produced a continuing succession of outstanding Australian rules footballers but have developed their own traditions of barracking and participation in the game.[68] Australian football has very deep roots among the sizeable Aboriginal population in many other communities as well. The only practical solution is to reform organised sport, to make it less racist as well as less sexist. Sporting culture, for better or worse, has become too important to too many Aborigines.

Sport also provides a popular theatre where the issue of racism has been raised. Nicky Winmar's dramatic gesture in a 1993 Australian football game, when he dealt with racist taunts by raising his guernsey and pointing to his black skin, achieved maximum media coverage and did much to place racism in popular culture more firmly on the public agenda.

9
ETHNICITY

T he role of ethnicity is a very rich theme in Australian sport, but one neglected until recently. Many in the past have tended to view what they define as 'ethnic' sports as inferior, existing on the margins of Australian sport. At its best 'ethnic' sport has been seen as quaint, harmless and peripheral: such is the case with the Scottish Highland Games, the German *turnverein* (gymnastic club) and Irish hurling. Since 1945 'ethnic' sport has been regarded by some in a more invidious light. Soccer violence between ethnically based clubs has been reported in the media regularly, and many believe it to be a blight on Australian sport. Many Australians believe that immigrants are unable to bury old rivalries, which continue to be played out in the theatre of Australian sport.

The debate on ethnic sport to date has been far too narrowly based because, in a sense, all Australian sport is 'ethnic' in that it has been (and continues to be) borrowed from a multitude of societies. Media definitions of some sports as 'ethnic' represents a way of marginalising certain sports and particular groups. This perception may be one reason why some forms of imported sport are incorporated more readily into the mainstream culture whereas others exist more on the periphery.

Patrick O'Farrell has suggested that the 'real history' of Australia, which has been 'monstrously neglected', is the 'history of the gradual growth and development, through confrontation and compromise, of a people of distinctive quality and character, derived from and produced by cultures—majority and minority—in conflict'.[1] Sport has been one area where important debates and contests have taken place between an English-oriented majority and a succession of so-called minorities. While the debates about Australian sporting culture have frequently been vigorous and bitter, they have, for the most part, been a creative exchange resulting in a stronger and more widely accepted sporting culture.

It is also worth exploring the different ways in which sporting culture has been imported. In some instances sport was brought to Australia by particular immigrant communities, such as the British or the Irish, as part of their cultural baggage. Sporting culture has been used by these immigrants to help establish an identity in a new society and to retain some link with its past. The 'Americanisation' of Australian sport, on the other hand, has occurred more indirectly and subtly, through the media (film and television) and advertising, together with more direct contact and closer political and economic ties which have provided a climate in which 'Americanisation' is more acceptable. The influence of Polynesia on Australian surfing culture has, by contrast, been more casual and indirect. Borrowing has occurred because of occasional contact, such as the visits of Tommy Tanna and Duke Kahanomoku.

There are many issues to be explored in regard to sport and ethnicity. What role does sport play in the community formation of immigrant groups? Are 'ethnic' sporting clubs creative expressions of multiculturalism or perpetuators of old tensions and focal points for violence? Have some sports, like soccer, suffered because of the association with immigrant groups—the 'wogball' stereotype? How, and under what circumstances, has American sport been imported to Australia? Are American sports and sporting practices replacing long-established British games?

Before World War I

British, and primarily English, notions of culture were dominant in Australia throughout the nineteenth century. The majority of the Australian population in the nineteenth century emanated from the United Kingdom; in fact as late as 1861 more than half the population were born there.[2] The colonial Establishment throughout this century was inspired by Anglo-Australian ideals—seeing itself as the colonial British. The close ties between the motherland and the colonies were reinforced through the successful transplantation of British culture, including games such as cricket and football, though the dominant winter sport in Victoria and other southern States was a domestic invention.

There were some variant sporting traditions to the British model. Scots, Welsh and Cornish immigrants attempted to perpetuate their particular sporting traditions in various ways. The Scots were one of the better-placed minorities because many who emigrated from the 1820s on were from the commercial middle classes or of gentry background and there was a relatively small number of Scottish convicts—they made up only 3.5 per cent of the convicts who came to Australia up to 1823. The Scottish-born and their descendants were a fairly small part of the colonial population, constituting less than 10 per cent. Many Scots were familiar and even comfortable with some elements of English culture, and some of the more affluent Scots gravitated from the Presbyterian to the Anglican Church. The Scots, like all other communities, were a heterogeneous group and there were also many more humble immigrants, large numbers of whom were produced in the 1840s by unemployment and the Highland 'clearances'.[3]

Malcolm Prentis, historian of the Scots in Eastern Australia, argues that Scottish immigrants had two cultural options. The first was to attempt to preserve intact distinctive Scottish cultural elements in Australia but to run the risk of trivialising their tradition as a caricature: an amalgam of 'tartan, golf, whisky, bagpipes and miserliness'. The other option was to contribute in a broader way to Australian culture.

The Scots in Australia did both. Caledonian societies, which were established in Sydney and Melbourne and in country towns, organised Annual Highland Gatherings, which included various Highland and other Scottish games, combining Scottish dancing with traditional sports such as throwing the caber and putting the stone. The twelfth such Games in Sydney were held on New Year's Day 1880 at the Sydney Cricket Ground and attracted a crowd of 5000. There were also separate Scottish sporting clubs such as the Scottish Rifle Volunteer Corps, begun in Queensland in 1886.[4]

The Scots contributed more to Australian sport through their patronage of particular sports which became popular, notably golf and soccer. Given the success with which the Scots moved into the Australian Establishment and were successful in commerce, politics and the professions, there was limited incentive for them to maintain separate sporting traditions. The introduction of golf to Australia was 'invariably associated with a Scot': they took the game to various parts of the country, founded clubs, established golf links and provided the leading professionals. Carnegie Clark (1881–1959), who emigrated from Carnoustie, was a dominant player, winning six Professional Championships and three Australian Opens. He also pioneered the manufacture of golf clubs and was the first to introduce the Vardon grip and the revolutionary Haskell ball.[5] One writer has suggested that the Scots were influential in the early history of soccer in New South Wales. Many of the first clubs, such as the Sydney clubs Caledonians, Scottish Rifles and Thistle, and the Newcastle clubs Minmi Rangers and Hamilton Athletics, were dominated by Scots.[6]

While the Scots found it relatively easy to assimilate into colonial culture, most of the Irish minority did not. A greater number of the Irish-born were from poorer and more working-class backgrounds, and a sizeable proportion of convicts came from Ireland—they made up 41 per cent of the convicts who had arrived in Australia by 1802. Most of the Irish were also Catholic.

Although they were as heterogeneous as the Scots—the 'Irish' included Gaelic Catholics, Anglo-Irish and Ulster Protestants and other groups—they became a more distinctive and separate group than the Scots. The Irish developed a measure of solidarity in part because the colonial Establishment entertained very deep prejudices against Irish-Australians, who were at times regarded as less than true and proper Australians.[7] At the more popular level sectarianism in its various forms, including conflict between Orangemen and Irish Catholics, furthered a sense of separateness in the second half of the nineteenth century.

Irish-Australians were also a large enough minority—while precise figures are difficult to ascertain they represented approximately a quarter of the Australian population in the nineteenth century—to consider creating separate cultural (including sporting) traditions. There were also many available models of aggressive Irishness, of maintaining a hatred for the English and things English in the colonies. The Gaelic Athletic Association (GAA) was founded in Ireland in 1884 to promote Gaelic games to challenge English games in Ireland. The GAA was an offshoot of Irish nationalism and demonstrated that sport was regarded as an important element of Irish national culture.[8]

The Irish, like the Scots, imported their distinctive culture and institutions. The hostility of the colonial Establishment provided even greater incentives to promote the Catholic Church and a separate Catholic educational system. Annual St Patrick's Day parades were a popular focal point, while the Catholic Church encouraged its flock to join the various branches of the Hibernian Society which were established from the 1870s. Although the Hibernian Society had English origins, the aim was to woo Catholics away from other benefit societies which were believed to have 'a secret or Masonic dimension'.[9]

Irish games such as hurling were also imported to Australia. There are references to hurling matches in Australia from the 1840s, and by the 1880s there were five clubs in Sydney, based on hotels. Interstate matches at the turn of the century attracted respectable crowds and patronage: Cardinal Moran was one of the 3000 spectators at a 1904 game. O'Farrell has suggested that one problem for the growth of this game was that most of the players were recent immigrants who were constantly on the move in search of employment, therefore providing 'no stable basis for either teams or organisation'.

A more important reason for the limited growth of separate Irish sports was the pressure to participate in 'Australian' sports: sport was one area in which the principle to 'Australianise or perish' applied. Campaigners for Irish sports made little headway in the schools because games were the way in which Catholic schools 'related to the rest of the Australian sporting community' and to abandon them would be to 'opt for the ghetto', isolating such schools from 'the mainstream of Australian life'.[10] So much importance has been placed on participation in British-inherited 'Australian' games that many Catholic schools and colleges became as famous as the non-Catholic colleges in the twentieth century as nurseries of cricket, rugby, rugby league and Australian football. Many regard 'Joey's' (St Joseph's) as the rugby school of Sydney.

O'Farrell has argued that those who subscribed to Gaelic or Anglo-Irish cultures in Australia did not revolt against English culture in anything like the same degree they did in Ireland. This was because the destructive hatred of things English did not develop as much in Australia. This occurred for several reasons. In spite of all the prejudice against Irish-Australians, there was the opportunity for many to progress in colonial society—materially, socially and politically. Australia frequently brought quick satisfactions for some immigrants. O'Farrell also says that while the continuing debate between the English-oriented majority and the Irish-oriented minority has been vigorous and even heated, it has not been divisive—the debate has been a 'unifying principle of Australian history'. English and Irish have participated in a 'creative exchange' about Australian culture. In spite of their subordinate status Irish-Australians have contributed markedly to Australian culture, including sport.[11]

While sport on the whole has had some part in reducing ethnic tensions within Australia and creating a broader common ground, it has on occasions reflected ethnic tensions and been associated with sectarianism. Such was the case in 1871 when Irish Catholic Larry Foley (1851–1917)—the 'Father of Australian Boxing'—fought Sandy Ross, who had militant Protestant links. This fight took place when the 'Irish pot was boiling' because of the reverberations of sending Fenian prisoners to Western Australia in 1869. O'Farrell, however, suggested that the fight between the champions of the Green and the Orange did not stir the pot further: in fact by 1871 the 'simmering animus had cooled to a degree where it was possible to sublimate it in a sporting contest'.[12]

While the Orange Lodge movement was relatively weak in Australia because extremists were unpopular,[13] sectarianism was a part of Australian life, and sport, well into the twentieth century. Sectarian antagonisms appeared in the Glebe Rowing Club in 1916, when they were fuelled by the conscription debate, and again surfaced at the 1928 annual general meeting when Catholics 'left the club en masse'. During the 1920s crew selection was often more influenced by 'religious persuasion than rowing ability'.[14]

Sectarianism occurred in cricket because the Australian Cricket Board was dominated by Freemasons and preferred that one of their own kind—Australia has had very few Catholic captains—should captain the national side.[15] Bill O'Reilly, a Catholic, believed that sectarianism was a factor when four of the five 'Irish' Catholic Test cricketers were hauled before the Australian Board of Control during the 1937–38 series. The precise reason for the meeting were never made clear, but the chairman of the board seemed to imply that the Irish contingent were 'representatives of an insubordinate and disloyal team of slackers and boozers'.[16]

Sport did at times appear to exacerbate, or at least provide a focal point, for tensions between the pro-Imperial English majority and the Irish Catholic minority. Such was the case during World War I when the divisive conscription referenda heightened differences between these two groups. Sport at this time, and boxing in particular, provided some expression for a 'frustrated minority'. Pugilist Les Darcy (1895–1917) also catered to the Irish need for heroes who could fill 'the need of a subordinate group for self-esteem'.[17]

Born into a working-class family from Maitland, Darcy came to Sydney in 1914 and defeated many prominent boxers, becoming Australian middleweight champion in 1915 and heavyweight champion in 1916. When he fled the country surreptitiously the day before the conscription referendum, he was vilified by middle-class supporters of conscription but became a symbol of Irish resistance, as important in a sense as the anti-conscription cleric Archbishop Mannix. Darcy's attempt to secure the world middleweight crown in North America was frustrated by officials and politicians. He died in Memphis not of a broken heart, as some suggested, but through blood poisoning from dental repairs after a 1916 fight. In death he became an Irish martyr and thousands viewed his body in Sydney and Maitland.[18]

Boxing has always been attractive to minority groups since it has been a sport by which 'outsiders' can demonstrate their physical prowess and fighting spirit, as has already been suggested in Chapter 8. The sport has long offered the promise of upward mobility for marginal groups. Darcy was a 'pure and simple hero, a good boy who loved and looked after his mother, went to daily Mass, said the rosary—and won:—"the power in his fists came straight from God"'.[19] Darcy symbolised the ambivalence of an ethnic minority in Australia who believed that he was cheated of a world title through jingoism and treachery. He epitomised the search for a martyr, which demonstrated the ambiguities of the Irish in Australia—in what Oliver McDonagh referred to as a 'double colonial' situation.

Smaller ethnic minorities, such as the Cornish, settled in particular pockets and regions of the country. Cornish settlers were prominent in a number of mining communities such as the Burra mines of South Australia in the mid-nineteenth century. Cornish wrestling was also popular in the Queensland mining community of Charters Towers.[20] The *South Australian* reported on 6 March 1848 that about 1000 had gathered to watch 'wrestling matches—the favourite amusement of Cornwall'.

Germans were also rather more prominent in South Australia where they formed social and sporting clubs, gymnastic and rifle clubs. The Adelaide Deutschen Turnverein, founded in 1864 and still operating at the turn of the century, was an ethnically exclusive club. While membership was open to any person of 'good repute' over the age of 17, business meetings were conducted in German and only members who had a 'knowledge of the German language' were entitled to vote.[21] The Chinese, from the time of the gold rush, brought their own sporting traditions, notably gambling games such as fan-tan and pak-a-pu and they created their own gambling establishments.[22]

The sports of these minority groups had virtually no influence on Australian sporting culture. Cornish, Welsh, German and Chinese sports existed in separate pockets of the country. The size and geographic distribution of these ethnic communities were undoubtedly the main reasons why community organisers preferred separate cultural organisations, though it is not known whether such groups also took part in mainstream sports.

One of the neglected themes of Australian sports history is how much swimming and surfing culture has been borrowed from Polynesia. This is in part because the links between sport in the two societies were slight and also because the innovations were adapted, improved and enhanced in Australia. The borrowing from various Pacific countries represented a very significant moving away from inherited British attitudes towards the sea.

Many Australian surfing and swimming traditions were borrowed from Polynesia. Captain Cook, who had discovered eastern Australia for the British in 1770, recorded his astonishment when he sailed into Kealakekua Bay, Hawaii, in 1778 to discover the local population swimming and board-riding in the surf.[23] Tommy Tanna, from the Marshall Islands, surfed at Manly Beach in 1889 and is credited with the introduction of body-surfing, which was taken up by the locals from the 1890s. Following his visit a number of Manly residents took up the sport, leading eventually to the challenge of archaic laws which prevented daylight surfing.[24] The 'Australian crawl', which revolutionised sprint swimming, was developed by Dick Cavill, who had observed the use of the stroke by Alick Wickham, a young Solomon Islander, resident in Sydney. Wickham also fashioned a board from a length of driftwood, while C. D. Paterson imported a genuine redwood *alaia* from Hawaii in 1912, but no one could ride it.[25]

The visit of the Hawaiian Olympic champion Duke Kahanomoku (1890–1968) in 1914–15 was seen as so important by the NSW Amateur Swimming Association that they delegated an official (and paid him a salary) to handle the tour. Ian Jobling has suggested that the primary motive of this association was to promote local swimming through the appearance of a popular international star. The association were even prepared to alter their rules to allow Kahanomoku to swim in local championships.[26]

Unable to import a surfboard to Australia, Kahanomoku made a longboard for himself which he rode at Freshwater Beach, Sydney. The 'Duke' did much to stimulate swimming and he was a pioneer of board-riding in Australia. Isabel Letham, who rode tandem with the Duke at Freshwater, became a prominent surfer. The Duke's board was given to a 15-year-old, Claude West, who became Australia's first surfboard champion.[27]

Australians have also been influenced indirectly by many other European and North American notions of sport and recreation. Scandinavians—notably miners from Norway—pioneered skiing in Australia in the 1850s at Kiandra; the Kiandra Ski Club was formed in 1879, largely by Norwegian and Austrian miners. After the sport received a boost in the twentieth century with the development of snow resorts, such as at Mount Kosciusko, European skiers, who were familiar figures on the Australian slopes from the 1920s, helped to develop the sport.

The rise of a national park movement, which drew inspiration from North America, was also influential. Walking and touring clubs, later known as bushwalking clubs, became very popular in the first decades of the twentieth century. The sport of orienteering—a sport combining bushwalking and map-reading—which was introduced from Sweden in 1969 was another sport based on the bush.

Asian sports such as kick-boxing and the martial arts became more prominent in Australia in the 1970s and 1980s. The growth of these sports reflects a greater Australian interest in things Asian—part of a growing regional consciousness together with increasing trade links—and an increase in Asian migration to Australia.

AMERICANISATION

There has been much recent discussion of the Americanisation of Australian sport. A number of American sports have enjoyed great popularity in recent times, most notably basketball, and to a lesser extent, baseball and American football. American sporting practice has also influenced Australian sports: there has been greater quantification in rugby league (tackle counts), female cheer-leaders, and even clothing such as baseball caps. The Americanisation of Australian sport is part of a wider Americanisation of Australian popular culture.[28]

Phillip and Roger Bell have suggested that the widely used concept 'Americanisation' is too simple because it assumes an American *cause* and an Australian *effect*.[29] They prefer to see American influence as modernisation, suggesting that America and Australia along with other Western capitalist nations are 'moving into the "modern" era for similar reasons'. It is part of a broader movement towards unfettered consumerism and a more global communications network. The Bells prefer the term 'modernisation' because it also allows for some degree of adaptation of American sporting practice to suit Australian needs. Many commentators, however, prefer to avoid the concept of tradition versus modernity because it implies that progress occurs through the agency of a modernising élite. Others have suggested that Americanisation is part of a broader globalisation of sport and other forms of popular culture as sport has become increasingly internationalised in the television era.[30]

However, it is more convenient to retain the term Americanisation since this refers to a particular form of modernisation or globalisation more prominent in Australia, and it is a term which is more familiar. For the most part Americanisation is not a matter of 'cultural aggression' but is bound up with fundamental technological and commercial changes which have created a climate in which American culture, along with investment and military alliances, is largely accepted without popular opposition.[31]

Although American sports have surfaced more prominently in recent decades there has been a long history of the Americanisation of Australian popular culture. The development of a distinctive North American city culture in the late nineteenth century provided Australians with an alternative to the British model. While the web of Australian popular culture consisted mostly of modified British strands, there was even then a surprising amount of borrowing from America: American vaudeville, minstrel shows, amusement parks (such as Coney Island and Luna Park) and the circus. Between 1875 and 1900 no fewer than six large American circuses visited Australia and some came more than once.[32]

Australians in this era appear to have drawn less inspiration from American sport, though there were some efforts to promote it. Albert Goodwill Spalding (1850–1915), wealthy American baseball entrepreneur and organiser, spared no effort and expense in his attempt in what was a missionary tour to Australia to promote baseball in the summer of 1888–89. Spalding's touring entourage included two American teams—his own Chicago team and a combined all-America side—who played exhibition games, a press corps to report the game, and several entertainers, a balloonist and a mascot to add to the colour. Spalding was an 'able and energetic booster of baseball', who believed in 'baseball, his business and America'. A successful tour would not only help spread the American game but would advance Spalding's thriving business, especially in baseball bats, balls, caps and uniforms.[33]

The tour, which was well organised and effectively promoted, was successful in part. Good crowds turned up to watch the exhibition matches at Melbourne, Sydney and some country centres such as Ballarat. Although baseball had been played in Australia before 1888, the tour stimulated a greater interest in baseball: new clubs and competitions were organised including intercolonial contests. An Australian baseball team toured America in 1897.

On the whole, however, the tour was unsuccessful in terms of establishing the game in Australia. The central problem was that baseball was in direct competition with the already-established summer game of cricket. Although the promoters of the tour were at pains to stress that cricket and baseball could complement rather than compete with each other, cricket also addressed the central political and social issue of the day: the relationship between the motherland and colonial Australia. An American game by definition had far less appeal in this era. There was also the problem that for all the superb organisation and smooth talking the tour was a direct attempt at cultural imperialism which was unlikely to work at this time. There may have been resistance then, even a backlash, to American sport. Roy Hay has noted that there has been a significant backlash over VFL/AFL attempts to Americanise Australian football in contemporary times and that there is also some similar resistance to North American norms in Australian soccer.[34]

If the impact of the Spalding tour was limited, Spalding did tap into the Australian sporting market at a later date. A. G. Spalding & Brothers established an agency in Sydney in 1909 which sold tennis and cricket equipment. While Australians were not yet ready to adopt American sports, they recognised the quality of American equipment and fashions.[35] There was also a continuing cultural negotiation between baseball and cricket. The best ball bowled by prominent cricketer M. A. Noble, who played first-class cricket from 1893–94 to 1919–20, was a 'curve ball which he had picked up from baseball'.[36] Baseball has long influenced Australian cricket fielding practice because it was the practice, until recently, for cricketers to play baseball in winter.

Baseball has enjoyed a resurgence in Australia in the 1990s, along with other American sports, basketball and gridiron. These sports have been introduced more indirectly to Australia, with Australians (along with some Americans) prominent in organisation and promotion. The growth of American sports undoubtedly reflects the decline of the English connection and a greater interest in things American or things modern and global. Money, in the form of huge potential contracts in one or another American league, has encouraged many young Australians to pursue a career in American sports.

Americanisation has been a more observable phenomenon in the twentieth century with the presence of American troops in Australia in wartime, the dominant role of Hollywood in cinema from the 1920s, the role of American television from the 1950s, and the influence of American advertising, technology and notions of consumerism, together with closer economic and political links.

Softball, which became largely a woman's game, was introduced by North Americans at the time of World War II. The game began in Australia in 1939 soon after Canadian Gordon Young became the director of physical education in New South Wales. From 1939 softball was taught at a summer school for primary teachers. The game benefited from the substantial US presence in Australia in wartime. It received an impetus from US Army Sergeant William Du Vernet, who organised recreation for his troops in parks and gardens, games which were sometimes watched by hundreds of people. One result was that Australian teams were formed to challenge the US nurses. Another American, Mack Gilley, introduced the game into Queensland in 1946.[37] It is ironic that while women's cricket struggled to gain recognition after 1945, the growth in softball for women was spectacular (see ch. 5).

The 'Open Tennis' controversy, which generated much heat in the 1950s and 1960s, provided a classic debate between British-derived amateur notions of sport and the more commercial American alternative. American entrepreneurs, including tennis promoter Jack Kramer and millionaire Lamar Hunt, lured many of the star Australian tennis-players to professional tennis, causing much public and media con-sternation (see ch. 11). It was not until 1968, when open tennis was introduced to Australia, that Australian tennis officials grudgingly accepted the coming of professional tennis.[38]

The American sport which grew most in the 1980s was basketball. Its rapid rise to media prominence in Australia has been due to very success-ful promotion which includes the establishment of national leagues (copied by other sports such as hockey and baseball), American razzmatazz such as the use of the public address system and a theatre organ to further excite the fans, and its presentation as an entertainment package. But slick promotion alone cannot explain why this game has been accepted by the public and has captured the imagination of many young people.

The rise of Australian basketball has yet to be adequately explored and explained, but a number of hypotheses are worth considering. A study of the Canberra Cannons has suggested that skilful marketing was an important ingredient in the success of the sport. Approximately a third of the club's budget was spent on marketing, and the National Basketball League (NBL) followed this lead when its director, Tony King, stated that 'more money has to be spent into putting people on seats rather than [just] getting good players'.[39] Since the introduction of satellite television broadcasting it has been relatively cheap and conveni-ent to broadcast American sport, and Australians have had the oppor-tunity to watch more and more of it. It is also possible that the game has become popular because Australian teams feature a large number of African-Americans. Black entertainers, whether they be musicians or sportspeople, have long held a special place in Australian society and have enjoyed a greater measure of acceptance than in North America.[40] It is also likely that basketball administrators have realised, rather sooner than other sports administrators, that many average consumers of sport like it to be presented as an entertainment package as much as a sport. A thoughtful article on the television presentation of the Olympic Games in America has suggested that, for better or worse, the techniques of soap opera are now influencing and even shaping Olympic telecasting. Rather than present an evening's telecasting as a succession of discrete sporting events—what a spectator in a stadium might witness—television programmers have attempted to script an integrated package of enter-tainment built around commercial breaks. This has been achieved by developing a montage which includes not only the events themselves but also audience briefing to build up suspense and focus on heroes.[41]

Another facet of Americanisation is that Australians have come to place greater emphasis on tilts with America. While Australian victories against the United States are celebrated with great gusto in Australia—as were defeats of the 'motherland'—they hardly cause a ripple in the United States. Along with some notable victories, particularly in Davis Cup tennis, defeats and disasters are equally celebrated, because they advance the popular myth of how difficult it is for Australians to get a fair go against the might of a superpower, and dramatise the ambivalence Australians feel towards what many view as their cultural masters. The chicanery of the big power is an enduring theme: many believed that both Les Darcy and Phar Lap were poisoned by the Americans, and the Australia II victory in 1983 was achieved despite the trickery of the officials of the New York Yacht Club. While many Australians continue to glory in the defeat of the 'motherland' in cricket, football and any other sport, many regarded victory in the America's Cup as the most significant victory of the twentieth century.

It is likely that Australian sport will become even more Americanised and globalised in the next century in the sense that our sporting culture and practice will become even more modernised and internationalised. Further growth of particular American sports in Australia is simply one facet of this process. It is unlikely that the Australian sporting map will ever be the same as the American—that American sports will replace Australian and British sports—because all imported sports will continue to be adapted to suit the Australian physical and social environment. It is likely that there will always be Australian variants of global sports.

IMPACT OF POST-1945 MIGRATION

Migration to Australia occurred on a more diverse scale than ever before after 1945. The Australian government believed that Australia needed to increase its population greatly if it were to hold its own against the perceived threat of the Asian hordes, and also that immigration would help develop the country. A stated aim of the Menzies government in the 1950s was to increase the population by 2 per cent each year, of which immigration would contribute 1 per cent. Although the government actively recruited British migrants, who were assisted financially to come to Australia, it had to look elsewhere to get sufficient numbers, and most immigrants were non-English-speaking (NES) people who came from Europe, with Greece, Italy and Yugoslavia providing the largest numbers. It was estimated for instance that 337 000 persons of Italian origin arrived in Australia between 1947 and 1970.[42]

The lot of the new immigrants, particularly the NES persons, was not an easy one. Many had to endure an initial period in unattractive settlement camps such as Herne Bay before they were able to establish their own housing. The dream of establishing a small business or making a good living in a short time was often far removed from the reality for many, which was working in sweat-shops or on the factory floor. Although immigrant communities soon established their own social networks, which were essential for survival, there were many problems for NES immigrants, such as understanding the culture of an alien society and gaining adequate political representation. These people were also visible because they tended to gravitate towards particular suburbs of Sydney and Melbourne which became immigrant enclaves—initially the poorer inner-city suburbs. Leichhardt in Sydney became known as 'Little Italy' and Marrickville as 'Greece', while Carlton, North Carlton and North Melbourne in Melbourne had a high proportion of the Italian-born and nearby Richmond and Collingwood were 20 per cent Greek-born by the 1970s. They were also subject to racism. While the government referred to them euphemistically as 'New Australians' many Anglo-Celtic Australians referred to them as 'dagos', 'wogs', 'wops', 'reffos' and 'spags'.

By the 1980s immigrants were coming from a wider source than ever before, with sizeable numbers from Arabic-speaking countries such as Lebanon and Egypt and more recently from Asia, notably Vietnam. By the 1990s the largest number of immigrants were coming from Asia, a fact which sparked considerable public debate. Some believed that moving away from an English-speaking, European and Christian population would lead to social problems. The Vietnamese too established enclaves in Sydney and Melbourne, though more in outer suburbs such as Sydney's Cabramatta, since the inner-city suburbs of Sydney and Melbourne had been reclaimed by the gentry.

Immigration has altered the Australian sporting landscape. The majority of NES immigrants were unfamiliar with most of the mainstream sports, cricket, Australian football and the rugby codes. Soccer was the one Australian game which many recognised initially. The population of some inner-city municipalities, which supported rugby league and Australian football clubs, was so altered by the 1980s that the suburbs no longer provided enough support for the existing clubs. Such was the case with one of the founding clubs of the NSW Rugby League, Newtown, which was axed in 1983. The problem for Newtown was that it was believed that the 'ethnic' newcomers preferred soccer to rugby league. Much of the Newtown territory came within the Marrickville municipality: in 1986 46 per cent of the municipal population was born overseas and most of these (40.3 per cent) were born in NES countries.[43] Suburbs in Melbourne such as Fitzroy now support a substantial NES population, and is one reason why the future of that Australian football club is problematical.

Sporting clubs (notably soccer) have provided important institutions for these new 'communities'. Soccer clubs, as Philip Mosely and Roy Hay have noted, preceded formal ethnic associations in some instances. Sport played a crucial role in community formation because it provided a largely accepted way for immigrant communities to organise themselves. It represented a way in which one immigrant community could relate to another and it was also a bridge between such a community and the wider Australian society through sport.

The involvement of NES immigrants in Australian soccer led to a dramatic shift in the organisation of the game, which had large implications. While soccer has had a long tradition of catering to minority cultures— British-born, miners, factory workers—most of the leading soccer teams were Australian-born and locality-based by the 1940s. From the 1950s there was a dramatic confrontation between the Anglo-Australian soccer establishment, the Australian Soccer Football Association Ltd, and a breakaway Soccer Federation movement, which was far more sympathetic to immigrant interests. Discontent surfaced initially because successful immigrant clubs, such as Hakoah in Sydney, believed that they were being discriminated against in the matter of promotion.[44]

For a short period the association and federation were in open competition, but the federation emerged victorious and took over the management of Australian soccer. Mosely has argued that the success of the federation represents an ethnic takeover of an Anglo-Australian game.[45] Hay, historian of the soccer split in Victoria, is more cautious. He believed that there were other factors behind the split as well as the migrant-versus-Anglo conflict. Hay has argued that there remained a strong Anglo presence in many ethnic clubs after the split and that the change in the 1950s was linked to a new generation of officials who sought to improve the organisation and professionalism of the game.[46]

From this time the stronger soccer clubs were based on ethnic organisations and identified as such by name. In the major cities of the country there were Dutch, German, Greek, Italian, Jewish, Maltese, Polish, Spanish, Croatian and Macedonian clubs. The principle of ethnically based soccer clubs was not limited to the creation of teams identified with one or another existing European nation, such as Greece, Italy or Yugoslavia. Clubs soon emerged such as Croatia Adelaide (1952) which was a focal point for a disaffected ethnic minority within Yugoslavia. While Preston Macedonia represented the people of one part of the former Yugoslav Republic, Heidelberg was the club of a section of Greek society, the Greek Macedonians.

There has been much controversy associated with the introduction of ethnically based soccer clubs. When a Croatian team first played Yugal in 1961, violence resulted and occurred on later occasions.[47] From this time many have seen ethnically based soccer as perpetuating violence. Some have argued that the existence of these clubs ran counter to the prevailing ideal that immigrants would assimilate into Australian society.

Some NES immigrant communities have looked to other sports as well as soccer. The Vietnamese community has encouraged young males to join martial arts clubs, as a conscious effort of community leaders to use sport as a tool in community formation.[48] Vietnamese youth also participate in Asian leagues outside mainstream soccer.

ETHNICALLY BASED SPORT: CONSTRUCTIVE MULTICULTURALISM?

There are a number of issues to explore in regard to immigrants and sport: their association with specific sports such as soccer and whether this has been a hindrance to this sport (the 'wogball' stereotype); the establishment of immigrant sporting clubs such as Marconi; and the degree of acceptance of immigrants in mainstream sports.

Soccer became so identifiable with NES communities that it became known popularly as 'wogball', a word that has achieved sufficient currency to be included in the *Macquarie Dictionary*. There has been continuing debate among the administrators who run the game and commentators as to whether this association has been beneficial or harmful to the growth of soccer. It has been argued by some that soccer's ethnic associations have locked it into a permanent minority status, accepted passionately by a minority of Australians but rejected by the majority. There have been many calls for soccer clubs to become based on districts, cities and regions—as is the case of most other codes—rather than on ethnic communities. The above argument underplays the drawing power of the Socceroos, who have been able to fill major stadiums for important internationals.

There have been regular attempts since the 1950s to de-ethnicise soccer, to remove and reduce the importance of ethnic attachments and symbols. There have even been attempts to promote non-ethnic clubs such as Canberra City, which was set up in the late 1970s to represent the 'people' of the national capital and was 'not connected with any ethnic group'. But in due course the club seemed to drift away from its stated ideals, becoming more of an 'ethnic English club'.[49]

There is the problem, first of all, of strong resistance from the ethnic clubs. There is also the issue of whether soccer authorities should cut their links with people who have supported the code so passionately. There have also been some attempts to ban ethnic symbols such as flags, which some regard as the trigger for violence. Such policies have proved difficult to enforce.

There has been much recent debate about whether ethnically based sporting clubs contribute in a positive sense to multiculturalism or whether they are to be blamed for importing and enhancing violence and ethnic tensions. Hay has argued that ethnically based soccer clubs have contributed positively: they have provided 'integrative services' for immigrant communities, helping immigrants to make their way in Australian society; they have met the deeper psychological needs of these communities and have actually helped to reduce the potential violence in Australian society. Soccer has helped provide immigrants with accommodation, jobs, networks and an introduction to Australian society. Such was the interest in improving the quality of many a local soccer team that many immigrants were recruited literally off the ship. The lot of NES immigrants was a difficult one in Australia in the 1950s and subsequent decades when racism was rampant. There was systematic denigration and discrimination leading to devaluation of the qualifications and experience of immigrants. Soccer clubs helped some working-class New Australians to survive.[50]

Hay thinks that the question of ethnic violence associated with soccer has been overstated. During the 1950s there were many instances of violence in other football codes as well as ethnic soccer, but while the former attracted limited attention the latter was big news since it fitted into racist and xenophobic stereotyping that many New Australians were a violent lot who could not forget their own enmities and assimilate into Australian society. Hughson believes that the media have created the mythology of soccer as a 'folk devil', a concept which suggests that perceived anti-social behaviour can be amplified to a form of 'moral panic'. Simply because of its ethnicity, hooliganism and violence were viewed as endemic in the 'folk devil' sport of soccer.[51]

The establishment of ethnically based sporting clubs could be viewed as part of a continuing discourse on what constitutes multiculturalism. Many have assumed that ethnic consciousness will fade in time and that second- or third-generation migrants will assimilate. While some degree of acculturation has taken place, studies of these clubs report a persistence of the ethnic self and identity. Drawing on the work of Michael Parenti, Philip Mosely has suggested that a more pluralist approach is preferable. While all immigrants acculturate to some extent, this need not mean jettisoning their past heritage. This dual identity was summed up by one Australian: 'My Soul to God. My Life to Australia. My Heart to Hungary.'[52]

Mosely has, in the past, been critical of the media perception of soccer violence as a hangover from European battles. He has argued persuasively that there were some other local factors in soccer violence. Misunderstandings sometimes developed from the different styles of play, the more robust British style popular in Australia versus the more refined Continental play. A more telling social factor has been that immigrants in Australia were subject to much abuse, racism, exploitation and even violence and the soccer field was the one place where they could vent their anger and even strike back. There were plenty of reasons closer to home for frustrated minorities to strike out. 'The game provided the European immigrant with the rare opportunity for expressing himself. He could stake out an area in society in which his voice bore weight and in which he had the chance to dominate. As such, there was freedom to release pent-up emotions, be they ambition, passion, frustration or aggression.'[53]

In his more recent work Mosely has emphasised some of the negative aspects of soccer violence and ethnic attachments. The conflict between Croatian and Serbian nationalists in Australia is a long-standing and bitter one which was imported to Australia. While there have been some positive multicultural aspects of these clubs—networking and preservation of cultural identity—both have become extremely politicised and have been a rallying point for intense nationalism. While it is also true that many successful football clubs are political to some extent, ethnically based soccer clubs have added a dimension to the politicisation of sport. The Yugal Football club benefited from support from the Yugoslav Consulate and Yugoslav Airlines, and was to some extent a front for Tito's Yugoslavia. Mosely concludes that Balkan-Australian clubs have used sport as a forum to air all manner of grievances against each other.[54]

Wray Vamplew has also emphasised that the perceived ethnic soccer violence represents the 'downside to multiculturalism'. While there is limited violence in Australian sport, compared to that of other societies, 'what occurs appears to be concentrated around its soccer grounds', and 'traditional homeland loyalties also included traditional homeland hatreds'. Vamplew's survey on violence in Australian sport confirmed that soccer was regarded as the most violent football code in the country and that crowd behaviour at soccer matches was rated as worse than that of any other sport.[55] Vamplew also noted that the problem is made worse because the 'ethnic mix in Australian cities means that the historical and contemporary political problems of Europe are condensed into a relatively small area'.[56]

NON-ENGLISH-SPEAKERS AND ANGLO SPORTS

There has been limited study of how, and under what circumstances, NES immigrants or their children gravitate to more established Anglo-Celtic sports.[57] It is not yet clear whether the natural assimilation that some assume has in fact occurred. Most second-generation Polish soccer-players in Melbourne retain an attachment and a preference for their ethnically based club.[58]

It is evident, however, even from a cursory glance that people from a NES background gravitate more into some sports than others, such as Australian football and rugby league. Australian football followers have long been used to a proliferation of non-Anglo-Celtic names and the fact that some of their star players, such as Alex Jesaulenko, were born overseas. By the 1980s there was the beginning of a second generation of Italian-Australians playing Australian football, with Stephen Silvagni emulating the deeds of his father Sergio for the Carlton Football Club. Non-Anglo-Saxons have also been prominent in rugby league, with Greek, Lithuanian and Croatian-Australians captaining the national side: Dr George Peponis, Tom Raudonikis and Max Krilich. Although there are fewer European immigrants in the more middle-class game of rugby the national team in the 1990s was served well by two Italian-Australian wingers, David Campese and Paul Carozza. In recent years there have been many rugby players, and even whole teams, from Islander communities. The inclusion in the national side of players of Tongan and Fijian origin such as Willie Ofahengaue and Ilie Tabua, as well as Zambian-born George Gregan, has implications both for the social status of rugby and for the wider social acceptance of immigrants from Oceania.[59]

Cricket, by comparison, has attracted relatively few European immigrants. It seems to be more difficult for people of NES backgrounds to acquire the skills of this game than any of the football codes. Cricket also carries more English trappings, which was a likely reason why Lennie Durtanovich changed his surname to Pascoe. Cricketer Geoff Lawson reported that the Chappell brothers made a habit of baiting Pascoe about his ethnic origins when they faced up to him.[60] During the 1980s Mike Veletta was the first Italian-Australian to reach the top ranks, but the bulk of the national team remains identifiably Anglo-Saxon.

It is too soon to ascertain whether World Series Cricket will attract greater support from NES immigrants and their children. By its greater promotion of limited overs cricket, rather than Test cricket, WSC may have enhanced cricket's appeal to non-Anglo-Celtic Australians. A 1979 survey of 434 students at a mainly working-class and multicultural school in Sydney, St Mary's (Cathedral) Christian Brothers High School, suggested that WSC may lead to a wider ethnic support for cricket. WSC cricket was nominated by 18 per cent of students as their favourite sport, ranking a close second to rugby league, which was nominated by 21 per cent. 'Establishment' cricket finished well down the list with a preferred rating of only 4 per cent.[60]

Undoubtedly sport has had some part in reducing ethnic tensions within Australia and creating a broader common ground of Australian identity, for example diminishing the tensions between the English-oriented majority and the Irish minority. Sport was such a compelling and attractive form of cultural discourse that the Irish could not afford to remain aloof. Irish-Australians have played some role in defining the character of mainstream Australian sport. In some areas of sporting culture, notably gambling, Irish-Australians have been rather more successful than Protestant wowser groups in having their voice heard.

Whether sport, and soccer in particular, has helped or hindered non-English-speaking immigrants in establishing themselves in Australia and in relating to other communities is still a matter of lively debate. No one would dispute that the ethnic sports club became a focal point for many NES communities in urban Australia and that these clubs have served useful social, economic and political purposes. But the cost of ethnically based soccer clubs—in terms of perceived violence, media and public stereotyping—has yet to be fully evaluated.

Media focus on 'ethnic' sports and ethnically based sports clubs may have caused them to lose sight of an opposite process: the ease and speed with which the sons (and to a much lesser extent, the daughters) of NES immigrants gravitate to established Anglo-Celtic sports. Ethnically based sporting clubs may well turn out to be transitional associations which will be discarded when they have served their purpose.

It is likely that future Australian sport will become more international and multicultural than before. Sporting culture has been drawn into a continuing debate about what it means to be an Australian. As Australian culture progressively becomes less Anglocentric, Australian sport too will change and evolve as it has done for the past two centuries.

10
THE MEDIA

It has become fashionable among critics to berate the media, blaming them for all that is perceived to be wrong with organised sport. Some see the sports media as too violent, sexist and racist and dominated by media tycoons, and even a central reason why sport has become 'corrupt'.[1] A problem with these perspectives is that the authors tend to see the media as separate from wider sporting practices. It has been argued that the view of television sport as a 'thing-in-itself' is a false one, that television sport is used by fans merely as part of their sporting culture—they also read, play, watch as live spectators, and talk about sport.[2] Audiences 'use', and even manipulate, the media in much the same way as the media attempt to direct them.

Much of the writing on sport and the media also suffers because it is ahistorical in that it assumes that sport has been transformed, usually for the worse, by television—ignoring how much earlier media technology influenced sport. Television sport did not emerge in a vacuum. Art, print media, radio, film, photo journalism have all contributed to new meanings and forms for sport. Television sport drew on all previous constructions of sport developed through other media forms. The distinctive and even revolutionary role of television sport can only be established by comparison with other media.

Organised sport was and is virtually a child of the media: the media gave and continue to give sport its shape, form and appeal. The arrival of the mass media, along with the emergence of photo journalism and the visual media, provided sport with new forms, images, ideologies, and greater popularity than before.

There are several questions that can be explored about sport and the media. In what ways did the media contribute to, and even shape, organised sport? Was this media transformation for better or worse? Has the media role in sport greatly altered since the coming of television? Is the language of the Australian sports media distinctive? In what ways have the media helped to create the moral universe of the sports follower?

THE COMING OF THE MASS MEDIA

The rise of the Australian mass media occurred at the same time that sport was beginning to enjoy unprecedented popularity in the three or four decades before World War I. The print media—tabloid newspapers, weekly papers and specialist sporting papers—were central to the expansion of sporting culture. The sporting press did more than record and disseminate information about an increasing number of sporting events: it interpreted and explained them, it invested them with shape, meaning and moral worth. The sporting press helped to construct and legitimate the new sporting universe that was organised sport. It created ideals and values for players and even defined appropriate behaviour for spectators.[3] It whetted the appetite of sporting followers to consume more sport.

The mass media and organised sport were the product of similar social and economic developments. The substantial rise in real incomes, increased leisure time, improved communications, transportation and literacy rates and the growth of urban society were all factors in the appearance of a more popular press. Improvements in technology and the growth of industry led to a reduction in the cost of newsprint and the cost of producing newspapers. With cheaper costs and potentially greater circulation, the price of newspapers dropped substantially from 9d or 1s earlier in the century to 1d or even less. Technological developments, in the form of lithography and photography, made newspapers more popular.

Newspapers became more accessible to the wider community from the 1880s. They began to cater to more specialist interests, including those of sports consumers. The *Referee*, founded in Sydney in 1886, was the first newspaper devoted to solely to sport. Other specialist papers followed such as the highly regarded *Melbourne Sportsman, Sydney Sportsman* and *Queensland Sportsman*. Some papers even catered for individual sports, such as *Queensland Cricketer & Footballer* and *Queensland Racing Calendar*.

These weeklies differed from the earlier 'sporting' newspaper *Bell's Life in Sydney and Sporting Reviewer*, which began in 1845. Unlike *Bell's Life*, which focused mainly on horse-racing, the *Referee* covered all major sports. *Bell's Life* was not an exclusively sporting newspaper in that it included politics and other forms of cultural entertainment.

Specialist newspapers appeared because daily and weekly papers, which devoted more and more columns to the increasing number of sports results, could not meet the demand for sports news and allocate sufficient space and to the growing number of sporting events. Chris Cuneen has also suggested that sport contributed to the appearance of Sunday newspapers, such as the *Sunday Times*, to convey news of Saturday afternoon sport. Such was the interest in sport that the *Referee* attracted quality writers, who were deeply committed to sport as a serious cultural enterprise. The overall tone of the *Referee* was 'solemn; there were no jokes, seldom any cartoons'. The writers, who regarded sport as a form of moral endeavour, included Richard Coombes, father of amateur athletics, John Corbett Davis (1869–1941), a knowledgeable cricket and football commentator, Alfred Arthur Greenwood Hales (1863–1936), who later became a war correspondent and novelist, and another novelist, Nat Gould. Richard Twopeny commented on the high calibre of Australian sports journalism of this era. He believed that the *Melbourne Sportsman* was 'the best sporting paper in the world'.[4]

Cunneen suggested that journalists had a part not only in shaping sporting agendas but also in creating sporting heroes and heroines. William Francis Corbett (1857–1923), who became a full-time journalist on the *Referee* in 1895, became an authoritative and popular sports writer over the next decades and helped in the creation of a 'golden age' of Australian sport from the 1890s to 1920. With his direct homely prose and his conversational technique, Corbett and other journalists helped to elevate a succession of working-class sports stars which included Victor Trumper in cricket, Dally Messenger in rugby league, Les Darcy in boxing, Annette Kellermann and the Cavills in swimming, and many others. While journalists alone did not create hero figures—they were a product of an expanding sporting culture, more working-class participation in sport, a public yearning for stars, and the greater sense of nationalism—Corbett and the Australian press did play an important part in the process of hero formation.

Claude Corbett (1885–1944), who carried on his father's sports journalism in the *Referee*, also helped to define a more nostalgic and less self-confident sporting atmosphere of the 1920s and 1930s. A romantic writer, Corbett reinforced his father's interpretation of the 'golden era'. One of his columns referred to the founders of rugby league in reverential tones: 'Did you ever stand in a room in the "dim, religious light" of a fading winter afternoon, surrounded by photographs of men whom you had known in the full bloom of their athletic manhood, and thought of them as they were—studied those pictures on the wall!'[5]

While many print journalists helped to elevate the people's heroes, to create sporting legends and to underpin the amateur view that sport should serve a serious moral purpose, the influence of sporting artists and photographers cannot be underestimated. Photo journalism and sporting art, along with artefacts like costumes, memorabilia, programs and souvenirs created powerful and attractive symbols which incorporated sporting values, extended the meaning of play and enhanced the appeal of games.

Historians have been slow to make use of visual sources even though photo journalism has been part of the media for over a century. While drawings, photographs and cartoons have been used to enhance and add to written monographs, they have not been seen as a source in their own right, which can be read, interpreted and understood. John Berger has said that visual images are a rich historical source because they appeal directly and immediately to a wide audience—literate and illiterate, adult and child—and provide 'direct testimony about the world which surrounded other people at other times': 'images are more precise and richer than literature'.[6]

Some of the first interpreters of sport were artists who produced sketches, engravings and paintings which, before 1850, provide some glimpses of sport and society, such as a series of scenes of recreation in Hyde Park painted by J. Rae in 1842. As sport became more prominent from the 1850s, there was an equivalent growth in sporting art. Samuel Thomas Gill (1818–80), the prolific goldfields painter, was one of the first artists to develop a distinctly Australian attitude and to paint ordinary life, which included life on the diggings, scenes of bush life, and Australian sport. His paintings of sport included scenes of some of the first intercolonial cricket matches along with McLaren's boxing saloon, Ballarat, (1854) and the Adelaide racecourse (1854). Geoffrey Dutton noted that Gill has been underrated as an artist partly because his sense of humour made him appear 'less serious' than other artists and because of a misconception that he was a 'rough customer in the knock-about, ultra-democratic Australian tradition, the world of pubs and racehorses'. Gill chose to record faithfully the culture of the ordinary person rather than painting the large landscapes which had established the reputation of earlier artists.[7]

Little is known about the influence of sporting art and how it was consumed.[8] Many of Gill's paintings focus on the atmosphere and crowd at cricket matches rather than the play itself. His paintings convey a romantic picture of a well-behaved and fashionably attired crowd and a colourful scene bathed in warm light and enlivened by gaily decorated tents and numerous trees. Painters such as Gill elevated sport and added to its appeal, depicting it in a romantic light and as a vibrant part of Australian culture. There were many others who chronicled the rise of sport, such as J. M. Crossland, who painted an Aboriginal cricketer at the Poonindie Mission, and two artists, Henry S. Glover and Henry Burn, who produced cricket illustrations of the 1861–62 English tour. Romantic pictures of star racehorses, such as Jorrocks and a succession of Melbourne Cup champions, helped install the horse as one of the great icons of Australian sporting culture.

Gill's cricket paintings, which are reminiscent of English paintings of rural cricket matches of the eighteenth century, tell us that he saw sport as a positive and civilising influence. Other paintings, notably his much-reproduced and admired 'McLaren's Boxing Saloon, Main Road Ballarat', conveyed the rich and vibrant culture of working-class sport pursued in a primitive hotel in this goldfields town and suggested that Australian sport was developing some distinctive forms.

Art provides an insight into changing attitudes towards sport. Geoffrey Dutton catalogues Australian perceptions of activities at the beach, swimming and surf bathing, body shapes, display and appropriate clothing.[9] Nineteenth-century paintings express the continuance of British attitudes towards the sun, sand and sea, with fully dressed ladies and gentlemen promenading (or sitting in deck-chairs) along the beach; twentieth-century art catalogues the Australian appropriation of the beach.

Improvements in the development of lithography and the invention of photography in the second half of the nineteenth century enabled sports illustration to become more prominent. Photography spawned weekly illustrated newspapers which appeared by the 1890s and by the turn of the century sport was reported almost as much by images as by words.

Whereas painters painted a whole sporting scene, lithographs in the sporting press were used increasingly to focus on the game itself, the players, the events and the techniques of sport. An 1878 lithograph, 'The Race of the Championship', in the Sydney Mail focused on the leading runner, who was seemingly oblivious to the plaudits of the crowd. The well proportioned and near-naked male runner, dressed in only running shorts and shoes, was presented in a heroic light. Lithography enabled greater attention to be paid to some of the stars of sport.

Although sporting art made great advances by the 1870s and 1880s, it was still fairly primitive. A lithograph of a football scrum in Sydney, from the Australasian Sketcher of 1879, while suggesting some of the pandemonium of this mêlée, was a rather stilted portrayal of the action. Artists found it even more difficult to depict play involving movement. In some such lithographs of the 1870s and 1880s the proportions—to the modern eye—are wrong and the sense of flow and movement jarring.

The arrival of photography greatly extended the media presentation of sport. While the first photographs of sport were still, it was not long before photographers had mastered the technique of 'action photography'. George Beldam, an English county cricketer, was one of its pioneers. Beldam took a succession of photographs at Hampstead Cricket Ground in October 1904 of Fred Spofforth. Although the 'Demon' bowler, aged 51, was well past his peak, Beldam's collection included a much-admired photograph, Spofforth's classic high leap in the action of bowling. So effective is this photograph of a perfectly balanced athlete, with his arm extended high, that some have assumed that this was the action of a bowler at the peak of his career.

From this time photography has an immense influence on the shape of sport and its ideologies: great moments, classic styles, celebrated events and champion teams have been republished frequently, adorned many walls, appeared in calendars and been reproduced as statues. One of the compelling images in cricket was the celebrated photograph of the lithe and daring Victor Trumper dancing down the wicket, which captured the athleticism and the adventurousness of Trumper's batting and conveyed the joy of cricket.

Photographs from this time have achieved many purposes. They have conveyed the athleticism of the stars in their most aesthetic and even balletic states, such as Roy Cazaly leaping high above the pack for a spectacular mark or the classic style of an Annette Kellermann dive. Particular photographs have also enabled the fan to admire the intricacies of a sport, such as the technique required for a square cut, the wedge shot from the bunker, or the perfectly timed leap of a line-out jumper. Photographs have also been used to express the approved ethics and ideologies of games. The end-of-game camaraderie between two mud-soaked opponents—the giant St George forward Norm Provan and the diminutive Western Suburbs five-eighth Arthur Summons—was one of the classic photographs of rugby league that was thought to epitomise the value of mateship. Such was the appeal of this photograph that it provided the design for the Winfield Cup.

With its ability to convey precise and realistic detail, photography also encouraged the sporting pose. Bodybuilding emerged in part from the photographic studio. Athletes, who attempted to imitate the classic poses of Greek sculpture, were decked out with accoutrements such as spears, shields and gladiators' boots.[10] Symbolic representation also became an important element of team photographs, with great attention paid to clothing and pecking order (see ch. 5).

There was very little criticism of sport, or any reference to its darker or more controversial sides, in the expanding visual media. Artists and photographers manufactured an idealised world of sport—an attractive and appealing moral universe—which could be sold to the public. They helped to manufacture an optimistic world of sport which was above criticism.

Sports journalism and illustration were only parts of the expanding media. During the second half of the nineteenth century there was an increased number of annuals—including the celebrated *Wisden* which began in 1864—along with prints, souvenirs, calendars, programs, memorabilia and all manner of artefacts. The rapid expansion of sporting ephemera was an important aspect of the media. Individuals and institutions began to establish their own libraries and museums, to create their own sports media and to appropriate sport for themselves.

The development of a distinctively Australian language and imagery of sport is another important aspect of sports media. While the language of sport, along with its culture, was at first imported, Australians developed their own rich vocabulary of sporting words, idioms and phrases: words such as 'mullygrubber', expressions such as 'Carn the Tigers' and 'Chewy on your boot', and a plethora of nicknames. One of the more famous expressions, 'Up there Cazaly!', which celebrated the high leap of footballer Roy Cazaly, became a rallying cry for diggers during World War II and the central theme of a Michael Brady song; it is now an AFL anthem. Sporting words and symbols, as Barry Andrews has suggested, are the means by which the media become part of popular culture in that the people themselves create expressions of sport.[11]

The language of sport is a rich part of Australian popular culture. It has intruded so effectively into all aspects of Australian cultural life, none more so than politics, that few people notice its extent. Meetings are 'kicked off', politicians have 'two bob each way' and preselections attract a 'Melbourne Cup field'. Politicians use sporting words and images to speak more in the language of the common person. In the process they add to the legitimacy of the sporting world. John Ryan has catalogued the many racing expressions familiar in everyday conversation which turn up in commerce, law, politics, education, the military, literature and even the church. An Anglican Church commentator stated that Bishop Harry Goodhew was the 'front runner in the field' for the Archbishopric of Sydney.[12]

FILM AND RADIO

One of the first Australian films ever made was of the 1896 Melbourne Cup. It was popular enough to run for three months. The film catered to the demand of a larger audience, unable to watch live, to participate in this important event. The race has been filmed and recorded in every subsequent year. The first films of the Cup were brief but they helped extend the Cup traditions. The film depicted horses and riders, and spectators arriving at Flemington; the fashionable atmosphere of this event—with images of women's hats and the vice-regal party—reflected the exalted status of this race-meeting. The brief filmed highlights extended the wider sporting 'imagined community' who took part.[13] It has been suggested that a sports film industry emerged over the next decades but faded away at the time of the Depression of the early 1930s.[14]

The tradition of filming and later replaying major sporting events was extended during the 1930s with the coming of sound and Cinesound Review newsreels, which began in 1931. Newsreels included a regular sporting segment in the weekly news report. It was the one way in which sports followers, before the era of television, could obtain a glimpse of a major event in another city.

While there have some sporting films—racecourse dramas, surf stories, and occasional sporting films such as *Dawn!* and *Phar Lap* and plays such as *The Club* made into films—the genre of the sporting feature film has not been influential or well developed. The same observation can be made of television mini-series such as *Bodyline* and the treatment of the life of Lionel Rose, which have been an occasional rather than a continuing genre. A lack of serious criticism of the sporting institutions and culture of this country may be the reason the genre of the sporting film and mini-series have failed to develop. To sustain the interest of an audience and to compete with a plethora of live sporting programs, sporting films need to achieve something more than simply celebrating sport.

One other possible reason for the limited development of sports films is the exclusion of women from them. The second Hollywood film of sporting star Annette Kellermann, *The Daughter of the Gods*, 'staggered America' when it was released after 1916 because it captured the dramatic action of Kellermann diving and swimming. Rather than featuring competitive sport, this movie represented action adventures which simply featured swimming and diving. The dismal failure of *Dawn!* (1978), 'a pseudo-documentary biography of Dawn Fraser', was in part, according to Richard Fotheringham, because the movie worked outside established genres and constructs.[15] Although there are some ambiguities and conflicts in the presentation of sport through film—*The Club* deals with conflict within a football club and Bruce Beresford's 1982 *Puberty Blues* represents a quirky 'paean to junior feminism'—film perpetuates dominant and masculine forms which largely exclude women.[16]

Sport has frequently been a *leitmotif* or a casual segment of many Australian films. It has also been an acceptable part of many documentaries because it has been used to sustain cultural myths. In feature films such as *Gallipoli* (1981), mythologies of war, sport and the bush intersected. The David Williamson script included two young sprinters who met at a sports carnival, the 'one country-bred and heroic, the other from the city and more self-centred'.[17]

Without question, radio was a more powerful sports medium than film, and did much to expand interest in sport. Within a relatively short period (less than a decade) there was sufficient advance in technology for a national radio hook-up in which listeners could follow live sporting events around the country. The first such national broadcast, of the controversial Bodyline series, did much to sell radio licences—which expanded from 1400 in 1924 to 370 000 by 1932. It also promoted the newly established Australian Broadcasting Commission (ABC).

Horse-racing benefited from radio more than other sports. The extension of the mass media from the printed page to the pictorial newspaper, cinema, newsreels and radio broadcasts caused a boom in racing from the mid-1920s. The greater coverage in turn resulted in record attendances such as over 90 000 patrons at Randwick in 1922 and the crowd of 126 000 which attended Flemington for the 1926 Melbourne Cup. One result of the boom in horse-racing and improvements in communications—in particular the rapid expansion of telephone services—was that the SP bookmaking industry also received an enormous boost. Radio and the telephone made betting easier for people such as women at home, who might not have been in the habit of attending a racecourse. It is likely that when conveniently located Totalisator Agency Boards (TABs) opened in the 1960s, there was a large, ready-made female gambling audience. This, at any rate, would explain why women were so prominent in TABs from their inception (see chs 5 and 11).[18]

While some sports administrators were concerned that radio broadcasts might reduce crowds, it soon became clear that the reverse was the case.[19] The ABC 1932–33 report concluded that 'experience has repeatedly shown that the broadcasting of descriptions is a most efficient

method of stimulating public interest and has almost invariably greatly
increased the numbers of spectators present on similar occasions there-
after'. The *Sydney Morning Herald* of 4 January 1933 suggested that
radio was extending the audience for cricket, since in 'thousands of
homes, the housewife who never went to a match is being educated
while the radio is turned on in the points and personalities of cricket'.

The sport benefited from the commentary of highly placed and articulate commentators, beginning with Sir Charles Moses, Michael Charlton
and former State player Alan McGilvray. With its imperial links and
long-established traditions, Test cricket gained a right of way over other
ABC programs, a position which it has largely retained to this day.
Broadcasting of other team-sports such as rugby league emerged more
slowly, with the first broadcasts not beginning until 1941. Although the
first broadcast of Australian football took place in 1925, radio coverage
was a 'pretty subdued affair' and its commercial potential was not recognised until after World War II.[20]

Radio also helped to extend sports consumption and establish new
conventions of sports spectatorship—that of staying up late at night to
listen to overseas sporting events. Such was the interest in receiving a
continuous and 'live' description of Test cricket in England that the
ABC introduced synthetic broadcasts in 1938. The system was based on
the transmission of cables at about five-minute intervals containing the
briefest of summaries of the events of that time. With the assistance of
a team who expanded the cable into commentary notes, provided up-
to-date maps of field positions, posted the score on a board, the commentators simulated a live broadcast. The commentaries were enhanced
by sound effects: a pencil tapped on wood indicated the sound of bat
meeting ball. Such was the professionalism of the commentators that
many listeners were convinced that the broadcasts were live, even
though the commentators went to some pains to explain the nature of
the synthetic broadcasts.[21]

Synthetic broadcasts distorted the game in a number of ways. Not
only were fictitious happenings invented to cover a break in the cables,
but occasionally the commentary even falsified the game. Ted a'Beckett
recalled one farcical situation when a commentator described how a
batsman was caught behind in regulation fashion whereas the batsman
had skied the ball which was taken by the keeper in the middle of the
pitch.[22] Radio also made cricket appear to be a faster-moving and more
exciting game than it was in that commentators filled in the gaps and dull
passages with reminiscences, anecdotes about players, or discussions of
the crowd, the weather, the birds and the morality and ideology of the
game. Chandler has noted that radio has greater potential to distort sport
than television: radio commentators can make a dull game seem exciting,
whereas television viewers can make up their own minds.[23]

The invention of the portable transistor radio by the early 1950s also
altered the consumption of sport. Many spectators took the transistor

to an event and listened to the expert commentary while watching it with their own eyes. Celebrated English journalist Neville Cardus was astonished that a family at the Sydney Test of December 1954 took their radio to cricket and 'turned it on full blast and—believe it or not—listened to the ABC commentators while looking at the actual play'. Cardus predicted that when television arrived people would want to take their sets to the ground and 'watch the screen vigilantly' to see if it corresponded to 'objective truth'.[24] Cardus was not far wrong, though he was not to know that spectators at the major grounds would watch on a giant video screen rather than their own sets. A purist, Cardus believed that spectators should watch a game intently and form their own judgements independently.

THE TELEVISION TRANSFORMATION OF SPORT

Sport was present at the birth of television in Australia. The 1956 Melbourne Olympics was an important reason why the Australian government finally decided, after a decade of debate, to introduce this new medium. The Olympics helped to sell television sets in the same way that the Bodyline series had popularised radio and the Melbourne Cup had enhanced the popularity of film.

There was much debate and controversy in 1956 on the role of television and the Olympics: whether the new medium should have priority over newsreel and film. While Olympic supremo Avery Brundage was attracted by the windfall profits from television contracts, which would enhance the status of the festival, he was ambivalent about delivering a more commercial Olympics. There was also considerable debate about whether the Games should be treated as a news event or an entertainment package.[25]

Although there was a honeymoon period in which the new medium was immensely popular, television sport did not make an impact until the 1970s. In its first decade and a half television sport was very limited and technologically primitive. Viewers could only watch live sporting events in their own city; coaxial cables between the various cities were not established until the 1960s. The 1956 Olympics were not broadcast live across Australia: viewers had to wait until film was flown from Melbourne. Filming was very primitive, with the cameras set at one fixed location. The impact of television on sport was therefore a limited one at first, and the audience was relatively small.

The technology of television improved rapidly in the 1970s. By the 1970–71 cricket series the ABC was able to organise a national television hook-up so that viewers around the country could watch live the entire thirty days of the Test series, 180 hours in all, though there were some broadcasting restrictions in the city where the Test was played. The introduction of colour television and slow-motion replays in the mid-1970s also enhanced television broadcasting. Designed in North

America so that spectators could watch action in ice hockey which was too fast for the naked eye, the replay proved immensely popular. Repeating the highlights of sporting action enabled greater explanation and understanding of the intricacies of complex and fast-moving actions—a great try, mark, catch and so forth.

The potential of television to alter the balance of the sporting world became clear by the 1970s. When the ABC broadcast the 1970–71 series against England to a national audience, there was an unprecedented television audience. While the series drew a very respectable total of 616 196 live spectators—an average daily figure of 20 279—the television audience for the later Tests was more than one million per day, approximately fifty times that of the live audience. Commercial television interests soon moved into the highly profitable area of television sport.

It did not take long for commercial interests to realise the profit to be earned from television sports broadcasting and that nationally packaged sports spectaculars could drive commercial television's profitable move to simultaneous programming.[26] The Australian cricket world was turned upside down when Kerry Packer of Channel 9 attempted a takeover of cricket to secure exclusive television broadcasting rights (see ch 11). Television sport proved to be a boon for many television station owners in that it provided a relatively cheap way of fulfilling their obligations for programs with Australian content.

Much of the debate on television and sport to this point has been narrowly focused, subjective and ahistorical. Most writers on the subject have simply assumed, more from personal observation than from any sustained historical analysis, that television sport has led to a decline in the quality of sporting culture. This view was set out starkly by North American Benjamin Rader, who argued that the once noble institution of sport had been degraded and trivialised by television coverage which had 'diminished the capacity of sports to furnish heroes, to bind communities, and to enact the rituals that contain, and exalt, society's traditional values'.[27] A number of Australian writers, such as Goldlust and Tatz, have developed similar arguments. Goldlust thought that the 'communal and ritual elements of spectator sport' had been swept away and replaced by sport as a 'commodity spectacle' and that high-performance sport had moved from 'play' to 'display'.[28]

These approaches leave many questions unanswered about sport and television. Few of these critics of television sport have delved into the subculture of the industry: 'how it works, who controls it, what questions those controllers ask, what pressures there are and, above all, how audiences respond to the product offered.'[29] There is also the assumption that the media exist as a separate and unified entity, whereas the media are 'a complex multiplicity of interests, groups, frameworks and instincts which might at once be competitive and complementary'.[30] There also needs to be much greater discussion of the specific ways in which television altered the sporting media and their consumption.[31]

An important task is to explore the changes and continuities in the sporting media before and after television. To what extent has television evolved out of previous media, drawing on and transforming existing sporting practices? Or, has television radically changed sports and their traditions, how they are played and consumed? Or, is television merely one of number of factors which are altering contemporary sporting practice?

Stoddart has listed six trends in the evolution of the media from print only to multi-electronic sportscasting.[32] This provides a useful starting-point for exploring changes and continuities in the sporting media after television. There has been a change, first, in the spatial dimensions of sportscasting, with column inches giving way to radio minutes and television seconds. Stoddart believes that this has led to a decline in the 'explanatory ability' of the media and that sports coverage has become increasingly superficial. While there is some truth in this, Stoddart may be in danger of comparing the quality print media with tabloid television. Perhaps, too, the more important issue with time and space is the change from words to pictures, the latter requiring far less explanation in that they can be 'read' by the viewer. With vast improvements in the technical quality and diversity of sports television pictures—filmed many times from every conceivable angle—viewers are presented with a wide range of sporting 'documents' from which they can make up their own mind about a particular aspect of play, whether a game is a good or bad one.

A second trend was that the coming of television sport not only ac-celerated the commercialism begun in the eras of print and radio but it transformed sport in that the networks discovered the advertising power of sport. This occurred because television led to a dramatic increase in the size of sporting audiences and the proportions of live versus home viewers. There has been a dramatic change in how sports obtained rev-enue in the television era, with gate-takings representing a diminishing amount compared with sponsorship and advertising revenue.[33] Such was the demand for media sport by the 1980s that advertisers paid huge sums to associate their product with an athletic festival. The nexus between sport and big business (see ch. 11) had much to do with television. Through television the corporate world was drawn into many forms of direct and indirect sponsorship of sports, teams and individual players.

Television has vastly altered the economic environment in which sport operates. Sports which are much in demand can now earn millions of dollars by selling the television rights for a season or a major series. The commercial rights to rugby league, for instance, for a term stretch-ing into the 1990s, fetched almost $50 million. The ABC can no longer afford to bid for the most popular sporting events such as the Olympic Games, international cricket and football. Since the 1970s it has lost the rights to televise many major sporting events.

Another trend, noted by Stoddart and many others, is that playing conditions and the practices of various sports have become increasingly calibrated by the media. The changed time-frame of sport in the television era is the most dramatic example of this. Whereas sport was largely confined to the weekend and public holidays and mostly occurred in daylight hours before the 1970s, television encouraged the expansion of night sport to coincide with the largest and most profitable viewing times. The popularity of television sport was also a reason why more sport was now being played on weekdays and nights and why sports events are now scheduled around the clock every day of the week. There has also been a sizeable increase in the amount of time devoted to media sport, which is now approximately 15 per cent of television time. Sport continues to occupy much time in radio, various forms of print media and video cassettes.

The search for larger television audiences has undoubtedly been a major reason, though not the only one, for the rise of more national leagues which began to replace suburban and city-based competitions by the 1980s. The introduction of more teams, playing in different time-zones, will enable more live television coverage of sport than before. The entry of Auckland and Perth into the 1995 national rugby league competition will make it possible for television to broadcast three and even four separate games on one day—as occurs in North America.

The greater payment of sports starts in the television era represented a fourth development. While some élite players enjoyed celebrity status and greater financial rewards through newspapers and radio exposure, the amounts were relatively minute when compared with the rich returns for celebrities in the television age. Golfer Greg Norman, for instance, has become a multimillionaire. The profitability of television sport has created an ever-increasing spiral of player salaries though rewards have been uneven, with a minority of players substantially better off. With television bringing more money to individual sports, there have been greater player demands to enjoy some of the fruits of increased profits. Larger player payments have also changed the face of Australian sport, making it more professional than ever before.

Another television trend of the past two decades has been that Australian sports tastes have been 'internationalised'. This development, Stoddart believes, has, 'possibly, undercut national identities'. With the introduction of satellite technology, broadcasting American sport became a relatively cheap way of expanding sports programming and extending it around the clock. However, it is also true that an increasing number of international sporting contests against a greater variety of opponents 'provide points of national identification'.[34]

The broadcasting of an increasing amount of international and particularly American sport has influenced Australian sporting practice. It has been an important factor in increased Australian borrowing from America of anything from clothing and rituals (cheer-leaders) to promotional techniques and spectator behaviour. Extensive television exposure is one reason why basketball is one of the fastest-growing sports in

Australia. The extent of television exposure does not fully explain the spectacular rise of basketball in the last two decades, which occurred because of the increasing Americanisation of Australian culture (see ch. 9).

The sixth development was that television, along with previous forms of sporting media, has preserved sport's status quo. Television interests have been decidedly conservative in that they have continued to favour those male sports which were well established before the era of television. In one sense television programmers have accepted entirely the sporting agendas and priorities which were established in the age of print and radio. It is ironic that while the impact of television has been radical and even revolutionary in some respects—altering sporting practice and consumption—television programmers have been conservative and reluctant to take any risks on promoting new sports which have the potential to attract large audiences. It has been suggested that television has been slow to recognise and to profit from the appeal of new sports, such as volleyball and soccer in the United States.[35]

Women's sports have suffered considerably from television's preference for the status quo because women's sports were relatively backward, in terms of their organisation as mass-spectator sports, at the beginning of the television era. Although netball is one of the fastest-growing sports in the country, with a participant base as large or larger than cricket and the various football codes, it has struggled (along with a host of other women's sports) to get any television exposure until recently.

Undoubtedly television has had a greater impact on sport than any previous medium. In many ways it has totally revolutionised the way in which sport is played, watched and consumed. It has helped to create a stronger link than before between sport as big business, transforming sport into a highly profitable and influential entertainment industry. Television has helped to create and legitimise a new professional world of sport and to sweep aside the last vestiges of amateurism.

It is also important to note that television, or earlier media for that matter, has never been the sole arbiter of sporting agendas and priorities. Research suggests that television follows as much as it leads sporting agendas: during the 1980s volleyball and soccer participation in North America has grown impressively despite negligible television coverage. During this period there was no equivalent growth in North America of the televised sports of gridiron, baseball and basketball.[36] Netball has enjoyed a similar growth, largely unaided by the media, in Australia.

DEBATES ABOUT TELEVISION AND SPORT

The corruption of sport   Many academics have been extremely critical of television as contributing to the corruption of sport, reducing the dignity and honour of sport to mere circus entertainment. They believe that media tycoons, along with the sponsors, are now too influential in setting sporting agendas. Tatz has argued that 'so often the sponsor men and the television men neither know, love, respect nor care about the games they show' and that together they have emasculated the rules of many games and contributed to a decline in the quality of play.[37] Tatz and others fear that sport will decline as a serious, moral and honourable contest. They point, as well, to many abuses which are associated with more television-driven corporate sport. To extend the market and make more profitable national competitions, the interests of long-standing fans have been neglected and established traditions have been overturned. Athletes also have to perform at inconvenient times, and, in the case of marathon runners, at some risk to their health.

While the 'corruption of sport' argument points to abuses in sport in the television era, it is an ahistorical view of the changes wrought to sport by television. It perpetuates a myth that sporting institutions were static and stable before television. This cultural conservative view also posits the existence of some golden age when sport was more pure than it is now, but the existence of any such golden age has yet to be identified. Behind this view is a yearning for the better aspects of the amateur ideal, which was a class-based and limited ideal.

It is also too easy to account for (and to blame) continuing changes in sporting traditions on television and sponsorship while ignoring the complex social reasons for them. Changes in time, work, leisure options, discretionary income and values along with new forms of community all have an impact on sporting traditions. The Americanisation of Australian culture, for instance, has been a powerful force for change in sporting culture. While the media have been the vehicle for the greater Americanisation of Australian sport, they have not been the sole cause of change. Similarly, the popularity of limited overs cricket cannot be explained simply by the influence of television and sponsorship. The immediate reason for this innovation in England in 1963 was the decline in attendances in three-day county games.

But there may be one sense in which sport can be regarded as having been corrupted. Unlike many other institutions of Australia, political, social and economic, sport has been placed on a pedestal above criticism by the general public. While individual players, clubs and institutions attract their share of criticism when they fail to win matches or to live up to the expectations of their followers, there is no broader criticism of the institution of sport itself. Such a climate has been conducive to some forms of corruption.

Violence   The 'technological determinist' view that television causes violence has long been popular. Vamplew has documented the existence of a widespread belief that the media glorify and condone violent sporting play: two-thirds to three-quarters of respondents affirmed this proposition in his study on sport and violence. The same people judged that television sports programs were more guilty of encouraging sports violence (76.4 per cent of respondents) than newspapers (72.2 per cent) and radio sports programs (62.6 per cent). There are some grounds, says Vamplew, for sympathising with the plea of the National Committee on Violence that the 'media avoid the gratuitous replay of violent incidents, refrain from glorification of violence and instead forcefully condemn it, and eschew metaphors of violence in the advertising of sporting events'.[38] And while aggression and even greed do feature prominently in television sporting language—commentators dwell on the 'big hit' or encourage the lust for a swag of medals at one or other Games—this is perhaps merely an aspect of television language generally. Vamplew also notes that many are to 'blame' for violence in sport—selectors, coaches, players and parents. It is all too easy to scapegoat the media for wider social problems.

Quantitative studies such as Vamplew's provide a less emotive and more objective context in which the links between sport, violence and the media can be discussed. Contrary to public and even some academic perceptions, there may well have been a decline rather than an increase in the level of violence in élite sport. Guttmann has argued that as sport has become more organised since the 1850s it has become more civilised and less violent.[39]

The popular belief that there is an increase in the level of sports violence may well occur because television, more than any previous medium, has helped to expose violence and place it more firmly on the sporting agenda. Television has helped to 'rip away the packaging in which the professional sports mystique used to be delivered' in that its close-ups reveal the 'angry scowl and vicious jab ... all starkly revealed' and replayed time and time again.[40] Edited highlights and replays, which focus on the more dramatic (and violent) aspects of play, may also help to create the false impression that violence is on the increase. Television coverage has certainly helped to place the issue of sports violence on the agenda. But the television camera may also help to diminish violence: video evidence at tribunals has been used to punish player violence.

The issue of sports violence in the media is a complex one. Vamplew has argued that the media may assume, incorrectly, that the sports fan enjoys a measure of violence in sports coverage. His research has suggested that the sports fan is far less interested in violence than is the prevailing media wisdom on the subject.[41]

Women's sports   There has been much debate, in the past decade, about media bias and limited coverage of women's sport. There have been a number of studies which have investigated the reasons for the negligible coverage and the steps that might be taken to change this situation.[42]

Women's sports continue to suffer because most were not well enough established at the dawn of television sport. Since then, the gap between the 'rich' and 'poor' sports has markedly widened. Women's sports are bedevilled by a catch-22: without regular television exposure it is more difficult for women's sporting authorities to build up their spectator support base; television authorities, uncertain about the potential drawing-power of women's sport, are unwilling to provide them with media exposure. There is also the problem that almost everyone who produces and constructs television sport—directors, programmers, photographers, commentators—are male and carry with them certain assumptions about what sport is and on the whole feel far more comfortable with male than with female sport.

It is all too easy to blame the media for their continuing limited coverage of women's sports. Unfortunately the media reflect widespread prejudices, long held in society as a whole, against women playing sport. Three long-standing negative images can be identified. A 'dolly-bird' style of reporting, where journalists concentrated on the appearances of female athletes, suggesting that their sporting achievements were trivial, has had a long history. A related feature is that only the more 'feminine' sports, such as diving, gymnastics, tennis and figure skating, which emphasise grace, rhythm and balance, have been promoted in the media.[43] The 'butch' image has been an even greater handicap for those women who dare trespass on any male territory of sport. Women who have taken up the male-dominated team-sports, such as cricket and football, have been categorised as closet males or 'butch' (see ch. 5). Women also have to put up with unfavourable comparisons with men's sport: a popular image is that women's sport is inferior sport. Media personality Don Lane reflected a widespread view when he commented that women's sport lacked the 'magnetism' of men's sport.[44]

The media have played a pivotal role in the rise of organised sport, creating the familiar images of sport and the moral universe in which sports operate. They have helped to popularise sport, extend its influence in Australian society and create virtually a separate moral and cultural world. Sport, the sports pages and sports segments on radio and television are a recognisable and distinct area of Australian life.

There is a curious disjunction between the writing of many academic critics of television sport and the approach of the majority of sports followers. While many academics lament what they see as the decline of sport in the television age, sport is more popular than ever before. While some commentators may believe that the sporting public has opted for 'inferior' sport, this is a partial and limited explanation. Television sport, for all its faults, has opened up many new sporting forms and alternatives, has played a greater educative role than any previous medium, has widened the audience for some sports, and has helped expose some inequities (and violence) in sports. In other words, television has helped to create and sustain a larger and more vibrant sporting culture than before.

There is a critical need for greater understanding and criticism of Australian sport given that the media have helped elevate sport to its current exalted status. Because so many public resources are devoted to sport, there are issues of equity and fairness which need to be raised concerning television sport which has discriminated, and continues to do so, against women's sports and many minor sports.

11
BIG BUSINESS

T he nexus between sport and big business has become readily observable in recent times with the display of company logos on costumes, the sponsorship of teams, cups and competitions, and the renaming of contests, such as the Foster's Melbourne Cup. Many have assumed that this is a new phenomenon, but there have been close links between sport and business for more than a century. To understand this continuing relationship, it is necessary to explore the broader historical context.

The links between sport and business have undergone three major changes in the past two centuries. Sport in Australia became more organised and commercialised from the 1850s, when gate-money sport became more prominent. The profitability of sport from that time attracted the interest of business concerns such as the Melbourne firm of Messrs Spiers & Pond who sponsored the first international cricket tour to Australia in 1861.

The coming of the mass media, and the rise of mass advertising from the 1880s, represented a second phase in that it provided an opportunity for closer links between sport and business. It also coincided with a spectacular expansion in spectator sport. Tobacco and liquor companies, along with providers of sports equipment and costumes such as Dunlop Rubber and Speedo, pursued sports sponsorship with increasing vigour.

The expansion of television sport from the 1970s represents a third stage in this continuing relationship between sport and business in that there have been even greater incentives for big business to become involved in sport. Sporting culture has greatly expanded in the television era, in terms of both media time and audience size. Sport has become a highly marketable commodity and big business has sought even more direct investment in it than before. Bob Stewart has argued that a new form of 'hyper-commercialised' sport emerged from the 1970s when sport evolved from modernity to postmodernity (see below).[1] Responding to this development, individual sports themselves became more corporatised.

Many questions can be raised about the relationship between sport and business. How commercialised was sport in the nineteenth century? Did business and the advertising industry alter the shape of sport? Has television changed, or merely extended, the nexus between sport and big business? Is the relationship between sport and big business beneficial or detrimental?

THE COMMERCIALISATION OF SPORT FROM THE 1850S

Sport in Australia became more organised and commercial from the 1850s. With the promise of larger audiences, grounds were enclosed and spectators charged for admission. Gate-money sport generated income which was used to develop sports facilities and to pay participants and administrators.

It did not take long for commercial interests outside sport to recognise that handsome returns could be made from investment in sport. After the second intercolonial cricket match between New South Wales and Victoria in 1857, there was some newspaper talk about raising funds to bring out an English team, but nothing eventuated. Two Melbourne publicans who became partners in the Café de Paris, Felix W. Spiers and Christopher Pond, recognised the potential return from an English cricket tour. They underwrote the 1861 tour and profited handsomely, earning £11 000.

As the sole sponsors of the tour, Spiers & Pond had a major say in the organisation of the venture. They sent to England their agent W. B. Mallam, who recruited 'the best team he could procure'. Local administrators bent over backwards to accommodate the sponsors by providing grounds free of charge and by enabling the sponsors to take all the gate-money and even enjoy the privilege of sub-letting booths at grounds. No Australian cricket body or cricketer received any profit from this venture. The sponsors were remarkably tight-fisted with their money and even quibbled over paying the Melbourne Cricket Club £175 for restoring their cricket ground despite a prior agreement to reimburse the club for damages incurred.[2] As the tour organisers and sponsors, Spiers & Pond dictated the shape of the tour. The sponsors were the dominant force in 1861 because the various cricket associations were still in their infancy and had limited capital.

Sponsorship was equally welcome in professional rowing. The leading scullers were supported by backers, which freed them from 'time and monetary constraints' and enabled them to improve their technique and physical fitness. The backer paid the sculler an agreed percentage of race earnings.[3] Sponsors also raised the necessary finance to send rowers overseas to compete in world titles, which was a vital service because professional sculling lacked any central organising body to fund these ventures. Little is known about the backers of the leading scullers. A publican, J. Deeble, supported Bill Beach, and pharmacists John and Thomas Spencer sponsored Henry Searle and John McLean.[4]

It would be unwise to exaggerate the degree of commercialism in sport before the 1880s. It was difficult to profit from the huge audiences which lined rivers to watch scullers, though there were a few primitive attempts to get some return. When Hanlan met Laycock at Penrith on 22 May 1884 for the world championship a temporary grandstand was erected at the finishing line to accommodate 6000 people. It was in turn enclosed by what must have been an unsightly 7 foot galvanised iron fence.[5]

Much of the sponsorship in this era was irregular and occasional. Although the 1861 English cricket tour yielded a handsome profit, Spiers and Pond did not invest in further sports sponsorship; rather they travelled to London and opened refreshment rooms. They brought the celebrated actor Charles Kean to Australia in 1863–64. Tours and exchanges were occasional events, and large and profitable crowds occurred inter-mittently. Major sporting events, in professional rowing for instance, were held 'spasmodically, not regularly'.[6] With the possible exception of horse-racing, which became commercialised rather more quickly than other sports, most sports were still run on a shoestring budget by part-time amateur officials.

It is also likely that it was not until the 1880s, when international tours in a number of sports became both regular and profitable, that the commercial potential of mass-spectator sport was recognised. After two English cricket teams visited Australia in 1861 and 1863, there was a gap before the third team arrived in the 1873–74 season. There were no sponsors of the 1878 Australian cricket team to England and various other countries, and the tour was self-funded—the players formed a joint stock company, each contributing £50. Some administrators were sceptical about whether the tour would be financially successful. Its commercial success—each player received a dividend of over £700— came as a surprise to all concerned.

The profitability of the tour raised questions which surfaced regularly in many sports over the next century. Who was to benefit from the profits generated? How much was to go into the pockets of the players, sponsors and administrators and how much was to be spent on the de-velopment of a sport? Who was to control a commercially successful operation?

Questions of money and power created division and dissension in many sports from this era. There was much debate about these issues in the Australian cricket world from 1878 to 1912, by which time the newly formed Australian Board of Control had asserted its authority (see ch. 7). The Australian cricket team, dissatisfied with the terms of-fered, virtually went on strike after the First Test of the 1884–85 home

series and were replaced by a second-string team for the Second Test. Six
of the leading players withdrew from the 1912 tour to England over a
wrangle which centred on the power of the newly created board to dic-
tate tour terms. The formation of the VFL in 1897, when a number of
teams broke away from the VFA, occurred largely because of a disagreement over player payments and the financial arrangement of clubs (see
ch. 3). Similar strains led to the Sydney rugby war of 1907. The debates
over money and power which racked many an amateur-minded sport
did not occur in horse-racing, where there was a franker acceptance
that sport was a business and was run as an industry.

THE MASS MEDIA AND THE ADVERTISING INDUSTRY

Advertising has a long history, but it was not until the late nineteenth
century that it became organised on a mass basis. It was a product of the
mature phase of the Industrial Revolution, when the mass of people
had greater potential consumer power with the gradual rise of real incomes. Advertising also became more profitable with increased literacy.
The emergence of the mass media provided a way by which products
could be promoted to an ever-increasing audience. The depression of the
1890s was an important factor in that the larger manufacturers who
survived tried to monopolise the market by regulating custom by brand-
names, display advertising and the press.[7]

The rise of an advertising industry led to closer links between monopoly capitalists and the mass media, and this altered the financial organisation of the media. Before then the bulk of newspaper revenue came
from actual sales, with classified advertising contributing a smaller
amount. The *Australian* in 1843 received only 40 per cent of its revenue
from advertising, which was mostly classified advertising. The situation
was reversed in the twentieth century: by the 1970s newspapers gained
three-quarters of their revenue from advertising.

Advertising profoundly affected sport. Because sport had become
one of the most popular forms of public discourse, advertisers turned to
it to sell all manner of products, particularly those directed to a male audience: cigarettes, alcohol and sporting goods. Advertisers participated
freely in sporting discourse and, in the process, reinforced the popularity
of sport. At the same time they also extended the sports media by association—suggesting, for instance, that sportsmen smoked and drank. Advertisers also helped to promote particular body types and shapes (see
chs 5 and 10).

Advertisers facilitated a closer relationship than before between sport
and big business. At first business merely attempted to profit from indirect sports association, but sport proved such a profitable means of

selling products that some companies sought a direct link with a sport, such as patronage of a particular event, which added greater recognition and authority to a product. From the 1890s Dunlop Rubber has had a long history of involvement with cycling, tennis and motor sports. Dunlop was a big winner from the cycling boom of the 1890s, gaining a near monopoly of bicycle tyre sales. The company worked hard to preserve its envied position by becoming the single greatest promoter of cycling activities in Australia; it even organised Dunlop Military Dispatch Rides, endorsed by the Department of Defence, between Adelaide and Sydney in 1909 and 1912 to demonstrate the potential role a bicycle might play in the defence of Australia.[8] Dunlop also profited from motorcycle and motor-car racing in the twentieth century and from tennis sponsorship. It employed a promising young tennis-player, Adrian Quist (1913–91) in its sportsgoods division from 1932. Quist, who won the national singles in 1936, 1940 and 1948, became general manager of the sportsgoods division in 1963.

Similarly, the Speedo company profited from the surfing boom in the early decades of the twentieth century. The liberation of the Australian beach also led to the reform of the Australian swimming-costume and the replacement of cumbersome and potentially dangerous attire with briefer and more practical swimwear.[9]

Not a great deal is known about the relationship between sponsors and sports administrators in this era. Undoubtedly the funds of sports were augmented by cigarette and liquor companies and by various firms involved in the provision of sporting goods and facilities. Less clear is the precise nature of the relationship between administrators and sponsors at this time. What was the pay-off for sponsors in return for promotion and sponsorship?

Research on advertising and the rise of commodity culture has suggested that the newfangled advertising industry met with little criticism and operated with few restrictions. There was an easy climate of acceptance, even an infatuation with this new industry, enabling advertisements for all manner of dubious products, such as quack medicines, to go unchecked. Psychologists, who referred to advertising as a science, helped provide legitimacy for the new industry.[10]

Cigarette-smoking, which came into vogue from the 1880s, 'was soon to sweep through Australia'.[11] Cigarettes benefited from advertising because the majority of Australian men smoked in the 1890s—perhaps four or five out of six. By contrast smoking for women met with disapproval. Because machines could produce thousands in a short time, cigarettes were more highly profitable than other forms of tobacco consumption.

The linking of smoking with sport was rarely questioned. Apart from criticism by wowser groups, smoking was generally accepted and came to be regarded as a 'recreation in itself'.[12] It seemed natural that this form of leisure should become an integral part of sport, accepted as it was in the workplace, where the 'smoko' became an institution. Smoking, like sport, was also defined as a manly activity, and this image was reinforced by advertisements which depicted members of the armed forces, especially naval officers, smoking.

Sport had long associations with alcohol and tobacco consumption. John Wisden, who published his first almanac in 1864, set himself up as a tobacconist in London in 1863 and a competitor, John Lillywhite, who published the *Young Cricketer's Guide*, sold tobacco products. It was not surprising that cigarette companies targeted sport to enhance the sale of their products. The link between sport and smoking was endorsed by leading sportspeople, many of whom were smokers, in advertisements.

Sport and smoking were accepted as separate male compartments from the 1880s and this was recognised by the creation of smoking stands at the major sports venues, such as the Sydney and Melbourne Cricket Grounds. A more formal link between cigarette companies and sports bodies did not emerge until the twentieth century when cigarette companies employed sportsmen on their staff, underwrote sporting competitions and even set up sports foundations, such as the Rothmans National Sport Foundation established in 1964.

Sport from this time became an attractive avenue of activity for entrepreneurs such as Sir James Joynton Smith (1858–1943), who became influential in all manner of sports. Born in England, Smith developed diverse interests ranging from founding hospitals, running hotels, starting newspapers—*Smith's Weekly*—controlling racecourses and furthering his boxing interests. He sold the Epping Racecourse to the NSW Rugby Union for £13 000 in 1907—a sale which helped the league indirectly—and drained a Kensington lake to establish the Victoria Park Racecourse. Smith was a lord mayor of Sydney and a New South Wales parliamentarian and was knighted for his services to business and politics in 1920.[13]

Although Smith was not one of the prime movers in the rugby split in 1907, he rescued the infant rugby league code after the financial failure of the first Kangaroo tour of England in 1908 had left the local league organisation in complete disarray. Smith helped the league organise a 'spectacular coup' when he guaranteed the 1909 Wallabies a substantial sum—of the order of £1500 to £1800—to switch to the league. It is likely that Smith, who was a 'flamboyant entrepreneur with a sharp eye for a quid', was motivated mainly by the 'sniff of a potentially successful business deal', rather than by any great feeling for the new code.[14] The *Bulletin*, which was no admirer of rugby league, was critical of Smith's coup, declaring that 'it is reducing football to private enterprise and making it a wild scramble for cash'.[15]

Hugh D. 'Huge Deal' McIntosh (1876–1942) was another influential sporting and theatrical entrepreneur and newspaper proprietor. A self-made man, he became involved in sport through selling pies at racetracks and prize-fights. McIntosh made a huge profit when he staged and refereed the world heavyweight bout between Jack Johnson and

Tommy Burns in a hastily erected open-air stadium at Rushcutter's Bay, Sydney, in 1908 (see ch. 9). McIntosh was an influential figure in Sydney sport and his involvements were varied. He ran a physical culture club at one point and was secretary of the League of Wheelmen in New South Wales from 1903 to 1907. His wife Marion was president of the NSW Ladies' Swimming Association in 1915–16 and before that had helped raise to funds for Fanny Durack and Mina Wylie to attend the Olympic Games in 1912.[16]

The man who headed a syndicate which bought the stadium from McIntosh in 1912 was Reginald Leslie 'Snowy' Baker (1884–1953), who excelled at a number of sports—boxing, swimming, water polo, athletics and rugby union—and won a boxing silver medal in the middleweight division in the 1908 London Olympics. Baker became a sports promoter and a coach. He moved to Hollywood and featured in films, which 'gave him ample opportunity to display his sporting skills in heroic fashion'. He capitalised on his name and physical attributes by opening fitness gyms and devising training programs.[17]

John Wren (1871–1953) was another prominent entrepreneur who had an extensive network of sports promotions and made a huge fortune from his various sporting enterprises. He operated more on the margins of respectable sport, first becoming famous for his illegal totalisator at Collingwood which operated from the 1890s. He later diversified his interests to promoting boxing—he built and owned stadiums—wrestling, motor-racing, pony-racing, trotting and horse-racing. Wren 'moved to distance himself from control of his racecourses' from the 1920s because of 'growing political opposition to him generally and to private racecourse ownership in particular'.[18] He was a controversial figure in Australian sport and was the subject of Frank Hardy's novel *Power Without Glory*.

Although money was far more freely accepted in horse-racing than in most other sports, racing and gambling 'co-existed in an inextricable but uneasy relationship' in the late nineteenth century.[19] Greater regulation of bookmaking, both on and off the course, was a matter of concern to those who ran the racing industry, as well as for the vocal Protestant lobby. Another concern from the 1880s was the proliferation of proprietary racing (pony-racing) companies, which catered more for working-class racing but, in the opinion of its critics, added to corruption in racing. Legislation in New South Wales and Victoria in the first decade of the twentieth century to restrict street betting and pony-racing was only partly successful. On-course totalisators proved more effective (see ch. 7).

COMMERCIALISM AFTER WORLD WAR I

Sport became even more profitable in the 1920s and 1930s, particularly with the greater interest generated by the expanded sports media though radio. Sporting facilities were extended at major grounds such as the

MCG, and larger attendances were recorded than ever before in many of the main spectator sports of the country. Increased money in sport continued to create tensions within sports and between administrators, players and sponsors.

The major sports of cricket, football and horse-racing boomed in the 1920s and the 1930s, and the controlling authorities benefited by the large crowds which attended. But it seemed that the Australian Cricket Board (ACB) was reluctant to allow players to profit much from the huge public interest in cricket, restricting opportunities for players to write for the press unless journalism was their main occupation. The star player of the era, (Sir) Donald Bradman, had a number of disagreements with the ACB. After the 1930 tour he was censured and fined £50 for allowing a version of his life story to be serialised in an English newspaper. Two years later he was again in conflict with the ACB over a three-tiered contract with F. J. Palmers, Radio 2UE and the *Sun* newspaper. It appeared likely for a time that Bradman would not play in further Test matches, but the matter was resolved when the *Sun* released Bradman from his contract. Bradman expressed his dissatisfaction in a letter to the ACB:

> If any player wishes to make a living in a channel which is not acceptable to the Board, he is not allowed to play for his country ... I most emphatically protest against the Board's being allowed to interfere with the permanent occupation of a player. To my mind the Board was never meant to have powers directing the business interests of players.[20]

The tensions created by commercialism in the 1930s—as cricket became a bigger and more profitable business—were a type of prelude for the cricket 'revolution' of the late 1970s.[21] Certainly the ACB at this time tried to keep a very tight rein on the finances of the game and were cautious of any elements of commercialism and professionalism. It is likely that the strength of amateurism in this era helped to maintain such a stance, as well as the reluctance of players to challenge the status quo.

This was equally the case in the VFL, which enjoyed continuing and spectacular expansion, with larger crowds and profits, from the 1920s to the 1960s except for the years of depression and war. Few footballers questioned the system as did ex-Fitzroy player Bert Clay, who expressed the view in 1952 that footballers were grossly underpaid. Clay stated that 'the League footballer is the worst paid fellow I know. We are top class entertainers. Why not top class money?'[22]

The continuing commercial tensions within the horse-racing industry in the twentieth century were of a different character. The problem of pony-racing was solved in New South Wales by a dramatic restructuring of racing by the McKell government in 1941 (see ch. 7). The issue of illegal off-course betting, which had expanded in the first half of the twentieth century, was resolved when TABs were created (see below and ch. 7).

While cricket authorities were able to contain the strains within the sport generated by commercialism—at least for a few decades—the sport of lawn tennis was split by the 'open tennis' debate from the mid-1950s to the mid-1970s. When it appeared that Frank Sedgman and Ken McGregor would defect to the American-run professional ranks, strenuous efforts were made to retain their services as amateurs: they were offered not only good employment prospects but even a chain of service stations. The situation was a particularly difficult one for the amateur-minded officials who ran the sport because it marked the beginning of the exodus of stars from the amateur ranks, with their 'whiz kid' replacements, Lew Hoad and Ken Rosewall, turning professional a few years later. Australia enjoyed a golden era of tennis success from 1946 to 1968 when it competed in the Challenge Round of the Davis Cup twenty-three times, winning on fifteen occasions. It was this very success which made the leading Australian stars more attractive to a succession of American promoters such as Jack Kramer and Lamar Hunt. The public debate was a heated one because it appeared to represent a stark choice between an American commercial conception of sport and a more nationalistic and British-inherited amateur view.

The evidence suggests that amateur-minded officials found it difficult to adjust to this new era of commercialism and professionalism. Some procrastinated and tried to avoid 'unpalatable alternatives', all of which only extended the duration of the crisis. But there may have been some method in their madness. Although the media loved to depict tennis officials as old fogies, long-standing administrators must have recognised that the introduction of American money and influence would lead to a decline in their influence, with many important tennis decisions being made outside Australia (see also ch. 9).[23]

While there was some criticism of Australian amateurs who turned professional, there was a partial acceptance of this move. Since they played for money, they were defined as 'lowly mercenaries' rather than as 'gentlemen' amateurs. However, as long as 'they did not encroach on or interfere with the amateur structure' there were few vehement attacks on them.[24] Perhaps the Australian tennis public and media, if not the officials, were moving towards a qualified acceptance of commercialism and professionalism in sport.

'HYPER-COMMERCIALISATION' FROM THE 1970S

New relationships were forged between sport and big business in the era in which television sport boomed from the 1970s. Money, business, the media, technology and the law were all factors which completely changed the form and character of organised sport. Bob Stewart has coined the term 'hyper-commercialisation' to describe the fundamental changes in leisure and recreation which occurred as the result of broader changes in economic structures which developed in advanced capitalist societies by the early 1970s.[25] While some have viewed this hyper-commercialisation as the work of television, Stewart believed that it was a reflection of changed and wider commercial and cultural practices:

this shift not only involved business organisations changing their work methods and employment practices, and customers changing their patterns of buying and consumption, but also artists, intellectuals and ordinary people more deeply embracing the consumerist ideology of capitalist society. These changing commercial and cultural practices constituted both a new way of viewing the world and a change in the structure of capitalism itself.[26]

Hyper-commercialisation reflected the change from a modern to a post-modern state. While the modern state emphasised values such as orderly process, rationality, achievement and efficiency, postmodernity stood rather more for the ephemeral, for instantaneity, volatility and image production. Ian Harriss has a similar explanation for the popularity of limited overs cricket:

> whereas cricket under modernism was characterised by rationalism, depth, order and constraint, cricket under the influence of post modernism had become geared to surface, spectacle and excess. Cricket was no longer ap-proached as a highly elaborate range of possible risk aversion strategies, but was instead an explosive, decentred, glossy spectacle, packaged ready for immediate consumption by both 'at ground' spectator and television viewer.[27]

While there is some criticism of this perspective (see below, World Series Cricket), both Stewart and Harriss rightly point out that change in sport-ing culture was not simply a product of altered media but was related to wider shifts in economic structures and cultural practice.

Stewart explained how hyper-commercialisation radically altered the structure of the VFL (now the AFL). The organisation of the game was fairly stable in the 1960s when the bulk of VFL club finances was derived from gate-receipts and memberships, which accounted for as much as 90 per cent of the income of a club. There was no corporate sponsorship or income from merchandising and minimal income from television rights. Players received a relatively small wage per game: the 1960 payment of $12 per match amounted to approximately a quarter of average male weekly earnings. With clubs largely dependent on the financial backing of their supporters, a strong and even primary link existed between the club and fans.

From the 1970s income from non-football sources began to increase. Money from sponsorship, merchandising and social club licensing rose from a negligible amount, less than 10 per cent in some clubs in 1960, to a third or a half of club income by 1980.[28] There was in the mid-1970s the beginning of large-scale corporate sponsorship, with Phillip Morris (Marlboro) sponsoring the finals series from 1976. With the ar-rival of colour television increasing sums were paid for television rights.

It was not until the 1980s that the nexus between football and busi-ness reached its peak when the VFL and the clubs regarded a close rela-tionship with the corporate world as desirable. Corporate logos became prominent and leading businessmen attached themselves to VFL football clubs. The VFL itself became a large-scale business enterprise. With larger audiences generated by television, player payments rose in advance of inflation from the 1970s. With the amount of money in the sport players were able to become professionals and a handful of them earned a good living from the game.[29]

An even more dramatic shift took place in the structure of the NSW Rugby League, which was made corporate in 1983. A more streamlined administration emerged in response to a crisis in the code which surfaced after the broadcasting of the 'Four Corners' program 'Big League', which alleged that there was widespread corruption in the sport. The president of the NSW Rugby League, Kevin Humphreys, resigned shortly afterwards. The new administration recognised that rugby league had of necessity to improve its structure and marketing if it wished to compete in a more highly competitive sporting world. Some of the reforms included the separation of the positions of president and executive director; the appointment of a general manager to run the code; the hiring of a management firm, W. D. Scott & Co., to restructure the administration; the incorporation of the NSW Rugby League; and the creation of a smaller and more efficient board of directors.[30]

Issues and debates

The closer relationship between big business and sport along with the media from the 1970s is a complex issue. A central question is whether big business is too dominant in sport and dictating too many sporting agendas. Another, which has been asked frequently, is whether 'corporate' sport has altered sporting culture for the worse.

World Series Cricket Issues relating to the World Series Cricket crisis of 1977–79 have been much debated because it seemed one of the starkest examples of the takeover of a sport by a media tycoon. Many believed that Packer's intervention forever altered the shape and priorities of a sport, that it led to a dramatic change in the way cricket was played, watched and covered by the media.

With its huge television audiences by the mid-1970s, it seemed that the game was ripe for takeover. Unable to secure exclusive television rights from the Australian Cricket Board, Packer signed up most of the leading international players and created his own cricket competition. Although the ACB battled on for two years, it had no choice but to make a truce with Packer in May 1979. Many historians believed that the ACB meekly caved in to Packer when it gave him exclusive television and marketing rights.[31]

There was scarcely a good word for Packer cricket in the media. Journalists, academics and former players were outraged by Packer's actions, which they believed were destroying the fabric of a traditional game. WSC was variously referred to as 'circus' and 'pyjama' cricket, suggesting that it trivialised the game. The Packer takeover was also referred to as a 'hijack', underlining its alleged illegitimacy. By contrast the cricket organised by the ACB was referred to as 'Establishment' cricket, suggesting it was the real thing. Unlike Packer, the ACB drew very little criticism as it was not seen as part of the 'problem'.

In spite of all this media outrage against WSC, bumper crowds turned up, particularly for limited overs night matches. When the lights were turned on for the first time at the Sydney Cricket Ground on 28 November 1978 the ground was bursting at the seams with a crowd of over 50 000. It is now clear that WSC 'won the hearts of Australians' in its second (1978–79) season.[32] By the time a truce was worked out between the warring parties, in May 1979, Packer cricket had established itself as a viable alternative which threatened the future of the established game.

In the decade and a half since then there have been a number of revisionist interpretations of what took place in 1977–79. The focus of many historians has widened. Most now agree that WSC was a product of broader media, economic and cultural change, and that Packer was the effect rather than the cause of change in cricket.

One view was that the Packer intrusion into cricket was a striking example of the 'corporate pitch': commercial cricket telecasts helped to 'socialise viewers to accept the values of capitalism'. Lawrence and Rowe argued that the public were the 'losers' since they were 'exposed to an increasingly aggressive spectacle, manipulated by commercial television for the benefit of advertisers'.[33] Cricket had been seduced by commercialism and capitalism.

Ian Harriss took this perspective further when he argued that WSC had reduced cricket to a form of soap-opera entertainment. Packer cricket offered 'the consumer the instant gratification which is so much a part of the consumer culture of late capitalism'. Harriss explained the shift to limited overs cricket as

> the emergence of an era in which the game is no longer based on the rational, calculating bourgeois individual. Indeed, the essence or 'depth' of Test cricket has given way to the glittering surface and spectacle of the highly commercialised commodity that is One-Day Cricket ... The one-day spectacle is packaged in much the same way as a one-hour television melodrama. There is some variation in each individual episode, but the conclusion is inevitably a hectic chase sequence.[34]

Brian Stoddart has challenged this view, offering the striking conclusion that 'far from degrading cricket, Packer gave it new dimensions by challenging outmoded visions of the game's social position'. Stoddart thinks that Packer needed the game 'to establish his channel as the leading sportscaster' in the country, to meet his 'legislatively required Australian content levels at an economically viable level' and to attract more high-level sponsorship. The game, however, also needed the media tycoon to 'deliver it a new audience share, boost its fragile economic base, and stimulate a new social popularity'.[35] The Packer 'revolution' in cricket occurred in part because the ACB was unable to deal adequately with structural changes in the world of cricket in the television age of the 1970s. The payment for élite players was inadequate. There was no recognition of the commercial potential of the limited overs game despite the fact that 46 000 turned up to a hastily organised match in Melbourne when the 1970–71 Melbourne Test was abandoned after the third day.

Packer cricket represented a remarkable shift in the culture of Australian cricket. The WSC upheaval helped strip away many of the Anglicist, clubby, gentlemanly vestiges of the game. The rule of the market-place dictated that cricket would become more Australian (and less Anglo-Australian) and more plebeian than before. So while Packer cricket was certainly market-driven, it did provide the game with a new dimension and even a new vision. For better or worse, Packer cricket has remade the culture of cricket into one more appropriate for a republican and multicultural Australia. The popular WSC anthem 'C'mon Aussie, c'mon', which became a hit in its own right, was symptomatic of the changed culture of cricket, which now took pop music and the youth culture on board.

Although Packer cricket reflected some degree of Americanisation or globalisation of Australian cricket, it became more unashamedly working-class and even chauvinistically Australian. While the ABC commentators continued to be fair and objective in their commentary, encouraging their audience to respect the best traditions of the game, to lose and win with dignity and to respect Australia's opponents, some Channel 9 and commercial radio commentators were far more excitable and stridently Australian and spoke with broader Australian accents. Packer cricket has indirectly spawned a range of tabloid radio journalists who broadcast cricket in the style of football commentary.

It may well be that in time Packer is seen as the catalyst rather than the cause of change in the structure of Australian and international cricket in the 1970s. As one writer put it,

> Once the bell cover over the era as a sporting incident is removed, and the event is examined in its historical and contemporary cultural context, it is clear that the era [of WSC] was one of progression rather than a radical revolution with television the vehicle for change rather than its cause. Put simply, WSC was a product of its times.[36]

Corporate football Goldlust, writing in 1987, lamented that corporate sport 'in which television operates as the principle entrepreneurial force seems poised to swallow up VFL football'. He argued that plans for expansion were engineered by an alliance of small groups, administrators, corporate sponsors and television networks who failed to consult, or take notice of the interests of, hundreds of thousands of the 'grass roots football supporters' of Melbourne.[37] Others, such as Sandercock and Turner, have viewed the greater commercialisation of Australian football as detrimental and a move away from the 'people's game'.[38]

Undoubtedly there is some truth in this perspective. The move of South Melbourne to Sydney was bitterly opposed by many members of the club, and the proposal to merge Fitzroy and Footscray created such a public outcry that it was shelved (see ch. 6). The NSW Rugby League showed little sympathy for one of its founding clubs, Newtown, which was axed from the competition in 1983, while another battling club, Western Suburbs, only survived through court action.

While it is true that there has been a massive change in sporting traditions, boundaries and allegiance in the television era, a continuing factor in the rise of organised sport from the 1850s has been the search for new markets and audiences. The first football clubs tapped into and enhanced a newly created tribalism of inner-city suburban communities. With the subsequent spread of cities, some of the inner-city rugby league teams were scrapped—Glebe and Annandale did not survive beyond the 1920s—and were replaced in time by outer suburban teams such as Canterbury-Bankstown (1934), Parramatta (1936), Penrith (1967) and Cronulla (1967).

Television has simply extended this search for new markets and larger audiences in that it has touched powerful community feelings in cities, regions and States. The move to more national competitions has proved successful in that the sense of interstate, intercity and regional rivalry is just as strong, if not stronger, than any rivalry between one suburban community and another. There are grounds for arguing that powerful suburban rivalries are no longer the force they once were (see ch. 6).

Many academic critics, such as Sandercock and Turner, yearn for a world that has passed, when administrators appeared more in touch with local supporters and where there was a strong link between a local suburban community and its players. This is an unrealistic and romantic view of sport and society. Communities are not static entities: the closely knit suburban communities where people lived, worked and played in the one suburban dormitory no longer exist. Australian society is now more mobile and individuals now participate in a number of work, residential and leisure communities. The newly created national competitions would not work as well as they do if they did not tap into some potential or existing communities (see ch. 6). Most sports now have national competitions in baseball, basketball, hockey, soccer and volleyball.

Totalisator Agency Boards (TABs)

Although the TAB was recommended as the solution to the problem of illegal off-course betting by a Royal Commission in South Australia in 1932, it was not until the 1960s that TABs were introduced throughout the country. They were set up primarily to enable the State to collect more gambling revenue, which was being lost to a multi-million pound

SP industry. The continuing success and expansion of the TABs demonstrate that in one area of sport and big business there has been a mutually beneficial and uncontroversial marriage between the interests of government, big business and the average punter.

The shape of the TAB in New South Wales was influenced by the findings of the Kinsella Royal Commission that legalised off-course betting should be made as unglamorous as possible. The initial TAB establishments in New South Wales were bare and even sterile, without seats, radio broadcasts and advertising. TABs were not located near churches, schools and licensed premises.[39]

Despite these restrictions, the public response to the TAB exceeded expectations and continued to grow spectacularly. From the start this legal alternative to SP bookmaking attracted many new punters. The TAB was a highly successful operation and governments underestimated the extent of revenue gained through it. While the South Australian government gained more than $3 million from its TAB in 1972–73, the New South Wales TAB contributed $37 806 870 to State revenue just two years later.[40]

While SP bookmaking continued to flourish, it is likely that the TAB attracted some of its clients who preferred a legal off-course alternative. There is evidence that the TAB attracted many new punters, particularly women, who found it convenient to patronise the TAB during the week while shopping. The use of computer technology in 1970s greatly expanded the operations of the TAB, providing increasing punting alternatives. John O'Hara has suggested that the arrival of the TAB, and its consolidation as a fixture of any suburban shopping centre, was 'a victory for the working-class bettor—the person who was less able or could least afford to attend race meetings'.[41]

PLAYER ASSOCIATIONS

One of the interesting sidelights of the growth of more professional sport in Australia from the 1970s has been the emergence of player associations in the major spectator sports which have attempted to express their views on remuneration, playing conditions and transfer arrangements. In a sense players' associations have been formed to counter the superior power of sports administrators. Within rugby league and the AFL they have been influential: collective action has modified the operations of the player draft.

Not all these player associations have succeeded. The main concern of the organisers of the six soccer associations from the late 1950s to the mid-1970s was their 'inferior position' under the retain and transfer system. Braham Dabscheck has suggested that they failed because the players involved participated in soccer part-time and were not able to generate enough income to employ full-time officials, as was the case with the British Professional Footballers' Association. As a result their stand was easily countered by their respective federations and clubs.[42]

Another association which failed to last was the Professional Cricketers Association of Australia, which was formed and registered in 1977. Although its office-holders were WSC players—Ian and Greg Chappell, Ross Edwards, Rod Marsh, David Hookes and Mick Malone—it did not want to confine its membership to Packer players and encouraged ACB players to join. Despite an initial burst of recruitment enthusiasm, the association was a spent force by 1982. Dabscheck believes that it failed to survive for three reasons: it did not attract sufficient numbers, particularly of Test non-Packer players; it failed to develop a bargaining position with the ACB; and it was difficult for an organisation with a small and scattered membership to organise effectively.

However, the demise of the players' association may also have occurred because it achieved some of its objectives. It helped to usher in two important changes in the structure of Australian cricket. The Cricket Sub-Committee—initially formed to ward off the impact of players' associations—proved an important body which liaised between administrators and players. The second change was to secure economic rewards for the top Australian cricketers through contracts, retainers and guaranteed minimum income, performance-related bonuses and provident fund payments.[43]

SPORTING VALUES IN A PROFESSIONAL AGE

The death of amateurism by the 1970s and 1980s left a void in sporting values and ethics. Amateurism, for better or worse, had provided a set of values and an ideology which defined the purpose of sport as something which should be enjoyed, and specific values of respecting one's opponent, winning and losing with dignity, playing within the rules and spirit of a game.

The task of developing appropriate sporting values for a more pragmatic, sceptical and litigious society will be more difficult. There is less respect now for the educators, clergymen, doctors, politicians and media personnel than there used to be—for those who articulated the amateur code and added their political weight behind its ethics. It is highly unlikely that there will be any equivalent wide-ranging ideal in the future.

One immediate result is that the law has been called upon to play an increasing role in defining acceptable and ethical behaviour in sport. This will mean disciplinary action for those who transgress the rules, settling disputes between players and administrators and other parties, dealing with all manner of sports violence, delineating the rights of players, clubs and administrators, and establishing conventions for a new sporting order. In the absence of any consensus about sporting ethics and behaviour, sports law has become a growth industry.

There have been attempts within individual sports to develop codes of conduct for players, coaches, clubs, parents and various other people involved in games. However, there remains a need for much further debate in the interests of reaching a broader consensus. There are a number of ways in which this can be achieved. Rather than a set of values, or codes of conduct, being handed down by administrators it would be preferable for administrators to consult with players, coaches and all those involved in sport itself to arrive at consensus. This approach has already proved successful in some sports. When a Professional Cricketers Association was formed in 1977 the ACB appointed a co-ordinator to liaise between itself and the players. Bob Merriman, an industrial relations specialist and a cricket administrator, was chosen for this role. Merriman, who was 'very keen to do the right thing by both parties', as Dennis Lillee put it, helped to provide effective liaison between the board and its players.[44]

Defining ethics and values for non-élite players, for that army of people who participate in school, junior and recreational sport, is a more difficult task but one that should not be ignored. Since juniors often imitate sporting practice at the élite level, the onus is on administrators to define appropriate goals. This is a critical area since schools and State education departments have increasingly opted out of school sport. The attempts to develop modified sport for children is a step in the right direction. The rugby league-modified games of mini footy and mod league recognised the special needs of children by developing a form of football with less body contact, greater co-operation and more enjoyment. A principle aim of kanga cricket was 'to provide the means and incentive to schools, with the minimum amount of organisation and material, and a maximum amount of fun' in a less competitive environment.[45] All young cricketers have an equal chance to perform with the bat and ball, as the game is organised on the principle that each player bat and bowl for an equal amount of time.

There is also a role for many people who write and speak critically on sport, including academics, administrators, journalists, educators and politicians and even those in the area of sports law. They should consciously help to define sporting values. A number of federal politicians have already had an important part in investigating issues of equity, fairness and discrimination in sport and in forming appropriate policy. Even though there is far less organised school sport, it is desirable that there should be some classroom discussion of the philosophy of sport and play—whether it is taught in politics, history or even life skills.

Business was present at the birth of organised sport in Australia. However, until Australian sport became hyper-commercialised, big business played a subsidiary role in most sports. This changed dramatically in the 1970s as Australia jettisoned its English model of sport for a more commercial one and the long-standing Australian prejudice against the professional and money in sport disappeared.

The new era of hyper-commercialisation has raised many issues about the purpose of sport and sporting ethics which are still being debated. Many commentators believe that the nexus between sport and big business has been detrimental. Sport is being 'constantly modified to suit its modern masters', serving the interests of corporate sponsorship and the advertising schedules of television networks.[46] Others lament the superficiality and commodification of sport in the postmodern era.

While there is a need for continuing criticism of the role of big business in a rapidly changing sporting order, it is futile to yearn for some past era when sport was less commercial and somehow more 'pure'. For better or worse, sport has become part of work and the mass-entertainment industry. Sport has transformed itself into business—indeed, a very big business. Any worthwhile critique of Australian sporting culture has to start from this reality.

This is far from suggesting that big business should monopolise sporting culture at the expense of players, spectators, administrators and government. There are issues other than money which should shape sporting priorities, such as health, equity and even tradition. Respect for existing sporting culture and for those with a long-standing interest in Australian sport may even generate larger profits.

12
AUSTRALIA: A PARADISE OF SPORT?

While Australia has inherited or borrowed much of its sporting culture, this culture has been transformed to such an extent as to have become distinctively Australian. Our culture of sport—the character of play, the behaviour of players and spectators, language, architecture and club identity—has become recognisably Australian, and its importance is generally agreed: most Australians would be surprised by any suggestion that sport was not a cornerstone of Australian life.

There are a number of historical reasons why Australia became a distinctive sporting paradise and why sport came to occupy such an important part of the Australian social, cultural and physical landscape from the 1850s. Sport was prominent at a formative stage in Australia's cultural formation. The character of Australian society was deeply influenced by the games cult from the 1870s, variously referred to as the 'Games Revolution', the 'Scramble for Sport' and the 'Great Sports Craze'. Strategically located and accessible land in new cities and country towns was dedicated to sport. The creation of cathedrals of sport in central locations reinforced the lofty status of sport. Abundant waterways and attractive beaches close to many of the major cities encouraged the development of outdoor sport.

Economic and political factors also contributed to the elevation of sport. Australia's prosperity after the gold rush provided the resources for an elaborate culture of sport: impressive stadiums, ovals, racecourses, pool-rooms, gymnasiums, swimming-pools and golf links were constructed. With the prosperity of a large section of the working class, the extension of the franchise and the strength of the union movement, working-class Australians were well placed to indulge their passion for sport.

A culture of sport also appealed to Australians for social and cultural reasons: the dearth of other forms of social cement which could bind new communities such as work and educational groups, neighbourhoods, suburbs and country towns. Australia had had no great war, no hostile neighbour or past tradition which could be used to unify the population. Communities were divided by religion (Protestant versus Catholic), ethnicity (English, Irish and others) and class. Sport provided a convenient and common cause which could be used to unite people.

Australia has also become a paradise of sport because it was male-dominated and sport was used to extend male hegemony. Implicit in much research on this subject is that Australia may have been more male-dominated, and more sporting, than was the case in equivalent societies. While it is difficult to establish this in any objective sense, the sexual imbalance in convict and frontier societies provides historical grounds supporting this view.

If Australia was a paradise of sport, it was more so for some Australians: for men more than women, and Anglo-Celtic Australians more than other immigrants and Aborigines. A sizeable number of women (and some men) have resented the dominant role of Australia's sporting culture.

While it is immensely difficult to compare sport (and the passion for sport) from one society to another, there are grounds for suggesting that the role of sport in Australian society may be so distinctive as to be unique.[1] Sport, for instance, occupies a more central place in the physical environment of Australian cities than in Britain. The cathedrals of sport in Melbourne—the Melbourne Cricket Ground, Flemington Racecourse and the Tennis Centre—are far grander and more imposing than sporting facilities in an old-world city such as London. Lord's, The Oval and Wembley are located more on the periphery of London.

The extent to which many intellectuals have resented it provides further evidence of the dominance of sport in Australia. Novelist Thomas Keneally remarked on a difference between Australian intellectuals and those of Britain and North America: many Australian intellectuals have a 'cultural twitch' about sport and so have failed to investigate some important institutions of Australian culture. Britain has had a succession of writers such as Neville Cardus and John Arlott who have moved easily from sports journalism to poetry, music and theatre criticism. America has had a long tradition of novelists such as Hemingway, Bellow, Mailer and others who have used sport as a vehicle for analysing American society. 'The sad thing', Keneally wrote, was that 'the Australian arts community in general—unlike the American one—has tended to resent and reject sport, to write little about it, and to exclude it from its imagery'.[2] The novelist Patrick White claimed that it 'seems as though life itself now depends on sport'. A few years later White elaborated his deep resentment of the role of sport in Australian culture:

> today, the sight of thugs writhing in the mud and bashing the hell out of one another in the name of sport has perhaps become part of our national 'colt-cher' ... A great number of Australians always seem to be running to or from

somewhere—city-to-surf in my native city—capital to capital ... This passion for perpetual motion: is it perhaps for fear that we may have to sit down and face reality if we don't keep going?[3]

Historian Beverley Kingston has argued that the rise of organised sport made Australia a more conservative, philistine and sexually segregated society:

> Organized sport clearly fostered Australian conformity and discouraged intellectual effort. Imperial ties were probably strengthened at the expense of national self-confidence. Republicanism was dealt a mortal blow ... Organized sport provided incentives and outlets for a handful of creative entrepreneurs. It also soaked up economic and emotional resources which might have produced different outcomes if directed elsewhere. Consider simply the money, skill, and imagination that was poured into innumerable and sometimes amazingly innovative forms of gambling. But the saddest effect of the pursuit of organized sport in the late nineteenth century appears in the way sport mirrored work by becoming sexually segregated. A problem already marked—the uneasiness and lack of communication between the sexes—was exacerbated by the segregation of leisure.[4]

Kingston has tried to counter what she regarded as the prevailing tendency of Australian historians to place an 'optimistic interpretation' on the growth of sport which stresses 'egalitarianism, national maturity, cohesiveness, pride'.[5]

Stoddart has endorsed some elements of this view, arguing that 'sport is amongst the most conservative of Australian social institutions' and '[Australian] sport quickly became deeply conservative in outlook'.[6] Stoddart is referring here to the fact that many who have promoted sporting institutions and defined sporting ideologies—administrators, politicians, doctors, educationists, clerics—did so for conservative reasons. It is important to note that when Stoddart refers to 'sport' it is a shorthand way of referring to the ideology attached to sporting culture.

Like health, however, sport is in itself neither conservative nor radical and can even be used by minority and oppositional groups to advance alternative perspectives. Sport was used at times by Irish-Australians to attack the values of the Anglican Establishment. Incoming migrants have also used sport to create a niche within an alien and at times hostile environment and to maintain their culture. Although sport has oppressed women on the whole, some women have used sport to challenge restricting gender boundaries. The militant Protestant lobby group active at the turn of the century suffered a succession of defeats as gambling became an accepted part of sporting culture. While middle-class notions have been prominent in many Australian sports, they have been modified and even changed by more working-class agendas. Ian Turner implied that 'the people' had a role in shaping the character of Australian football.[7]

For better or worse, sport has become central to Australian life and the business of being Australian. Sporting culture is accessible and pro-

vides continuing satisfaction for many Australians. It is immensely popular and also addresses some of the central issues of Australian life. For
as Keneally has written, sport mimics life and is a 'paradigm for war, the
family, real estate, politics', adding that 'the arts and sport are akin in
many aspects—in both, talent expresses itself through instinct rather
than through rational thought. Both of them, at their best, possess an
unconscious yet divine grace'.[8] Sport is the regular theatre for ordinary
Australians or as historian Manning Clark put it, when referring to Australian football, it is the ballet for the ordinary person.

Nothing is likely to be achieved by disapproval of sport or by defining the Australian passion for all things sporting as an 'obsession'.[9] The
word implies that this passion is somehow unworthy or politically incorrect and that it is better channelled into art, politics, religion or intellectual effort. Such a judgement is élitist and undemocratic. To label
sporting passion as obsession is to attach a pejorative label which denies
many Australians the satisfaction they derive from sport.

There is an urgent need for Australian intellectuals to take off the
gloves and criticise and scrutinise our sporting culture. Because many intellectuals have chosen to resent and ignore sport, it has been an area of
life above criticism. While politicians, business and many other leaders
have been criticised, sport has been elevated and romanticised. Teams,
coaches, individual players have been chastised but not sport itself. The
task at hand is to modify this paradise, making it more accessible, equit-
able and fair for all Australians who wish to participate in it, and less
corrupt, racist and sexist. There is also an urgent need to reflect on the
desirable future for the Australian paradise of sport in an ever-changing
world.

NOTES

Note: Titles of books and journal articles are given in short form only; full titles will be found in the bibliography. *OCAS* references are to the entry, not the author of an entry.

PREFACE

1 See, for instance, Dunstan, *Sports*.
2 See bibliography: Lemon, *History of Australian Thoroughbred Racing*; Stremski, *Kill for Collingwood*; Tatz and Stoddart, *The Royal Sydney Golf Club*; Painter and Waterhouse, *The Principal Club*; Cashman and Weaver, *Wicket Women*; O'Hara, *A Mug's Game*; Tatz, *Aborigines in Sport*; Goldlust, *Playing for Keeps*; Stell, *Half the Race*; Fotheringham, *Sport in Australian Drama*; Howell and Howell, *The Genesis of Sport in Queensland*.
3 Nankervis, *Boys and Balls*, p. 21.
4 Gruneau, *Class, Sport and Social Development*.
5 Stoddart, *Saturday Afternoon Fever*, p. 8.
6 Drawing on the tradition of Rigauer, *Sport and Work*.

1 THE BRITISH INHERITANCE

1 See Brailsford, *British Sport*. Brailsford is critical of those sports historians who deny any meaningful connection between ancient contests and modern sporting competition (p. 2). The continuity of sporting culture from earlier to more recent times is also a theme of Birley, *Sport and the Making of Britain*.
2 Terms coined by W. F. Mandle at the first ASSH Conference in 1977 and John Lowerson, *Sport and the English Middle Classes*.
3 Brailsford, 'Geography of Eighteenth Century English Spectator Sports'.
4 Brookes, *English Cricket*, p. 38.
5 Bale, 'Rustic and Rational Landscapes', p. 5.
6 O'Hara, *A Mug's Game*, p. 4.
7 Nauright, 'Reclaiming Old and Forgotten Heroes', p. 138.
8 Brailsford, *Bareknuckles*.
9 Brailsford, 'Geography of Eighteenth Century English Spectator Sports', p. 42.

10 McKendrick et al., *The Birth of a Consumer Society*
11 Cunningham, *Leisure*, p. 12.
12 Walvin, *Leisure in Society*.
13 Buckley, *Fresh Light on 18th Century Cricket*, p. 21.
14 Lowerson, in Tony Mason, ed., *Sport in Britain*, p. 189.
15 Bale, *Sport and Place*, p. 70.
16 Arlott, *From Hambleton to Lord's*, p. 10.
17 See Vamplew, *Pay Up and Play the Game*.
18 Bowen, *Cricket*, p. 54.
19 Harris, *Sport in Britain*, pp. 79–80.
20 See Itzkowitz, *Peculiar Privilege*.
21 Holt, *Sport and the British*, p. 8.
22 Shirley H. S. Reekie has concluded that only a minority of women from any class took part in sport. See McCrone, *Playing the Game*.
23 Flint and Rheinberg, *Fair Play*, p. 16.
24 Holt, *Sport and the British*, pp. 89–90.
25 Delves, 'Popular Recreation and Social Conflict in Derby 1800–1850', p. 89.
26 Harris, *Sport in Britain*, p. 106.
27 See Malcolmson, *Popular Recreations*; Thomas, *Man and the Natural World*.
28 Clark, *The English Alehouse*, p. 199.
29 Brailsford, 'Sporting Days in Eighteenth Century England', p. 52.

2 AN UNLIKELY PARADISE

1 This objective has been challenged by theories like that of Robert J. King, who proposes that the real reason for the British establishing a settlement in the southern continent was the need for a base from which to challenge Spanish colonial supremacy in the Pacific. See *The Secret History of the Convict Colony: Alexandro Malaspina's report on the British Settlement of New South Wales*, Allen & Unwin, Sydney, 1990.
2 Cumes, *Their Chastity was not too Rigid*, p. 15.
3 O'Hara, *A Mug's Game*, p. 4.
4 Barry Collett, *Wednesdays Closest to the Full Moon: A History of South Gippsland*, Melbourne University Press, Melbourne, 1994, p. 21.
5 See Salter, Games and Pastimes of the Australian Aboriginal.
6 Jim Poulter, Marn Grook. Blainey (*A Game of Our Own*, pp. 95–6) concluded that it is unlikely that any Aboriginal football game influenced the evolution of Australian football.
7 Robertson, 'Sport and Play in Aboriginal Culture—Then and Now', pp. 1–16.
8 Howell, Howell and Edwards, 'Wrestling Among the Australian Aborigines'.
9 See Nicholas et al., *Convict Workers*.
10 Dunning, 'Convict Leisure and Recreation', pp. 12–13.
11 Raszeja, *Decent and Proper Exertion*, p. 30.
12 *ADB*, vol. 2; Lemon, *History of Australian Thoroughbred Racing*, vol. 1, pp. 95–6.
13 Mason, 'Football on the Maidan', pp. 142–3.
14 Allen, *Plain Tales from the Raj*, p. 156.
15 O'Hara, *A Mug's Game*.

16 See Daly, *Elysian Fields*.

17 See Scott, *Early Cricket in Sydney*.

18 *Australian*, 30 April 1827.

19 See Hickie, *They Ran with the Ball*.

20 Blainey, *A Game of Our Own*, pp. 29–30.

21 Ibid., pp. 152–3.

22 This figure excluded the military and their families.

23 *ADB*, vol. 1.

24 de Serville, *Port Phillip Gentlemen*, p. 58.

25 Adair, 'A Social History of Public Houses', p. 101.

26 Scott (*Early Cricket in Sydney*, p. 32) has provided a long list of innkeeper-cricketers: John Beeson, Arthur Devlin, Richard Driver, Edward Flood, Joseph Flood, Henry F. 'Toby' Green, James Hamilton, David Hill, William Hill, George Morris, John Rowley and Richard Tress.

27 There is reference to a Cumberland Hunt Club in 1812.

28 Australian Aquatic Racing Club (1830), Regatta Club (1839), Royal Yacht Club (1840), Hunt Club (1830s).

29 de Serville, *Port Phillip Gentlemen*, p. 58.

30 See Lemon, *History of Australian Thoroughbred Racing*, vol. 1.

31 Daly, *Elysian Fields*, p. 36.

32 Ibid.

33 The terms derived from the two forms of currency which operated in New South Wales at the time. 'Currency' referred to bills or notes which were issued by private individuals and which were sometimes convertible into British currency, sterling.

34 Scott, *Early Cricket in Sydney*, p. 47.

35 Riess, *City Games*, p. 16.

36 Lemon (*Australian Thoroughbred Racing*, vol. 1, p. 188) notes, however, that the boundary between gentleman and trader was more often in the imagination than in cold fact.

37 Quoted in Cumes, *Their Chastity was not too Rigid*, p. 82.

38 Scott, *Early Cricket in Sydney*, p. xiii.

39 Ibid., p. 80.

40 Stell, *Half the Race*, p. 4.

41 Ruszeja, *Decent and Proper Exertion*, p. 34.

42 Brailsford, 'Sporting Days in Eighteenth Century England', pp. 51–2.

43 Cashman, 'Horse Racing in Mid-19th Century Marrickville', pp. 29–33.

44 Harte, *SACA*, p. 42.

45 Cashman, 'Violence in Sport in Sydney', pp. 1–9.

46 Painter and Waterhouse, *The Principal Club*, p. 12.

47 Blainey, *A Game of Our Own*, p. 30.

48 *ADB*, vol. 5.

3 City Games

1 Frost, *Australian Cities in Comparative View*, pp. 15–17.

2 Lee and Fahey (*Labour History*, no. 50, May 1986), have noted that while average and aggregate earnings increased during the Long Boom, the increase in real earnings was often erratic because of the importance of

seasonality in the economy and short-terms swings due to unemployment or underemployment.

3 Fitzgerald, *Rising Damp*.
4 Blainey, 'History of Leisure', p. 10.
5 Harte, *SACA*, p. 40.
6 Davison, 'Punctuality and Progress', pp. 169–91.
7 Blainey, 'History of Leisure', p. 7.
8 See Howell and Howell, *Genesis of Sport*, pp. 140–1.
9 Smith, *Australian Painting*, p. 48.
10 See McCarthy, Training the Body or the Mind?
11 See Riess, *City Games*.
12 Blainey, *A Game of Our Own*, pp. 14–15.
13 Gregory, Recreation and Community, pp. 41, 43, 90.
14 Keating, *Surry Hills*, pp. 37–7, 46.
15 Tatz and Stoddart, *Royal Sydney Golf Club*, p. 110.
16 McKenry, 'Parks for the People', p. 23.
17 Cunneen, '"Hands off the parks!"', pp. 105–19; McKenry, 'Parks for the People', pp. 23–35.
18 McKenry, 'Parks for the People', p. 23.
19 Frost, *Australian Cities*, p. 40.
20 For a longer discussion, and supporting evidence, of this theme see Cashman and Hickie, 'Divergent Sporting Cultures of Sydney and Melbourne'.
21 Lemon, *History of Australian Thoroughbred Racing*, vol. 1, p. 195.
22 Twain, *Following the Equator*, pp. 161–3.
23 O'Hara, *A Mug's Game*, pp. 71–2.
24 See Bennett, 'Professional Sculling'.
25 Adair, '"Two Dots in the Distance"', p. 56.
26 Bennett, *The Clarence Comet*, pp. 71–94.
27 Adair, '"Two Dots in the Distance"', 74–8.
28 See *OCAS, s.v. Boxing*.
29 See Mason, *Professional Athletics in Australia*.
30 See Sissons, *The Players*
31 See David Montefiore, *Cricket in the Doldrums*.
32 Blainey, *A Game of Our Own*.
33 Hickie, *They Ran with the Ball*.
34 Howell and Howell, *Genesis of Sport*.
35 See Hibbins, 'English Origins of Australian Rules Football'.
36 Cashman and Hickie, 'Divergent Sporting Cultures of Sydney and Melbourne', pp. 42–3.
37 Hickie, *They Ran with the Ball*, pp. 125–6.
38 *OCAS, s.v. Australian Rules Football*.
39 Stremski, review of Blainey, in *International Journal of the History of Sport*.
40 Dunne, The Development of Coogee, pp. 217–30.
41 Doepel, Emergence of Surf Bathing, pp. 34–59.
42 Phillips, 'Ethnicity and Class at the Brisbane Golf Club', p. 206.
43 Tatz and Stoddart, *Royal Sydney Golf Club*, pp. 29–33.
44 *OCAS s.v. Lawn Bowls*.
45 See Roberts, 'An Ancient Game'; McCarthy, Testing the Bias.
46 See Cashman, 'The Australian Sporting Obsession'.

4 AMATEUR VERSUS PROFESSIONAL

1 See Mangan, *Athleticism in the Victorian and Edwardian Public School.*
2 Brown, 'Muscular Christianity in the Antipodes', pp. 173–87.
3 *Bell's Life in Victoria*, 30 March 1861.
4 Swain, *A Quarter Past the Century*; Hickie, Origins of Rugby Football.
5 Stewart, 'Athleticism Revisited', p. 40.
6 See Sherington, *Shore.*
7 See Connellan, *Ideology of Athleticism.*
8 See Brown, 'The Legacy of British Victorian Social Thought'.
9 Waddy, *Stacy Waddy*, p. 19.
10 See Scott, 'Cricket and the Religious World in the Victorian Period'; Sandiford, 'Cricket and Victorian Society'.
11 Gregory, Recreation and Community, pp. 56-7.
12 Phillips, 'Ethnicity and Class at the Brisbane Golf Club'.
13 Howell and Howell, *Genesis of Sport*, p. 72.
14 Solling, *Boatshed on Blackwattle Bay*, pp. 23–8.
15 Ibid., p. 12.
16 Lane and Jobling, 'For Honour and Trophies', pp. 3–4.
17 Ibid., pp. 6–11.
18 Moore and Phillips, 'The Sporting Career of Harold Hardwick, p. 62.
19 Ibid., pp. 70–1.
20 Mason, *Professional Athletics in Australia*, p. v.
21 Cashman, *'Ave a Go Yer Mug!*, pp. 32–3.
22 Harte, *SACA*, pp. 64, 105, 118.
23 McKernan, 'Sport, War and Society', pp. 12–13.
24 Corris, *Lords of the Ring*, p. 69.
25 See Solling, *The Boatshed on Blackwattle Bay.*
26 Pollard, *Australian Cricket*, p. 1131.
27 Harte, *SACA*, pp. 72–128.
28 Mancini and Hibbins, *Running with the Ball*, p. 2.
29 *ADB*, vol. 8; *OCAS s.v.*; Moore, 'One Voice in the Wilderness'; Henniker and Jobling, 'Richard Coombes and the Olympic Movement in Australia'.
30 Gordon, *Australia and the Olympic Games*, p. 47.
31 *ADB*, vol. 7.
32 Stewart, 'Athleticism Revisited', p. 44.
33 See Crawford, 'Athleticism, Gentlemen and Empire in Australian Public Schools'.
34 See Mason, *Professional Athletics in Australia.*
35 *OCAS s.v.* Athletics.
36 White and Harrison, *100 Years of the New South Wales AAA.*
37 Ibid., p. 22.
38 Ibid., p. 128.
39 See Montefiore, *Cricket in the Doldrums*; Grace, 'The Rise and Fall of the Australasian Cricket Council'.
40 See Sharp, Sporting Spectacles.
41 Hickie, Origins of Rugby Football, pp. 364–69.
42 Phillips, 'Ethnicity and Class at the Brisbane Golf Club', pp. 201–13.
43 *OCAS s.v.* Golf; Tatz and Stoddart, *Royal Sydney Golf Club*, p. 213.

44 Kinross Smith, 'Privilege in Tennis and Lawn Tennis', pp. 189, 197.
45 Ibid., p. 207.
46 *OCAS s.v.* Amateurism.
47 Mandle in Cashman and McKernan, eds, *Sport: Money, Morality and the Media*, p. 8.
48 O'Hara, *A Mug's Game*, pp. 80–3.
49 This is implied by O'Hara in ibid., p. 83.
50 McKernan, 'Sport, War and Society', pp. 1–2.
51 O'Farrell, Open Tennis, pp. 173–4.

5 GENDER

1   *OCAS s.v.* Gender.
2   Quoted in Nankervis, *Boys and Balls*, p. 157
3   Quoted in ibid., pp. 157–8.
4   Bryson, 'Sport and the Oppression of Women'.
5   Dunning, 'Sport as a Male Preserve'.
6   Springhall, *Youth, Empire and Society*.
7   Richards, *Commodity Culture of Victorian England*.
8   See Bratton, *Impact of Victorian Children's Fiction*.
9   Riess, 'Sport and the Redefinition of American Middle-class Masculinity'.
10 Ibid., p. 11.
11 Thomson, 'The Geographical Conditions of City Life', pp. 5—6.
12 Todd, Conceptualisations of the Body, p. 25.
13 See Cunneen, '"Hands off the parks!"'.
14 Lake, 'The Politics of Respectability'.
15 Connell, *Which Way is Up?*, p. 20; Connell, 'An Iron Man'.
16 West, 'Boys: Sport and Ideology'; West, 'Do Men Make the Rules?'
17 Scott, *Early Cricket in Sydney*, p. xiv.
18 Nauright, 'Sport and and the Image of Colonial Manhood'.
19 Park, 'Biological Thought, Athletics and the Formation of a "Man of Character"', p. 10.
20 White, *Inventing Australia*, pp. 154–6.
21 Murray, '"Boys will be Boys"', p. 31.
22 McCalman, *Struggletown*, p. 140.
23 See Dutton and Laura, 'Towards a History of Bodybuilding'.
24 Broome, 'The Australian Reaction to Jack Johnson', p. 308.
25 Howell, Howell and Brown, *The Sporting Image*, p. 108.
26 See Hickie, *They Ran with the Ball*.
27 Booth, 'Swimming, Surfing and Surf-Lifesaving', p. 1.
28 Stell, *Half the Race*, pp. 191–2.
29 Howell, 'Australia's First Female Olympians', pp. 17–29.
30 Guttmann, 'Eros in Sport', p. 139
31 McKay, *No Pain, No Gain?*, p. 170.
32 Riess, *City Games*, pp. 5–6.
33 Cunneen, 'Elevating and Recording the People's Pastimes', p. 165.
34 Cashman and Weaver, *Wicket Women*, p. 189. There are many other questions about sport and sexuality which need to be explored further. Leonie Randall, in a review of works on women's sport (*Sporting Traditions*, vol.

8, no. 2, May 1992, pp. 210–25), commented on the existence of lesbian sporting teams.

35 *Independent Monthly*, March 1994, p. 69.
36 Leonie Randall made a brief reference to lesbian sporting teams in 'Women's Sport', p. 217.
37 'Conversations with Netball Players and Administrators', p. 88.
38 Guttmann, *Women's Sport*, p. 105.
39 McCarthy, Training the Body or the Mind?, p. 41.
40 Quoted in Lilienthal, Tea, Talk and Tennis, p. 19.
41 Vertinsky, *Eternally Wounded Woman*, p. 15.
42 McCarthy, Training the Body or the Mind?, pp. 87–91.
43 Ibid. p. 60.
44 Stell, *Half the Race*, p. 26.
45 Crawford, 'Sport for Young Ladies'; 'English Influences on Australian Physical Education'.
46 See Stell, *Half the Race*.
47 Lilienthal, Tea, Talk and Tennis.
48 Stell, *Half the Race*.
49 Raszeja, *Decent and Proper Exertion*, p. 22.
50 Rose Scott did not want Fanny Durack and Mina Wylie to attend the 1912 Olympic Games because it would involve them swimming in from of a mixed audience. She resigned from the NSW Ladies' Amateur Swimming Association over this issue. See Allen, *Rose Scott*.
51 Stell, *Half the Race*, p. 1.
52 Guttmann, *Women's Sport*, p. 100.
53 Roper, 'Inventing Traditions in Colonial Society', p. 35.
54 Stell, *Half the Race*, pp. 8–11
55 Ibid., p. 17.
56 Resources had been allocated earlier for female swimming-baths, but this represented a form of fashionable leisure rather than sport.
57 See Raszeja, *Decent and Proper Exertion*.
58 Ibid.
59 O'Farrell, draft chapter on Women and Tennis, kindly supplied to the author.
60 Fitzpatrick, 'The Spectrum of Australian Bicycle Racing', p. 336.
61 Raszeja, *Decent and Proper Exertion*, pp. 23–4.
62 See Cashman and Weaver, *Wicket Women*
63 Embrey, Batter Up!
64 See Edman, The Commercialisation of Women's Sport; Jobling and Barham, 'Development of Netball'.
65 Anne Sargeant, History of Netball video.
66 'Conversations with Netball Players and Administrators', pp. 9, 10, 16.
67 Broomhall, A Feminist Analysis of New Zealand Netball.
68 Randall, *A Fair Go?*, p. 78.

6 COMMUNITY AND PLACE

1 See Bennett, 'Regional Sentiment and Australian Sport', p. 94.
2 Ibid., p. 98.
3 See Mandle, 'Cricket and Australian Nationalism'.

4 Bale, *Sport and Place*; Brailsford, 'Geography of Eighteenth Century English Spectator Sports'.
5 Stremski, *Kill for Collingwood*, pp. 1–2.
6 Ibid., p. 11.
7 McCalman, *Struggletown*, pp. 139–42.
8 Parsons, 'Labour, Rugby League and the Working Class'
9 Blackwell, 'Class, Community and Rugby League'.
10 Gregory, Recreation and Community, pp. 50–8.
11 Bonnell, Cashman and Rodgers, *Making the Grade*, pp. 7–9.
12 Derriman, *True to the Blue*, pp. 64–70; Harte, *SACA*, p. 137.
13 Hickie, *The Game for the Game Itself*, ch. 3.
14 Heads, *History of Souths*, p. 7.
15 Stremski, 'The Community Fights Back', pp. 33–4.
16 See Mosely, Social History of Soccer.
17 Mosely, 'Factory Football', p. 33.
18 Tatz and Stoddart, *Royal Sydney Golf Club*, p. 15.
19 Forster, 'Sport, Society and Space'.
20 Buley, *Australian Life in Town and Country*, p. 143.
21 Quoted in *Bell's Life in Victoria*, 23 November 1861.
22 O'Hara, draft manuscript kindly supplied to the author.
23 Daly, *Elysian Fields*, p. 149.
24 See Gillett, Where the Big Men Fly.
25 Ibid., p. 120.
26 'Austral', *Lawn Tennis in Australasia*, p. 185.
27 Forster, 'Sport, Society and Space', p. 28.
28 *OCAS s.v.* 'Country Show Sports'.
29 Blainey, 'History of Leisure', p. 17.
30 *OCAS s.v.* Sheep-shearing.
31 Blainey, 'History of Leisure', p. 17; Howell and Howell, *Genesis of Sport*, p. 220.
32 *OCAS s.v.* Sharman, Jimmy.
33 See Corris, *Lords of the Ring*, pp. 74–90.
34 Howell and Howell, *Genesis of Sport*, p. 266.
35 See Thomson, '"Hurricane Bob" Skene'.
36 Howell and Howell, *Genesis of Sport*, p. 229.
37 Stell, *Half the Race*, p. 143.
38 Daly, *Elysian Fields*, p. 144.
39 O'Hara, *A Mug's Game*, pp. 66–7.
40 Howell and Howell, *Genesis of Sport*, pp. 241, 271–3.
41 Ibid., p. 274.
42 Daly, *Elysian Fields*, pp. 45, 145, 162, 181.
43 Headon, 'To See a Racecourse', pp. 141, 143.
44 *Bulletin*, 31 December 1898.
45 Headon, 'To See a Racecourse', p. 143.
46 Herbert, *Poor Fellow My Country*, pp. 65, 68.
47 Howell and Howell, *Genesis of Sport*, p. 216.
48 Mandle, 'Cricket and Australian Nationalism'.
49 *Bulletin*, 19 March 1898.
50 Mandle, 'Cricket and Australian Nationalism', pp. 225–45.
51 *Australasian*, 27 May 1871.

52 There is some evidence that the New Zealand sporting relationship is assuming larger proportions partly as a reaction to anti-Australian feeling emanating from across the Tasman. It was reported that a sizeable group of Australians, watching a rugby Test between England and New Zealand in the early 1990s, barracked strongly for the England team.
53 Whimpress, *The South Australian Football Story*, p. 99.
54 Montefiore, *Cricket in the Doldrums*; Stobo, Australian Nationalism and Cricket.
55 Montefiore, *Cricket in the Doldrums*, p. 80.
56 Grace, 'Rise and Fall of the Australasian Cricket Council', p. 45.
57 Jaggard, *Garth*, p. 19.
58 Bennett, 'Regional Sentiment', p. 107.
59 Bennett, 'Cannons and Canberra', pp. 2–22.
60 Ibid., p. 17.
61 Headon, '"Putting Soul into the Cemetery with Lights"'.

7 POLITICS

1 Harte, *SACA*, pp. 30, 43.
2 Adair, '"Two Dots in the Distance"', p. 68.
3 Derriman, *True to the Blue*, pp. 34–6, 130–8.
4 Harte, *History of Australian Cricket*, p. 583.
5 Corcoran, draft thesis on rugby league in NSW, kindly supplied to the author.
6 Mosely, Social History of Soccer, pp. 80–7.
7 Booth, 'War Off Water', pp. 143–4.
8 Stoddart, 'Sport and Society', pp. 656–7.
9 Tatz and Stoddart, *Royal Sydney Golf Club*, pp. 28, 74.
10 Phillips, 'Ethnicity and Class', p. 205.
11 Lawson, *Brisbane in the 1890s*, p. 210.
12 Ibid.
13 Dent, Australia's Participation, p. 28.
14 Ibid., p. 51.
15 Moore, Concept of British Empire Games, pp. 141–3.
16 Dent, Australia's Participation, ch. 9.
17 Bailey, Melbourne Olympics, p. 12.
18 Ibid., p. 90.
19 Gordon, *Australia and the Olympic Games*, pp. 195–200.
20 Ibid.
21 *OCAS s.v.* Olympic Games 1956 (Melbourne)
22 Sissons and Stoddart, *Cricket and Empire*.
23 See Toohey, Politics of Australian Elite Sport.
24 Selth, *The Prime Minister's XI*, p. 16.
25 *Wisden*, 1963, pp. 67–73.
26 Stoddart, *Saturday Afternoon Fever*, p. 66.
27 See Semotiuk, 'Commonwealth Government Initiatives'; Armstrong, 'Sport and Recreation Policy'.
28 McCoy, 'Sport as Modern Mythology', p. 40.
29 O'Hara, *A Mug's Game*, p. 182.

30 McCoy, 'Sport as Modern Mythology', p. 43.
31 *Australian Magazine*, 24–5 October 1992.
32 Semotiuk, 'Commonwealth Government Initiatives', p. 154.
33 Harte, *History of Australian Cricket*, pp. 595, 601, 602.
34 Ibid., pp. 571, 654; Haigh, *Cricket War*, pp. 23, 26, 27.
35 *OCAS*, *s.v.* Australian Institute of Sport.
36 Hartung, 'Sport and the Canberra Lobby', pp. 209–10.
37 Tatz, 'Race, Politics, and Sport', p. 28.
38 See *Age*, 28 June 1971 and *Sunday Australian*, 27 June 1971 quoted in Ward, 'Trifling with Their Games'.
39 Tatz, 'Sport in South Africa'.
40 Harte, *Two Tours and Pollock*.
41 See Deane, 'Melbourne Press and the Moscow Olympics'; Young, 'The Melbourne Press and the 1980 Moscow Olympic Boycott Controversy'.
42 Howell and Howell, *Aussie Gold*, p. 304.
43 Harte, *History of Australian Cricket*, pp. 552, 572.

8 ABORIGINES AND ISSUES OF RACE

1 Broome, 'Professional Aboriginal Boxers', p. 53. By 1994 Aborigines had achieved 65 national titles
2 Howell and Howell, *Genesis of Sport*, pp. 69–70.
3 Lemon, *History of Australian Thoroughbred Racing*, vol. 1, p. 176.
4 Blades, Australian Aborigines, Cricket and Pedestrianism, pp. 28–34.
5 See Whimpress, 'Poonindie, Cricket and the Adams Family'; Daly, '"Civilising" the Aborigines'.
6 Blades, Australian Aborigines, p. 40.
7 Mulvaney and Harcourt, *Cricket Walkabout*, p. 37.
8 Ibid., p. 170.
9 Ibid., p. 21.
10 Blades, Australian Aborigines, p. 144.
11 Fotheringham, *Sport in the Australian Drama*, p. 36.
12 Mulvaney and Harcourt, *Cricket Walkabout*, p. 12.
13 Ibid., pp. 132–48.
14 Blades, Australian Aborigines, p. 144.
15 Quoted in ibid., p. 106.
16 The actual figures quoted were in dollars ($25 000 and $500) since this story emanated from America. Written for *Police News*, Boston, by an Australian correspondent, 12 March 1890.
17 Blades, Australian Aborigines, pp. 112–24.
18 Ibid., pp. 95, 109–10.
19 *Referee*, 25 March 1903.
20 *Referee*, 20 April 1904.
21 Broome, *Aboriginal Australians*, pp. 87–100.
22 Tatz, *Aborigines in Sport*, p. 14.
23 Roth, Annual Report of the Chief Protector of Aborigines for 1904, p. 20, quoted in Blades, Australian Aborigines, pp. 69, 86, 136; *ADB*, vol. 11.
24 Blades, Australian Aborigines, p. 142.

25 See Tatz, *Aborigines in Sport*, pp. 120–1.
26 Broome, *Aboriginal Australians*, pp. 78, 80–4.
27 Blades, 'Australian Aborigines' pp. 80–5.
28 Howell and Howell, *Genesis of Sport*, p. 108.
29 Broome, 'Australian Reaction to Jack Johnson', p. 343.
30 Ibid., p. 363.
31 It is likely that had a more deferential black been the opponent of Burns there would have been no such outcry because African-Americans such as the stage performer Irving Sayles have long held a special place in Australian society. African-Americans belonged to unions and married 'white' women and no one complained.
32 Harte, *SACA*, pp. 191–2, 262–3.
33 *Referee* 9 June 1916.
34 Blades, Australian Aborigines, pp. 73–4.
35 Stoddart, *Saturday Afternoon Fever*, p. 166.
36 Blades, Australian Aborigines, pp. 72–5.
37 Whimpress, 'Few And Far Between'; 'The Marsh-MacLaren Dispute'.
38 Whimpress, 'The Marsh-MacLaren Dispute'.
39 Tatz, *Australian Aborigines*, p. 70.
40 Broome, Review of *Aborigines in Sport*, *ASSH Bulletin*, no. 7, April 1988, p. 25.
41 Broome, 'Professional Aboriginal Boxers', p. 49
42 Ibid., p. 57.
43 Ibid., p. 68.
44 Tatz, *Australian Aborigines*, p. 47.
45 Broome, 'Professional Aboriginal Boxers', p. 69.
46 Tatz, *Australian Aborigines*, p. 39.
47 Broome, 'Professional Aboriginal Boxers', p. 58.
48 Tatz, *Australian Aborigines*, p. 50.
49 Interview by Richard Broome at Cherbourg Aboriginal reserve, Queensland: Broome, 'Professional Aboriginal Boxers', p. 67.
50 Cashmore, *Black Sportsmen*.
51 The team was (* = international players): *Dale Shearer, David Liddiard, *Tony Currie, *Mal Meninga, *John Ferguson, *Steve Ella, Scott Gale, *Cliff Lyons, Jeff Hardy, Ron Gibbs, *Sam Backo, Mal Cochrane, Paul Roberts. Reserves: Ricky Walford, *Craig Salvatore.
52 Quoted in Tatz, *Australian Aborigines*, pp. 80, 141.
53 Ibid., p. 80.
54 Ibid..
55 Testimony of Steve Hall, who is himself Aboriginal, and who is the coaching and development manager for the Far Western District of New South Wales.
56 Dave Nadel, 'Aborigines and Australian Football', p. 61.
57 Charles Perkins, *A Bastard Like Me*, pp. 39–73.
58 Stell, *Half the Race*, pp. 236–9.
59 Ibid., p. 236.
59 McGrath, *Born in the Cattle*, pp. 49–67.
61 Paraschak, 'Aborigines and Sport in Australia'.
62 Tatz, *Australian Aborigines*, pp. 83–4.
63 Nadel, 'Aborigines and Australian Football'.

64 Tatz, Australian Aborigines, p. 73.
65 Tatz 'Aborigines: A Return to Pessimism'.
66 Tatz, Aborigines in Sport, p. 129.
67 Broome, Review of Aborigines in Sport, p. 25.
68 Black Magic (videorecording) produced by Paul Roberts in conjunction with the Southern Aboriginal Corporation, c. 1988.

9 ETHNICITY

1 O'Farrell, The Irish in Australia, p. 10.
2 52 per cent (612 531) of the Australian population in 1861 (1 168 149) were born in the United Kingdom.
3 Sherington, Australia's Immigrants, pp. 10, 40.
4 Prentis, The Scots in Australia, pp. 194–218.
5 OCAS s.v. Golf.
6 Mosely, Social History of Soccer, pp. 15, 18–20.
7 See O'Farrell, Catholic Church and Community in Australia, ch. 5.
8 Mandle, Gaelic Athletic Association, pp. 14–15.
9 O'Farrell, The Irish in Australia, p. 173.
10 Ibid., pp. 185–7.
11 Ibid., pp. 5–17.
12 Ibid., p. 213.
13 Ibid., pp. 101–5, 262.
14 Solling, Boatshed on Blackwattle Bay, p. 124.
15 Harte, History of Australian Cricket, p. 305. Derriman noted, in the Sydney Morning Herald, 17 June 1993, that there had been a gap of sixty years from the time Percy McDonnell led Australia (in 1889) to the next Catholic captain, Lindsay Hassett (1949).
16 O'Reilly, 'Tiger', pp. 157–60.
17 O'Farrell, Irish in Australia, p. 262.
18 See Moore, In Memory of the Martyred Boxer Darcy.
19 O'Farrell, Irish in Australia, pp. 101–5, 262.
20 Howell and Howell, Genesis of Sport, p. 261.
21 Daly, Elysian Fields, pp. 45, 95–6.
22 O'Hara, A Mug's Game, pp. 76–7, 121.
23 Cashman, Headon and Kinross-Smith, The Oxford Book of Sporting Anecdotes, pp. 1–3.
24 See Doepel, Emergence of Surf Bathing.
25 OCAS s.v. Surfing.
26 Jobling, Duke Kahanomoku. Further research on the funding of this tour will be undertaken by Jobling to ascertain whether making money from the tour was a relatively minor motivation.
27 OCAS s.v. Surfing.
28 See White, 'Americanization and Popular Culture', pp. 3–21; Waterhouse, 'Popular Culture and Pastimes', pp. 238–85.
29 Bell and Bell, Implicated, pp. 1–16.
30 Nauright, NZ Physical Education Newsletter.
31 White, 'Americanization and Popular Culture', p. 20.

32 Waterhouse, 'Popular Culture and Pastimes', pp. 257–66.
33 Mitchell, 'Baseball in Australia', pp. 2–24.
34 pers. comm., 7 April 1994.
35 O'Farrell, draft thesis on the social history of tennis, 1874–1929.
36 Robinson, *On Top Down Under*, p. 90.
37 *OCAS s.v.* Softball. I am also indebted to Lynn Embrey who provided me with an outline of her research project on the history of Australian softball.
38 O'Farrell, Open Tennis.
39 Bennett, 'Cannons and Canberra', p. 7.
40 Waterhouse, *Black and White Minstrel*, pp. 145–51
41 Chandler, Telecasting the Olympics, pp. 11–12.
42 Sherington, *Australia's Immigrants*, p. 143.
43 Cashman and Meader, *Marrickville*, p. 58.
44 Hay, 'Marmaras' Oyster or Seamonds' Baby', p. 5.
45 *OCAS s.v.* Soccer; Mosely and Murray, 'Soccer'.
46 Hay, 'Marmaras' Oyster or Seamonds' Baby', pp. 19–29.
47 Philip Mosely, 'Balkan Politics in Australian Soccer'.
48 See McCoy, 'The Influence of Structural Factors'.
49 Harrison, 'What's in an Ethnic Name', pp. 32–3.
50 Hay, 'British Football', pp. 58–60.
51 Hughson, 'The Wogs are at it Again'; Cohen, *Folk Devils and Moral Panics*.
52 Mosely, Issues and Approaches, p. 12; Parenti, 'Ethnic Politics'.
53 Mosely, Social History of Soccer, pp. 313–14.
54 Mosely, 'Balkan Politics in Australian Soccer', pp. 33–43.
55 Vamplew, *Sports Violence in Australia*.
56 Vamplew, 'Violence in Australian Soccer'
57 See, for instance, Dew, Ethnic Involvement in Sport—Geelong.
58 Unikoski, *Communal Endeavours*.
59 Ticher, 'Notional Englishmen', pp. 87–90.
60 Lawson, *Henry*, p. 45.
61 Unpublished paper by Tony Luff, see Cashman, *'Ave a Go, Yer Mug!*, p. 166.

10 THE MEDIA

1 See, for instance, Tatz, 'The Corruption of Sport'; Goldlust, *Playing for Keeps*; McKay, *No Pain, No Gain*.
2 Chandler, TV Sport.
3 Guttmann, *Sports Spectators*, p. 88.
4 Cunneen, 'Elevating and Recording the People's Pastimes', p. 163.
5 Ibid., p. 171.
6 Berger, *Ways of Seeing*, p. 10.
7 Dutton, *S. T. Gill's Australia*, p. 7.
8 See Jobling, 'Pastimes, Games and Sport'.
9 Dutton, *Sun, Sea, Surf and Sand*.
10 Dutton and Laura, 'Towards a History of Bodybuilding', pp. 30–2.
11 Andrews, '"Tugging Four Bits off the Deck at the WACA"', p. 150.
12 John Ryan, *AJC Racing Calendar*, October 1993, p. 12.

13 Miller, 'Dawn of an Imagined Community', pp. 49–51.
14 Fotheringham, *Sport in Australian Drama*, p. 159.
15 Ibid., pp. 181, 183–4.
16 Miller, 'Dawn of an Imagined Community', p. 54.
17 Fotheringham, *Sport in Australian Drama*, p. 169.
18 Sean Brawley, *Beating the Odds*.
19 Cashman, *'Ave a Go, Yer Mug!*, pp. 93–4.
20 Sandercock and Turner, *Up Where Cazaly?*, pp. 156–7.
21 Inglis, Sport and the Australian Broadcasting Commission.
22 Cashman, *'Ave a Go, Yer Mug!*, p. 102.
23 Chandler, Television and National Sport, p. xii.
24 *Sydney Morning Herald*, 22 December 1954.
25 See Wenn, 'Lights! Camera! Little Action'.
26 Cunningham and Turner, eds, *The Media in Australia*, p. 30.
27 Rader, *In Its Own Image*.
28 Goldlust, *Playing for Keeps*, pp. 172–4; Tatz, 'Corruption of Sport'.
29 Stoddart, Sport and Television, p. 5.
30 Ibid., p. 7.
31 Chandler, *Television and National Sport*.
32 *OCAS s.v.* Media
33 Stewart, 'Economic Development of the Victorian Football League'.
34 O'Regan, *Australian Television Culture*, p. 80.
35 Chandler, TV Sport.
36 Ibid.
37 Tatz, 'Corruption of Sport', p. 13.
38 Vamplew, *Sports Violence in Australia*, pp. 37, 46.
39 Guttmann, *Sports Spectators*, pp. 122–3.
40 Chandler, *Television and National Sport*, pp. xi–xii.
41 Vamplew, *Sports Violence in Australia*, p. 46.
42 For example, Working Group on Women in Sport, *Women, Sport and the Media*.
43 King, 'Sexual Politics of Sport', p. 68.
44 Cashman and Weaver, *Wicket Women*, ch. 8.

11 BIG BUSINESS

1 Stewart, Theoretical Framework.
2 Scott, Cricket Matches, pp. 7–19.
3 Adair, '"Two Dots in the Distance"', p. 53.
4 Bennett, 'Professional Sculling in New South Wales', p. 129.
5 Adair, 'Professional Sculling', p. 68.
6 Ibid., p. 74.
7 See Windschuttle, *The Media*.
8 Fitzpatrick, 'Spectrum of Australian Bicycle Racing', p. 338.
9 Doepel, Emergence of Surf Bathing, pp. 60–1.
10 Richards, *Commodity Culture of Victorian England*.
11 Blainey, 'History of Leisure', p. 19.
12 Walker, *Under Fire*, p. 6.
13 Heads, *True Blue*, pp. 84–5.

14 Ibid.
15 Quoted in ibid., p. 88.
16 *ADB*, vol. 10.
17 Fotheringham, *Sport in Australian Drama*, pp. 160–2.
18 *OCAS s.v.* Horse-racing.
19 Waterhouse, *Principal Club*, p. 40.
20 Rosenwater, *Sir Donald Bradman*, p. 172.
21 See Sharp, Professionalism and Commercialism.
22 Sandercock and Turner, *Up Where Cazaly?*, pp. 143–4.
23 O'Farrell, Open Tennis.
24 Ibid., p. 3.
25 Stewart, Theoretical Framework.
26 Ibid., p. 3.
27 Harriss, 'Packer, Cricket and Post Modernism', quoted in Stewart, Theoretical Framework, p. 21.
28 Stewart, *Australian Football Business*, p. 74.
29 Stewart, 'Economic Development of the Victorian Football League'.
30 Heads, *True Blue*, pp. 395–7.
31 See, for instance, Harte, *History of Australian Cricket*, pp. 606–29.
32 Ibid., p. 598.
33 Lawrence and Rowe, eds, *Power Play*, pp. 164, 177.
34 Harriss, 'Packer, Cricket and Post Modernism', pp. 117–18.
35 Stoddart, 'Sport and Television', pp. 13–14.
36 Quick, World Series Cricket, p. 196.
37 Goldlust, *Playing for Keeps*, p. 170.
38 Sandercock and Turner, *Up Where Cazaly?*
39 Brawley, *Beating the Odds*.
40 O'Hara, *A Mug's Game*, pp. 223–4.
41 Ibid., pp. 195–6.
42 Dabscheck, 'Early Attempts'.
43 Dabscheck, 'Professional Cricketers Association of Australia'.
44 Ibid., pp. 2–26.
45 *Cricketer*, March 1984.
46 Lawrence and Rowe, *Power Play*, p. 173.

12 AUSTRALIA—A PARADISE OF SPORT?

1 Cashman's article 'Australian Sporting Obsession' pointed out the problems in comparing sporting passion from one society to another. Since this time the author has shifted his opinion to accept that there may have been some distinctive and even unique features of Australian sport.
2 'Good Weekend', *Sydney Morning Herald*, 5 March 1988.
3 Quoted in *OCAS s.v.* Literature.
4 Kingston, Oxford History of Australia, vol. 3, p. 198.
5 Ibid, p. 198.
6 Stoddart, *Saturday Afternoon Fever*, pp. 13–14, 22.
7 Sandercock and Turner, *Up Where, Cazaly?*
8 'Good Weekend', *Sydney Morning Herald*, 5 March 1988.
9 This view, enunciated by Keith Dunstan in *Sports*, has been influential.

SELECT BIBLIOGRAPHY ON AUSTRALIAN SPORT*

* This bibliography includes the full citations of all the books which appear, in shorter form, in the notes. For a more complete bibliography on individual sports, see Wray Vamplew, Katharine Moore, John O'Hara, Richard Cashman, Ian Jobling, eds, *The Oxford Companion to Australian Sport*, OUP, Melbourne, revised edition 1994.

Adair, Daryl, 'Respectable, Sober and Industrious': A Social History of Public Houses and Alcohol in Early Colonial Adelaide, 1836–c.1870, BA Hons thesis, Flinders University, 1989
——, '"Two Dots in the Distance": Professional Sculling as a Mass Spectacle in New South Wales, 1876–1907', *Sporting Traditions*, vol. 9, no. 1, November 1992, pp. 52–83
Allen, Charles, *Plain Tales from the Raj*, Century Publishing, London, 1985
Allen, Judith A., *Rose Scott: Vision and Revision in Feminism*, OUP, Melbourne, 1994
Andrews, Barry, '"Tugging Four Bits off the Deck at the WACA": Australian Sport and Australian English' in Cashman and McKernan, eds, *Sport: Money, Morality and the Media*, pp. 136–61
Arlott, John, ed., *From Hambleton to Lord's: The Classics of Cricket*, Johnson, London, 1948
Armstrong, Tom, 'Sport and Recreation Policy: Will She be Right', *Sporting Traditions*, vol. 3, no. 2, May 1987, pp. 162–72
Bailey, Ray, The Melbourne Olympics and its Place in 20th Century Australian History, MA thesis, University of Sydney, 1992
Bale, John, *Sport and Place: A Geography of Sport in England, Scotland and Wales*, C. Hurst, London, 1982
——, 'Rustic and Rational Landscapes in Cricket', *Sports Place*, vol. 2, no. 2, 1988, pp. 5–18
Bell, Philip, and Roger Bell, *Implicated: The United States in Australia*, OUP, Melbourne, 1993
Bennett, Scott, 'Professional Sculling in New South Wales', *Journal of the Royal Australian Historical Society*, vol. 71, pt. 2, October 1985, pp. 127–42
——, 'Regional Sentiment and Australian Sport', *Sporting Traditions*, vol. 5, no. 1, November 1988, pp. 97–111

——, 'The Cannons and Canberra', *Sporting Traditions*, vol. 3, no. 1, November 1986, pp. 2–22

——, *The Clarence Comet: The Career of Henry Searle 1866–89*, Sydney University Press, Sydney, 1973

Berger, John, *Ways of Seeing*, Penguin, Harmondsworth, 1972

Birley, Derek, *Sport and the Making of Britain*, Manchester University Press, Manchester, 1993

Black Magic (video recording), produced by Paul Roberts in conjunction with the southern Aboriginal Corporation, c. 1988

Blackwell, Linda, Class, Community and Rugby League, BA Hons thesis, Macquarie University, 1984

Blades, Genevieve Clare, Australian Aborigines, Cricket and Pedestrianism: Culture and Conflict, 1880–1910, BHMS Hons thesis, University of Queensland, 1985

Blainey, Geoffrey, *A Game of Our Own: The Origins of Australian Football*, Information Australia, Melbourne, 1990

——, 'The History of Leisure in Australia: The Late-Colonial Era', *Victorian Historical Journal*, vol. 49, 1978, pp. 7–22

Bonnell, Max, Richard Cashman, James Rodgers, *Making the Grade: 100 Years of Grade Cricket in Sydney 1893–94 to 1993–94*, NSWCA, Sydney, 1994

Booth, Douglas, 'Swimming, Surfing and Surf-Lifesaving', in Vamplew and Stoddart, eds, *Sport in Australia*, pp. 231–54

——, 'War Off Water: The Australian Surf Life Saving Association and the Beach, *Sporting Traditions*, vol. 7, no. 2, May 1991, pp. 135–62

Booth, Douglas, and Colin Tatz, '"Swimming with the Big Boys": The Politics of Sydney's 2000 Bid', *Sporting Traditions*, vol. 11, no. 1, May 1994, pp. 3–23

Bowen, Rowland, *Cricket: A History of its Growth & Development throughout the World*, Eyre & Spottiswoode, London, 1970

Brailsford, Dennis, *Bareknuckles: A Social History of Prize-Fighting*, Lutterworth Press, Cambridge, 1980

——, *British Sport: A Social History*, Lutterworth Press, Cambridge, 1992

——, 'Sporting Days in Eighteenth Century England', *Journal of Sport History*, vol. 9, no. 3, Winter 1982, pp. 41–54

——, 'The Geography of Eighteenth Century English Spectator Sports', *Sport Place*, vol. 1, no. 1, Winter 1987, pp. 41–56

Bratton, J. S., *The Impact of Victorian Children's Fiction*, Croom Helm, London, 1981

Brawley, Sean, *Beating the Odds: Thirty Years of the Totalizator Agency Board of New South Wales*, Focus, Sydney, 1994

Brookes, Christopher, *English Cricket: The Game and its Players*, Weidenfeld & Nicolson, London, 1978

Broome, Richard, 'The Australian Reaction to Jack Johnson, Black Pugilist, 1907–9' in Cashman and McKernan, eds, *Sport in History*, pp. 343–63

——, *Aboriginal Australians: Black Response to White Dominance 1788–1980*, Allen & Unwin, Sydney, 1982

——, 'Professional Aboriginal Boxers in Eastern Australia 1930-1979', *Aboriginal History*, vol. 4, nos 1–2, June 1980, pp. 49–71

Broomhall, Jayne, A Feminist Analysis of New Zealand Netball, B. Phys. Ed. thesis, University of Otago, 1993

Brown, David W., 'Muscular Christianity in the Antipodes: Some Observations on the Diffusion and the Emergence of a Victorian Ideal in Australian Social Theory', *Sporting Traditions*, vol. 3, no. 2, May 1987, pp. 173–87

——, 'The Legacy of British Victorian Social Thought: Some Prominent Views on Sport, Physical Exercise and Society in Colonial Australia', *Sport & Colonialism in 19th Century Australasia*, ASSH Studies in Sports History, no. 1, ASSH, 1986, pp. 19–41

Buley, E. C., *Australian Life in Town and Country*, Newnes, London, 1905

Bryson, Lois, 'Sport and the Oppression of Women', *Australian and New Zealand Journal of Sociology*, vol. 19, no. 3, November 1983, pp. 413–26

Buckley, G. R., *Fresh Light on 18th Century Cricket: A Collection of 1,000 New Cricket Notices from 1697 to 1800 A.D.*, Cotterell & Co., Birmingham, 1935

Cashman, Richard, *'Ave a Go Yer Mug! Australian Cricket Crowds from Larrikin to Ocker*, Collins, Sydney, 1984

——, 'Horse Racing in Mid-19th Century Marrickville: Petersham Racecourse, Newtown Steeplechase and Barwon Park Turf Club', *Heritage*, no. 5, 1989, pp. 29–33

——, 'The Australian Sporting Obsession', *Sporting Traditions*, vol. 4, no. 1, November 1987, pp. 47–55

——, *The "Demon" Spofforth*, NSWUP, Sydney, 1991

——, 'Violence in Sport in Sydney Prior to 1850', *ASSH Studies in Sports History* no. 7, ASSH, Campbelltown, 1992, pp. 1–9

Cashman, Richard, David Headon and Graeme Kinross-Smith, *The Oxford Book of Australian Sporting Anecdotes*, OUP, Melbourne, 1993

Cashman, Richard, and Tom Hickie, 'The Divergent Sporting Cultures of Sydney and Melbourne, *Sporting Traditions*, vol. 7, no. 1, November 1990, pp. 26–46

Cashman, Richard, and Michael McKernan, eds, *Sport in History*, UQP, Brisbane, 1979

——, eds, *Sport: Money, Morality and the Media*, NSWUP, Sydney, 1981

Cashman, Richard, and Chrys Meader, *Marrickville: Rural Outpost to Inner City*, Hale & Iremonger, Sydney, 1990

Cashman, Richard, and Amanda Weaver, *Wicket Women: Cricket & Women in Australia*, NSWUP, Sydney, 1991

Cashmore, Ernest, *Black Sportsmen*, Routledge & Kegan Paul, London, 1982

Chandler, Joan M., Telecasting the Olympics to the United States, unpub. paper, ASSH/NASSH Conference, Hawaii, 1993

——, *Television and National Sport: The United States and Britain*, University of Illinois Press, Urbana, 1988

——, TV Sport: Programming for Pleasure and Profit, unpub. paper, ASSH Conference, Canberra, 1991

Cohen, Stanley, *Folk Devils and Moral Panics*, Granada, London, 1973

Clark, Peter, *The English Alehouse: A Social History 1200–1830*, Longman, London, 1983

Coleman, Robert, *Seasons in the Sun: The Story of the Victorian Cricket Association*, Hargreen, Melbourne, 1993

Connell, R. W., *Which Way is Up?: Essays on Sex, Class and Culture*, Allen & Unwin, Sydney, 1983

——, 'An Iron Man: The Body and Some Contradictions in Hegemonic Masculinity', in M. Mesner and D. Sabo, eds, *Sport, Men and the Gender Order: Critical Feminist Perspectives*, Human Kinetics, Champiagn, Illinois, 1990

Connellan, Mark, *The Ideology of Athleticism, Its Antipodean Impact, and Its Manifestations in Two Elite Catholic Schools*, ASSH Studies in Sports History, no. 5, 1988

Corris, Peter, *Lords of the Ring: A History of Prize-fighting in Australia*, Cassell, Sydney, 1980

Crawford, Ray , 'Athleticism, Gentlemen and Empire in Australian Public Schools: L.A. Adamson and Wesley College, Melbourne', *Sport & Colonialism in 19th Century Australasia*, ASSH Studies in Sports History, no. 1, ASSH, 1986, pp. 42–64

——, English Influences on Australian Physical Education: The Morris Sisters at Melbourne Girls' Grammar School, 1898–1913, unpub. paper, VII Commonwealth and International Conference on Sport, Physical Education, Recreation and Dance, Brisbane, 1982

——, 'Sport for Young Ladies: The Victorian Independent Schools 1875–1925', *Sporting Traditions*, vol. 1, no. 1, November 1984, pp. 61–82

Cumes, J. W. C., *Their Chastity was not too Rigid: Leisure Times in Early Australia*, Longman Cheshire, Melbourne, 1979

Cunneen, Chris, 'Elevating and Recording the People's Pastimes', in Cashman and McKernan, eds, *Sport: Money, Morality and the Media*, pp. 162–76

——, '"Hands off the parks!" The provision of parks and playgrounds' in Jill Roe, ed., *Twentieth Century Sydney: Studies in Urban and Social History*, Hale & Iremonger, Sydney, 1980, pp. 105–19

Cunningham, Hugh, *Leisure*, Croom Helm, London, 1980

Cunningham, Stuart, and Graeme Turner, eds, *The Media in Australia: Industries, Texts, Audiences*, Allen & Unwin, Sydney, 1993

Dabscheck, Braham, 'Early Attempts at Forming Soccer Player Unions in Australia', *Sporting Traditions*, vol. 10, no. 2, May 1994, pp. 2–27

——, 'The Professional Cricketers Association of Australia', *Sporting Traditions*, vol. 8, no. 1, November 1991, pp. 2–26

Daly, John, '"Civilising" the Aborigines: Cricket at Poonindie, 1850–1890', *Sporting Traditions*, vol. 10, no. 2, May 1994, pp. 59–67

——, *Elysian Fields: Sport, Class and Community in Colonial South Australia 1836–1890*, The author, Adelaide, 1982

——, *Feminae Ludens: Women's Competitive Sport in South Australia, 1936–1956 and the Influence of Sports Reporter Lois Quarrell*, Openbook Publishers, Adelaide, 1994

——, *Quest for Excellence: the Australian Institute of Sport in Canberra*, Australian Government Publishing Service, Canberra, 1991

Davison, Graeme, 'Punctuality and Progress: The Foundations of Australian Standard Time', *Australian Historical Studies*, no. 99, October 1992, pp. 169–91

Deane, John, 'The Melbourne Press and the Moscow Olympics', *Sporting Traditions*, vol. 1, no. 2, May 1985, pp. 27–42

Delves, Anthony, 'Popular Recreation and Social Conflict in Derby 1800–1850', in Yeo, Eileen and Stephen, eds, *Popular Culture and Class Conflict 1590–1914: Explorations in the History of Labour and Leisure*, Harvester, Sussex, 1981

Dent, William Wallace, Australia's Participation in the Olympic and British Empire Games, 1896-1938, MA Hons thesis, University of New England, 1987

de Serville, Paul, *Port Phillip Gentlemen and the Good Society in Melbourne before the Gold Rushes*, OUP, Oxford, 1980

Derriman, Philip, *True to the Blue: A History of the New South Wales Cricket Association*, Richard Smart, NSWCA, Sydney, 1985

Dew, Stephanie, Ethnic Involvement in Sport – Geelong, MA thesis, Deakin University, 1992

Doepel, Mark, The Emergence of Surf Bathing and Surf Life Saving at the Holiday Resort of Manly 1850–1920: Currents of Conflict, BA Hons thesis, University of NSW, 1985

Duncan, Marina, Conversations with Netball Players and Administrators: Oral History Pilot Project, unpub. manuscript, AANA, 1994

Dunne, Lawrence, The Development of Coogee and other Sydney Seaside Resorts up to 1920, MA Hons thesis, University of NSW, 1988

Dunning, E., 'Sport as a Male Preserve: Notes on the Social Sources of Masculine Identity and its Transformations', in N. Elias and E. Dunning, *Quest for Excitement*, Blackwell, Oxford, 1986, pp. 267–83

Dunning, T. P., 'Convict Leisure and Recreation: The North American Experience in Van Dieman's Land 1840–1847', *Sporting Traditions*, vol. 9, no 2, May 1993, pp. 3–15.

Dunstan, Keith, *Sports*, Cassell, Melbourne, 1973

Dutton, Geoffrey, *S.T. Gill's Australia*, Macmillan, Melbourne, 1981

——, *Sun, Sea, Surf and Sand—the Myth of the Beach*, OUP, Melbourne, 1985

Dutton, Kenneth R., and Ronald S. Laura, 'Towards a History of Bodybuilding', *Sporting Traditions*, vol. 6, no. 1, November 1989, pp. 25–41

Dyer, Ken, *Challenging the Men: The Social Biology of Female Sporting Achievement*, UQP, Brisbane, 1982

Edman, D. T., The Commercialisation of Women's Sport: Netball as a Case Study, B. Soc. Sc. Hons thesis, University of NSW, 1986

Embrey, Lynn, Batter Up! Fifty Years of Softball in Australia, unpub. NASSH paper, Saskatoon, 1994

Finlay, Ric, *Island Summers: A History of Tasmanian Representative Cricket*, St David's Park Publishing, Hobart, 1992

Fitzgerald, Shirley, *Rising Damp: Sydney 1870–90*, OUP, Melbourne, 1987

Fitzpatrick, Jim, *The Bicyle and the Bush: Man and Machine in Rural Australia*, OUP, London, 1980

——, 'The Spectrum of Australian Bicycle Racing: 1890-1900', in Cashman and McKernan, eds, *Sport in History*, pp. 331–8

Flint, Rachael Heyhoe, and Netta Rheinberg, *Fair Play: The Story of Women's Cricket*, Angus & Robertson, London, 1976

Forster, Clive, 'Sport, Society and Space: The Changing Geography of Country Cricket in South Australia 1836–1914', *Sporting Traditions*, vol. 2, no. 2, May 1986, pp. 23–47

Fotheringham, Richard, *Sport in Australian Drama*, CUP, Melbourne, 1992

Frost, Lionel, *Australian Cities in Comparative View*, McPhee Gribble, Melbourne, 1990

Georgakis, Steven, Pan-Hellenic Soccer Club 1957–1976: A Study of Ethnic Supported Soccer in N.S.W., B.Ed. thesis, University of Sydney, 1994

Gillett, Rodney Allan, Where the Big Men Fly: An Early History of Australian Football in the Riverina Region of New South Wales, B. Litt. thesis, University of New England, 1983

Goldlust, John, Playing for Keeps: Sport, Media and Society, Longman Cheshire, Melbourne, 1987

Gordon, Harry, Australia and the Olympic Games, UQP, Brisbane, 1994

Grace, Radcliffe, 'The Rise and Fall of the Australasian Cricket Council 1892–1900', Sporting Traditions, vol. 2, no. 1, November 1985, pp. 37–46

Gregory, Philip, Recreation and Community: A Study of the Development of the St George Area to 1914, MA thesis, University of NSW, 1981

Guttmann, Allen, 'Eros in Sport', in Donald G. Kyle and Gary D. Stark, eds, Essays on Sport History and Sport Mythology, Texas A & M University Press, Arlington, 1990, pp. 139–54

——, Sports Spectators, Columbia University Press, New York, 1986

——, Women's Sport: A History, Columbia University Press, New York, 1991

Gruneau, Richard, Class, Sport and Social Development, University of Masachussets Press, Amherst, 1983

Gruneau, Richard, and David Whitson, Hockey Night in Canada: Sport, Identities, and Cultural Politics, Garmond Press, Toronto, 1993

Haigh, Gideon, The Cricket War: The Inside Story of Kerry Packer's World Series Cricket, Text, Melbourne, 1993

Harris, H. A., Sport in Britain: Its Origins and Development, Stanley Hall, London, 1975

Harrison, Graham, 'What's in an Ethnic Name: Soccer Clubs in Australia', Canberra Anthropology, vol. 2, no. 2, October 1979, pp. 23–35

Harriss, Ian, 'Packer, Cricket and Post Modernism', D. Rowe and G. Lawrence, eds, Sport and Leisure: Trends in Australian Popular Culture, Harcourt Brace Jovanovich, Sydney, 1990, pp. 109–21

Harte, Chris, A History of Australian Cricket, Andre Deutsch, London, 1993

——, SACA: A History of the South Australian Cricket Association, SACA, Adelaide, 1990

——, Two Tours and Pollock: The Australian Cricketers in South Africa 1985–87, Sports Marketing, Adelaide, 1988

Hartung, Greg, 'Sport and the Canberra Lobby', in Cashman and McKernan, eds, Sport: Money, Morality and the Media, pp. 194–215

Hay, Roy, 'British Football, Wogball or the World Game? Towards a Social History of Victorian Soccer', in O'Hara, ed., Ethnicity and Soccer in Australia, pp. 44–79

——, 'Marmaras' Oyster or Seamonds' Baby: The Formation of the Victorian Soccer Federation, 1956-64', Sporting Traditions, vol. 10, no. 2, May 1994, pp. 3–24

Headon, David, '"Putting Soul into the Cemetery with Lights": The Canberra Raiders Phenomenon', Sporting Traditions, vol. 9, no., 2, May 1993, pp. 31–46

——, 'To See a Racecourse Become a Pandemonium: Horse Racing in the Northern Territory in the First Decades of White Settlement', Sporting Traditions, vol. 3, no. 2, May 1987, pp. 137–51

Heads, Ian, The History of Souths 1908–1985, South Sydney District Rugby Football League Club, Sydney, 1985

——, *True Blue: The Story of the NSW Rugby League*, Ironbark Press, Sydney, 1992

Henniker, Garth, and Ian Jobling, 'Richard Coombes and the Olympic Movement in Australia: Imperialism and Nationalism in Action', *Sporting Traditions*, vol. 6, no. 1, November 1989, pp. 2–15

Herbert, Xavier, *Poor Fellow My Country*, Collins, Sydney, 1975

Hibbins, G. M., 'The English Origins of Australian Rules Football', in J. A. Mangan, ed., *The Cultural Bond: Sport, Empire, Society*, Cass, London, 1992, pp. 108–28

Hickie, Tom, 'The Origins of Rugby Football in Sydney to 1880', Ph.D. thesis, University of NSW, 1991

——, *The Game for the Game Itself: The Development of Sub-District Rugby*, Sydney Sub-District Rugby Union, Sydney, 1983

——, *They Ran with the Ball*, Longman Cheshire, Melbourne, 1993

Holt, Richard, *Sport and the British: A Modern History*, Clarendon Press, Oxford, 1993

Howell, Max, Reet Howell and David Brown, *The Sporting Image: A Pictorial History of Queenslanders at Play*, UQP, Brisbane, 1989

Howell, Maxwell L., Reet A. Howell and Kenneth Edwards, Wrestling Among the Australian Aborigines, unpub. paper, ASSH-NASSH Conference, Hawaii, 1993

Howell, Reet, and Max Howell, *Aussie Gold: The Story of Australia at the Olympics*, Brooks Waterloo, Albion, 1988

——, *The Genesis of Sport in Queensland: From the Dreamtime to Federation*, UQP, Brisbane, 1992

Howell, Reet A., 'Australia's First Female Olympians', *Olympic Sientific Congress Official Report 1984*, pp. 17–29

Hughson, John, 'Australian Soccer – "Ethnic" or "Aussie": The Search for an Image', *Current Affairs Bulletin*, vol. 68, no. 10, March 1992, pp. 12–16

——, 'The Wogs are at it Again': Media Reportage of Australian Soccer Riots, unpub. draft chapter

Inglis, Ken, Sport and the Australian Broadcasting Commission 1932–1945, unpub. paper, ASSH Conference, 1979

Itzkowitz, D. C., *Peculiar Privilege: A Social History of Fox-Hunting, 1753–1885*, Harvester Press, London, 1975

Jaggard, Ed, *Garth: The Story of Graham McKenzie*, Fremantle Arts Centre Press, Perth, 1993

James, Alf, *Ratu Kadavu's Fijian Cricket XI in Australia 1907/08*, The Author, Sydney, 1993

Jobling, Ian F., Duke Kahanomoku – Hawaiian Olympian: Outcomes of His Visit to Australia in 1914–15, unpub. paper, ASSH-NASSH Conference, Hawaii, 1993

——, Pastimes, Games and Sport in Australian Painting, unpub. paper, ASSH Conference, Launceston, 1993

Jobling, Ian, and Pamela Barham, 'The Development of Netball and the All-Australia Women's Basketball Association (AAWBBA): 1891–1939', *Sporting Traditions*, vol. 8, no. 1, November 1991, pp. 29–48

Keating, Christopher, *Surry Hills: The City's Backyard*, Hale & Iremonger, Sydney, 1991

King, Helen, 'The Sexual Politics of Sport', in Cashman and McKernan, eds, Sport in History, pp. 68–85

Kingston, Beverley, *The Oxford History of Australia*, vol. 3, 1860–1900, OUP, Melbourne, 1988

Kinross Smith, Graeme, 'Privilege in Tennis and Lawn Tennis: The Geelong and Royal South Yarra Examples but not Forgetting the Story of the Farmer's Wrist', *Sporting Traditions*, vol. 3, no. 2, May 1987, pp. 189–216

——, *The Sweet Spot: One Hundred Years of Life and Tennis in Geelong*, Melbourne, 1984

Lake, Marilyn, 'The Politics of Respectability: Identifying the Masculinist Context', *Historical Studies Australia and New Zealand*, vol. 22, no. 86, April 1986, pp. 116–31

Lane, David G., and Ian F. Jobling, 'For Honour and Trophies: Amateur Rowing in Australia, 1888–1912', *Sporting Traditions*, vol. 4, no. 1, November 1987, pp. 2–26

Lawrence, Geoffrey, and David Rowe, eds,. *Power Play: The Commercialisation of Australian Sport*, Hale & Iremonger, Sydney, 1986

Lawson, G., *Henry—The Geoff Lawson Story*, Ironbark Press, Sydney, 1983

Lawson, Ronald, *Brisbane in the 1890s: A Study of an Australian Urban Society*, UQP, Brisbane, 1973

Lemon, Andrew, *The History of Australian Thoroughbred Racing*, 2 vols, Classic Reproductions, Melbourne, 1987 and Southbank Communications Group, Melbourne, 1990

Lilienthal, Sonja, Tea, Talk and Tennis: An Early History of Women's Sport at the University of Sydney 1882–1918, B. Ed. thesis, University of Sydney, 1987

Lowerson, John, *Sport and the English Middle Classes 1870–1914*, Manchester University Press, Manchester, 1993

——, 'Golf', in Tony Mason, ed., *Sport in Britain: A Social History*, pp. 187–214

Lynch, Rob, 'A Symbolic Patch of Grass: Crowd Disorder and Regulation on the Sydney Cricket Ground Hill', in O'Hara, ed., *Crowd Violence at Australian Sport*, pp. 10–48

McCalman, Janet, *Struggletown: Public and Private Life in Richmond 1900–1965*, MUP, Melbourne, 1985

McCarthy, Louella, Testing the Bias: Sex, Class and Lawn Bowls, BA Hons thesis, University of NSW, 1988

——, Training the Body or the Mind? Debates about 'Higher Education' of Girls in late-19th century New South Wales, MA thesis, University of NSW, 1991

McCoy, Al, 'Sport as Modern Mythology: SP Bookmaking in New South Wales 1920–1979', in Cashman and McKernan, eds, *Sport: Money, Morality and the Media*, pp. 34–67

McCoy, Damien, 'The Influence of Structural Factors on the Emergent Ethnicity of Immigrant Groups: The Vietnamese in Sydney, Australia', *Ethnic Groups*, 1992, vol. 19, pp. 247–65

McCrone, Kathleen E., *Playing the Game: Sport and the Physical Emanicpation of English Women 1870–1914*, University of Kentucky Press, 1988

McGrath, Ann, *'Born in the Cattle': Aborigines in Cattle Country*, Allen & Unwin, Sydney, 1987

McKay, Jim, *No Pain, No Gain? Sport and Australian Culture*, Prentice Hall, New York, 1991

McKay, J. and T. Miller, 'From Old Boys to Men and Women of the Corporation: The Americanisation and Commodification of Australian Sport', *Sociological of Sport Journal*, vol. 8, 1991, pp. 86–94

McKendrick, Neil et al. *The Birth of a Consumer Society: The Commercialization of Eighteenth-Century England*, Indiana University Press, Bloomington, 1982

McKenry, Keith, 'Parks for the People', *Victorian Historical Journal*, vol. 49, 1978, pp. 23–35

McKernan, Michael, *The Makers of Australia's Sporting Traditions*, MUP, Melbourne, 1993

——, 'Sport, War and Society: Australia 1914–18', in Cashman and McKernan, eds, *Sport in History*, pp. 1–20

Malcolmson, R. W., *Popular Recreations in English Society*, CUP, Cambridge, 1973

Mancini, A., and G. M. Hibbins, *Running with the Ball: Football's Foster Father*, Lynedoch, Melbourne, 1987

Mandle, W. F., 'Cricket and Australian Nationalism in the Nineteenth Century', *Journal of the Royal Australian Historical Society*, vol. 59, pt. 4, December 1973, pp. 225–45

——, 'Sport and Money: Introduction, in Cashman and McKernan, eds, *Sport: Money, Morality and the Media*, pp. 7–9

——, *The Gaelic Athletic Association & Irish Nationalist Politics 1884–1924*, Christopher Helm, London, 1987

Mangan, J. A., *Athleticism in the Victorian and Edwardian Public School*, CUP, Cambridge, 1981

Mason, Percy, *Professional Athletics in Australia*, Rigby, Adelaide, 1985

Mason, Tony, ed., *Sport in Britain: A Social History*, CUP, Cambridge, 1989

——, 'Football on the Maidan', in J. A. Mangan, ed., *The Cultural Bond: Sport, Empire and Society*, Cass, London, 1992

Matthews, J.J. 'Building the Body Beautiful', *Australian Feminist Studies*, no. 5, Summer 1987, pp. 17–34

Miller, Toby, 'The Dawn of an Imagined Community: Australian Sport on Film', *Sporting Traditions*, vol. 7, no. 1, November 1990, pp. 48–59

Mitchell, Bruce, 'Baseball in Australia. Two Tours and the Beginnings of Baseball in Australia, *Sporting Traditions*, vol. 7. no. 1, November. 1990, pp. 2–24

Montefiore, David, *Cricket in the Doldrums: The Struggle between Private and Public Control of Australian Cricket in the 1880s*, ASSH Studies in Sports History, no. 8, ASSH, Campbelltown, 1992

Moore, Andrew, 'The Curse of the Kalahari: The North Sydney Bears and the Ghosts of 1921-1922', *Sporting Traditions*, vol. 5, no. 2, May 1989, pp. 148–72

——, 'Testosterone Overdose: Popular Culture and Historical Memory', *Sporting Traditions*, vol. 10, no. 1, November 1993, pp. 2–22

Moore, Katharine, 'One Voice in the Wilderness: Richard Coombes and the Promotion of the Pan-Britannic Festival Concept in Australia 1891–1911', *Sporting Traditions*, vol. 5, no. 2, May 1989, pp. 188–203

——, In Memory of the Martyred Boxer Darcy, ASSH Conference, 1991

——, The Concept of British Empire Games: An Analysis of Its Origin and Evolution from 1891 to 1930, Ph.D. thesis, University of Queensland, 1986

Moore, Katharine, and Murray Phillips, 'The Sporting Career of Harold Hardwick: One Example of the Irony of the Amateur-Professional Dichotomy', *Sporting Traditions*, vol. 7, no. 1, November 1990, pp. 61–76

Mosely, Philip, A Social History of Soccer in New South Wales 1880–1957, Ph.D. thesis, University of Sydney, 1987

——, 'Balkan Politics in Australian Soccer', in O'Hara, ed., *Ethnicity and Soccer in Australia*, pp. 33–43

——, *Ethnic Involvement in Australian Society: A History 1950–1990*, Australian Sports Commission, Canberra, 1994

——, 'Factory Football: Paternalism and Profits', *Sporting Traditions*, vol. 2, no. 1, November 1985, pp. 25–36

——, Issues and Approaches to Migration, Ethnicity and Sport, unpub. paper

Mulvaney, John, and Rex Harcourt, *Cricket Walkabout: The Australian Aborigines in England*, Macmillan, Melbourne, 1988

Murray, Maree, '"Boys will be Boys": The Construction of the Men of League', *Sporting Traditions*, vol. 10, no. 1, November 1993, pp. 24–36

Murray, William, *Football: A History of the World Game*, Scolar Press, Aldershot, 1994

——, *The Old Firm: Sectarianism, Sport and Society in Scotland*, John Donald, Edinburgh, 1984

Nadel, Dave, 'Aborigines and Australian Football: The Rise and Fall of the Purnim Bears', *Sporting Traditions*, vol. 9, no. 2, May 1993, pp. 47–63

Nankervis, Brian, *Boys and Balls*, Allen & Unwin, Sydney, 1994

Nauright, John, 'Sport and and the Image of Colonial Manhood in the British Mind: British Physical Deterioration Debates and Colonial Sporting Tours, 1878–1906', *Canadian Journal of History of Sport*, vol. 23, no. 2, December 1992, pp. 54–71

——, 'Reclaiming Old and Forgotten Heroes: Nostalgia, Rugby and Identity in New Zealand', *Sporting Traditions*, vol. 10, no. 2, May 1994, pp. 131–9

Nicholas. Stephen et al. *Convict Workers*, CUP, Melbourne, 1989

O'Farrell, Patrick, *The Irish in Australia*, NSWUP, Sydney, 1987

——, *The Catholic Church and Community in Australia*, Thomas Nelson, Melbourne, 1977

O'Farrell, Virginia, Open Tennis: The Australian Debate c 1955– c 1975, BA Hons thesis, University of NSW, 1982

O'Hara, John, *A Mug's Game: A History of Gaming and Betting in Australia*, NSWUP, Sydney, 1988

——, 'An Approach to Colonial Sports History', in Vamplew, ed., *Sport and Colonialism*, pp. 3–18

——, ed., *Crowd Violence at Australian Sport*, ASSH Studies in Sports History no. 9, Sydney, 1992

——, ed., *Ethnicity and Soccer in Australia*, ASSH Studies in Sports History no. 10, Sydney, 1994

O'Regan, Tom, *Australian Television Culture*, Allen & Unwin, Sydney, 1993

O'Reilly, Bill, *'Tiger': Sixty Years of Cricket*, Fontana/Collins, Sydney, 1985

Painter, Martin, and Richard Waterhouse, *The Principal Club: A History of the Australian Jockey Club*, Allen & Unwin, Sydney, 1992

Paraschak, Vicky, 'Aborigines and Sport in Australia', *ASSH Bulletin*, no. 17, September 1992, pp. 15–19

Parenti, Michael, 'Ethnic Politics and the Persistence of Ethnic Identification', in Henry J. Pratt, ed., *Ethno–Religious Politics*, Schenkam, Cambridge, Mass., 1974

Park, Roberta J., 'Biological Thought, Athletics and the Formation of a "Man of Character"', in J. A. Mangan and James Walvin, eds, *Manliness and Morality: Middle-class Masculinity of Britain and America 1800–1940*, Manchester University Press, Manchester, 1987

Parsons, T.G., 'Labour, Rugby League and the Working Class – the St George District Rugby League Football Club in the 1920's, *Teaching History*, vol. 12, pt 2, August 1978, pp. 22–35

Pearson, Kent, *Surfing Subcultures of Australia and New Zealand*, UQP, Brisbane, 1979

Perkins, Charles, *A Bastard Like Me*, Ure Smith, Sydney, 1975

Phillips, Dennis, *Australian Women at the Olympic Games*, Kangaroo Press, Sydney, 1992

Phillips, Janet, and Peter Phillips, 'History from Below: Women's Underwear and the Rise of Women's Sport', *Journal of Popular Culture*, vol. 27, no. 2, Fall 1993, pp. 129–48

Phillips, Murray, 'Ethnicity and Class at the Brisbane Golf Club', *Sporting Traditions*, vol. 4, no. 2, May 1988, pp. 201–13

Pollard, Jack, *Australian Cricket: The Game And the Players*, Angus & Robertson, Sydney, 1988

Poulter, Jim, Marn-Grook – Original Aussie Rules, unpub. paper

Prentis, Malcolm D., *The Scots in Australia: A Study of New South Wales, Victoria and Queensland, 1788–1900*, Sydney University Press, Sydney, 1983

Quick, Shayne P., World Series Cricket, Television and Australian Culture, Ph.D. thesis, Ohio State University, 1990

Rader, Benjamin, *In Its Own Image: How Television Has Transformed Sport*, Free Press, New York, 1984

Randall, Leonie, *A Fair Go? Women in Sport in South Australia 1945–1965*, ASSH Studies in Sports History, no. 6, Flinders University, 1988

——, 'Women's Sport: A Review Article', *Sporting Traditions*, vol. 8, no. 2, May 1992, pp. 210–25

Raszeja, Veronica, *A Decent and Proper Exertion: The Rise of Women's Competitive Swimming in Sydney to 1912*, ASSH Studies in Sports History, no. 9, Campbelltown, 1992

Richards, Thomas, *The Commodity Culture of Victorian England: Advertising and Spectacle, 1851–1901*, Stanford University Press, Stanford, 1990

Rigauer, Bero, (trans by Allen Guttmann), *Sport and Work*, Columbia University Press, New York, 1981

Riess, Steven A., *City Games: The Evolution of American Urban Society and the Rise of Sports*, University of Illinois Press, Urbana, 1989

——, 'Sport and the Redefinition of American Middle-class Masculinity', *International Journal of the History of Sport*, vol. 8, no. 1, May 1991, pp. 5–27

Roberts, Alan, 'An Ancient Game in a New Land: Bowling and Society in N. S. W. to 1912, *Journal of the Royal Australian Historical Society*, vol. 65, pt 2, September 1979, pp. 109–26

Robertson, Ian, 'Sport and Play in Aboriginal Culture—Then and Now', *Salisbury College of Advanced Education, Paper no. 8, 1975*, pp. 1–16

Robinson, Ray, *On Top Down Under: Australia's Cricket Captains*, Cassell, Sydney, 1975

Roper, M., 'Inventing Traditions in Colonial Society: Bendigo's Easter Fair, 1871–1885', *Journal of Australian Studies*, vol. 17, November 1985, pp. 31–40

Rosenwater, Irving, *Sir Donald Bradman: A Biography*, Batsford, London, 1978

Ryan, John, 'Racing and Australian Language', *ASSH Bulletin*, no. 20, June 1994, pp. 1–6

Sandiford, Keith, 'Cricket and Victorian Society', *Journal of Social History*, vol. 17, no. 2, Winter 1983, pp. 303–17

Salter, Michael Albert, Games and Pastimes of the Australian Aboriginal, MA thesis, University of Alberta, 1967

Sandercock, Leonie, and Ian Turner, *Up Where Cazaly? The Great Australian Game*, Granada, London, 1981

Scott, Jas, Cricket Matches: Played by English Teams in Australasia and Australian Teams on Tour, unpub. manuscript, NSWCA Library, pp. 7–19

——, *Early Cricket in Sydney 1803 to 1856* edited by R. Cashman and S. Gibbs, NSWCA, Sydney, 1991

Scott, P., 'Cricket and the Religious World in the Victorian Period', *Church Quarterly*, 3, 1970

Selth, Don, *The Prime Minister's XI: The Story of the Prime Minister's XI Matches Menzies to Hawke*, The Author, Canberra, 1990

Semotiuk, Darwin M., 'Commonwealth Government Initiatives in Amateur Sport in Australia 1972–1985', *Sporting Traditions*, vol. 3, no. 2, May 1987, pp. 152–62

Sharp, Martin, Professionalism and Commercialism in Australian Cricket during the 1930s: The Origins of the Cricket Revolution, BA Hons thesis, University of NSW, 1981

——, Sporting Spectacles: Cricket and Football in Sydney 1890–1912, Ph.D. thesis, Australian National University, 1986

Sherington, Geoffrey, *Australia's Immigrants 1788-1988*, 2nd edn, Allen & Unwin, Sydney, 1990

——, *Shore: A History of Sydney Church of England Grammar School*, SCEGS, Sydney, 1983

Sissons, Ric, *The Players: A Social History of the Professional Cricketer*, Pluto, Sydney, 1988

Sissons, Ric, and Brian Stoddart, *Cricket and Empire: the 1932–33 Bodyline Tour of Australia*, Allen & Unwin, London, 1984

Smith, B. *Australian Painting 1788–1970*, OUP, London, 1971

Solling, Max, *The Boatshed on Blackwattle Bay: Glebe Rowing Club 1879–1993*, GRC, Syndey, 1993

Solling, Max, and Harry Wark, *Under the Arches: A History of the Glebe District Hockey Club to 1993*, Glebe Hockey Club, Sydney, 1994

Springhall, J.O., 'Adolescence, Work and Family Relationships, 1880–1914', *Newsletter, Social History Society*, Spring 1980

——, *Youth, Empire and Society: British Youth Movements*, Croom Helm, Connecticut, 1979

Stell, Marion K., *Half the Race: A History of Australian Women in Sport*, Angus & Robertson, Sydney, 1991

Stewart, Bob., A Theoretical Framework for Analysing the Commercial Development of Australian First Class Cricket, unpub. paper, ASSH Conference, Launceston, 1993

——, 'Athleticism Revisited: Sport, Character Building and Protestant School Education in Nineteenth Century Melbourne', *Sporting Traditions*, vol. 9, no. 1, Nov. 1992, pp. 35–50

——, *The Australian Football Business: A Spectator's Guide to the VFL*, Kangaroo Press, Sydney, 1983

——,'The Economic Development of the Victorian Football League 1960–1984', *Sporting Traditions*, vol. 1, no. 2, May 1984, pp. 2–26

Stobo, Richard, Australian Nationalism and Cricket in the Nineteenth Century, BA Hons thesis, University of Sydney, 1989

Stoddart, Brian, *Invisible Games: A Report on the Media Coverage of Women's Sport*, Sport and Recreation Minister's Council, Canberra, 1994

——, *Saturday Afternoon Fever: Sport in the Australian Culture*, Angus & Robertson, Sydney, 1986

——, 'Sport and Society 1890-1940: A Foray', in C. T. Stannage, ed., *A New History of Western Australia*, UWAP, Perth, 1981

——, Sport and Television: Reflections upon a Cultural Phenomenon, unpub. paper.

Stremski, Richard, *Kill for Collingwood*, Allen & Unwin, Sydney, 1986

——, Review of Blainey, *A Game of Our Own, International Journal of the History of Sport*, vol. 8, no. 1, May 1991, pp. 160–1

——,'The Community Fights Back: The Resurrection of the Footscray Football Club', *NASSH Proceedings*, 1991, pp. 33–4

Swain, Peter L., *A Quarter Past the Century: A History of Newington College 1863–1988*, Newington College, Sydney, 1988

Tatz, Colin, *Aborigines in Sport*, ASSH Studies in Sport No. 3, Adelaide, 1987

——, Aborigines: A Return to Pessimism, 1989, unpub. paper.

——, *Aborigines: Sport, Violence and Survival*, Research Report of the Criminology Research Council, Sydney 1994

——, *Obstacle Race*, NSWUP, Sydney, 1995

——, 'Race, Politics, and Sport', *Sporting Traditions*, vol. 1, no. 1, November 1984, pp. 2–36

——, 'Sport in South Africa: The Myth of Integration', *Australian Quarterly*, vol. 55, no. 4, Summer 1983, pp. 405–20

——, 'The Corruption of Sport', *Current Affairs Bulletin*, 59, 4, September 1982

Tatz, Colin, and Brian Stoddart, *The Royal Sydney Golf Club: The First Hundred Years*, Allen & Unwin, Sydney, 1993

Thomas, Keith, *Man and the Natural World: Changing Attitudes in England 1500–1800*, Allen Lane, London, 1983

Thomson, David, '"Hurricane Bob" Skene—an Australian Polo Legend', *ASSH Bulletin*, no. 20, June 1994, pp. 7–12

Thomson, J.P., 'The Geographical Conditions of City Life', *Proceedings and Transactions of the Royal Geographical Society of Australasia*, Queensland, vol. 14, 1898–99

Ticher, Mike, 'Notional Englishmen, Black Irishmen and Multicultural Australians: Ambiguities in National Sporting Identity, *Sporting Traditions*, vol. 11, no. 1, November 1994, pp. 75–91

Todd, J., Conceptualisations of the Body in Australia c. 1880–c. 1925, BA Hons thesis, University of NSW, 1991

Toohey, Kristine Margaret, The Politics of Australian Elite Sport: 1949–1983, Ph.D. thesis, Pennsylvania State University, 1990

Twain, Mark, *Following the Equator*, 1897

Unikoski, Rachel, *Communal Endeavours: Migrant Organisations in Melbourne*, ANU Press, Canberra, 1978

Vamplew, Wray, *Pay Up and Play the Game: Professional Sport in Britain, 1875–1914*, CUP, Cambridge, 1988

———, ed., *Sport and Colonialism in Nineteenth Century Australasia*, ASSH Studies in Sports History, no. 1, ASSH, Flinders University, 1986

———, *Sports Violence in Australia: Its Extent and Control*, A Report for the National Sports Research Program, ASC, 1991

———, 'Violence in Australian Soccer: The Ethnic Contribution', in O'Hara, ed., *Ethnicity and Soccer in Australia*, pp. 1–15

Vamplew, Wray, and Brian Stoddart, eds, *Sport in Australia: A Social History*, CUP, Melbourne, 1995

Vertinsky, Patricia, *The Eternally Wounded Woman: Women, Doctors and Exercise in the Late Nineteenth Century*, Manchester University Press, Manchester, 1992

Waddy, Ethelred, *Stacy Waddy: Cricket, Travel and the Church*, Sheldon Press, London, 1938

Walker, Robin, *Under Fire: A History of Tobacco Smoking in Australia*, MUP, Melbourne, 1984

Walvin, James, *Leisure in Society 1830–1950*, Longman, London, 1978

Ward, David, 'Trifling with Their Games': Australian Reactions to the 1971 South African Rugby Tour, BA Hons thesis, UNSW, 1993

Waterhouse, Richard, *Black and White Minstrel: The Australian Popular Stage 1788–1914*, NSWUP, Sydney, 1990

———, 'Popular Culture and Pastimes', in Neville Meaney, ed., *Under New Heavens: Cultural Transmission and the Making of Australia*, Heinemann, Melbourne, 1989, pp. 238–85

West, B.P., 'Do Men Make the Rules or do the Rules Make Men', *Mens Studies Review*, Autumn 1992

Wenn, Stephen R., 'Lights! Camera! Little Action: Television, Avery Brundage, and the 1956 Melbourne Olympics', *Sporting Traditions*, vol. 10, no. 1, November 1993, pp. 24–36

Whimpress, Bernard, 'Few And Far Between: Prejudice and Discrimination among Aborigines in Australian First Class Cricket 1869-1988', *Journal of the Anthropological Society of South Australia*, vol. 30, nos 1 & 2, December 1992, pp. 57–70

———, 'The Marsh-MacLaren Dispute at Bathurst 1902 and the Politics of Selection', *Sporting Traditions*, vol. 10, no. 2, May 1994, pp. 45–58

———, 'Poonindie, Cricket and the Adams Family', *Sporting Traditions*, vol. 10, no. 2, May 1994, pp. 69–76

———, *The South Australian Football Story*, South Australian National Football League, Adelaide, 1983

White, R.P.B., and Malcolm Harrison, *100 Years of the NSW AAA: The Official Centenary History of the N.S.W. Amateur Athletic Association 1887–1987*, Fairfax Library, Sydney, 1986

White, Richard, 'Americanization and Popular Culture in Australia', *Teaching History*, vol. 12, pt. 2, August 1978, pp. 3–21

———, *Inventing Australia*, Allen & Unwin, Sydney, 1981

Windschuttle, Keith, *The Media*, 2nd edn, Penguin, Ringwood, 1990

Working Group on Women in Sport, *Women, Sport and the Media*, AGPS, Canberra, 1985

Young, Michael, 'The Melbourne Press and the 1980 Moscow Olympic Boycott Controversy', *Sporting Traditions*, vol. 4, no. 2, May 1988, pp. 184–200

INDEX

commercialisation 4, 5, 48, 188–90, 193–7
Commonwealth Games 118–19, 126
Confederation of Australian Sport 125
Connell, Bob 72, 76
Coombes, Richard 63, 171
Corbett family 171
Cornish sport 23, 104, 156
corruption 52, 136, 182–3
costume, sporting 79, 84, 87–8
Coulthard, Faith 135, 147
cricket 1–10, 23–4, 48, 61, 66, 96, 105–7, 132–3, 167–8, 177–8, 188–90
    women's 85–6, 88
Crossland, John Michael 133, 172
croquet 40, 87–8
Cunneen, Chris 171
cycling 52–3, 88

Dabscheck, Braham 201, 202
Darcy, Les 47, 60, 156
Davis, J.C. 141, 171
Devery, Keeley 90
Dick, Harriet 38, 86
Dickinson, Evelyn 85
Driver, Richard 24, 62, 115
Dunlop company 191
Durack, 'Fanny' 50, 80, 87
Duras, Fritz 121
Dutton, Geoffrey 172–3

electorate cricket 96–7
Ella family 145, 147
Ellicott, Bob 124
entrepreneurs, sporting 38, 188–9, 192–3
ethics 202–3
ethnic symbols 164–7
Eton College 10, 49

feminism 84–5
femininity 82–5, 88–90
    see also women
Fijian cricket tour 140–1
film, sporting 175–6
Flemington racecourse 30–1, 41, 42, 43

Foley, Larry 47, 155
Foster, David 101
Fotheringham, Richard 176
football 12–13, 32, 48–50, 67–8
    see also individual codes
Footscray Australian Football Club 97, 200
fox-hunting 2, 10–11
Fraser, Malcolm 124
Freeman, Cathy 146

gambling 3, 15, 17–18, 21, 42, 48, 54, 61, 122–3, 136
gate-entry charges 2, 4, 5
Geelong
    Grammar 37, 64, 102
    Tennis Club 68
Gilbert, Eddie 135, 141
Gill, S.T. 36, 103, 172
Gillam Holden, Frances 83
Glebe Rowing Club 59, 61–2
goldfields 47, 51, 103–4, 172
Goldlust, John 179, 199
golf 1, 6, 38, 51, 67, 87–8, 153
Goolagong (Cawley), Evonne 146–7
Grand Prix, motorcycle 126
Great Public Schools (GPS) 56, 66
Guttmann, Allen 80
gymnastics 84

Hale, Rev. Mathew 132
Hambleton Cricket Club 2, 7, 8
Hammersley, W.J. 49, 62
Hanlan, Edward 115
Hardwick, Harold 60
Harrison, H.C.A. 57, 62
Harriss, Ian 196, 198
Hawke, Bob 120, 124
Hay, Roy 159–60, 163–6
Henry, Albert 135, 139, 141
Herbert Xavier 104–5
hockey 83, 88–90
holiday, half 35, 43
homosexuality 12, 81–2
horse-racing 1, 2, 4, 5, 6, 7, 9, 19–20, 43–5, 104–5, 122–3, 132, 194
Howe, Jackie 101
Hughes, Kim 128
Hughes, Thomas 55, 74, 76

Newtown Rugby League Club 95,
163, 200
Nicholls, Sir Doug 139, 142, 148
Norman, Greg 181
North Queensland Cowboys 109
Northern Territory sport 104–5

O'Farrell, Patrick 151, 154–5
O'Hara, John 3, 98–9, 201
Olympics, The 118–20, 128–9, 161,
178

Packer, Kerry 115–16, 124, 179,
197–9
parks 40, 75, 158
parochialism, regional 106–8
Paraschak, Vicky 148
Parsons, George 95
Paterson, Banjo 104
Perkins, Charles 146
Pewtress, Margaret 89
photography 74, 78, 171–4
player associations 201–2, 203
polo 102
Polynesia 157, 167
Poonindie Mission 132–3
Powlett, F.A. 22
professionalism 42, 48, 58, 64–71,
195
Protestant lobby 121–2
publican, role of 13, 22–5
Purnim Bears 146, 149

Queensland
Amateur Athletic Association 137
Cricket Association 141
Rifle Association 117
Turf Cub 45

Rader, Benjamin 179
racial politics and theory 75–7, 103,
137, 140–1, 146
radio 176–8
Randwick racecourse 32, 41, 43, 114
rebel tours 128
Referee 61, 63, 170, 171
Richards, Ron 142, 144
Riess, Steven 74
rifle clubs 117–18
riots 61, 103

Riverina 99
rodeo 102
Rose, Lionel 142, 143, 144, 147
Roth, Dr Walter Edmund 138
Rothmans National Sports
Foundation 129, 130, 192
rowing 64–5
Royal
Adelaide Golf Club 68, 117
Melbourne Gold Club 68, 117
Queensland Golf Club 117
Sydney Golf Club 39, 51, 68, 98,
117
royal prefix 117
rugby 48–50, 67–8, 97, 167
rugby league 49, 67, 77, 95, 107–8,
130, 145, 167, 192
rural sport 3–4, 12–4, 98–103
Ryan, John 175

Salter, Michael 16
Samuels, Charlie 47, 136
Sandercock and Turner 199, 200
Sandow, Eugen 78
Scharleib, Dr Mary 83
Scotch College 37, 39, 64
Scots 152–3
Scott, Rose 85
sculling 46–7, 188–9
Searle, Henry 46
sectarianism 155
sexuality 80–2
Sharman, Jimmy 101
sheep-shearing 100–1
shows, country 100–1
skiing 157–8
soccer 49, 97–8, 116, 153, 163–4
Social Darwinism 54–6, 137, 138
softball 88–9, 160
South African sporting contacts 124,
127–8
South Australian
Cricket Association 35, 61, 62,
97, 114–15
Football Association 62
Football Club 61
Jockey Club 43, 45
Southern Rugby Football Union 50,
63
Smith, James Joynton 67, 192